Arthur Mackay Ellis

A Guide to the Income Tax Acts for the Use of the English Income

Tax Payer

Arthur Mackay Ellis

A Guide to the Income Tax Acts for the Use of the English Income Tax Payer

ISBN/EAN: 9783337715731

Printed in Europe, USA, Canada, Australia, Japan

Cover: Foto ©Suzi / pixelio.de

More available books at **www.hansebooks.com**

A GUIDE

TO THE

INCOME TAX ACTS

FOR THE USE OF THE

ENGLISH INCOME TAX PAYER.

BY

ARTHUR M. ELLIS, LL.B. (Lond.),

SOLICITOR,

Author of "A Guide to the House Tax Acts."

———

THIRD EDITION.

———

LONDON:

STEVENS AND SONS, LIMITED,

119 & 120, CHANCERY LANE,

Law Publishers and Booksellers.

1893

LONDON :

PRINTED BY C. F. ROWORTH, GREAT NEW STREET, FETTER LANE—E.C.

PREFACE TO THIRD EDITION.

———◆———

A THIRD EDITION having been called for, the
Acts of Parliament which have been passed,
and the Cases which have been decided relating
to Income Tax, since the last edition was published, have been noted in the present Edition.

A. M. E.

August, 1893.

a 2

PREFACE TO SECOND EDITION.

THE fact of a Second Edition having been called for within a year of the publication of the first makes me hope that the Work has been found useful. This Edition has been carefully revised, and I hope that it may be found free from errors, although the task I have set myself, of giving a connected reading of more than twenty-four Acts of Parliament, the language of which is not more free from ambiguity than such language usually is, is no easy one. The cases which have been decided since the last Edition was published are noted in the present Edition. The cases given as "unreported" are to be found in a series of reports printed for the use of the Inland Revenue Office, but not in the reports generally accessible to the public. I have been indebted for useful information on some points to the new edition of "Bourdin's Land Tax," recently edited by Mr. Shirley Bunbury, Assistant Registrar of Land Tax.

A. M. E.

February, 1886.

PREFACE TO FIRST EDITION.

My aim in writing this book has been to provide the income tax payer in England with a guide to the enactments scattered through, at least, four-and-twenty Acts of Parliament, in pursuance of which that tax is assessed and levied. I have divided the book into four chapters; the first describes the officials concerned in assessing, charging, and collecting, the tax; the second deals with the properties and profits which are the subjects of the tax; the third describes the methods of assessment and collection; and the fourth treats of the allowances, abatements, and relief, which the income tax payer may claim on one ground or another, and of the modes in which assessments erroneously made are corrected. In treating of these topics I have used, as far as possible, the very words of the Acts of Parliament; and I hope it will be found that I have brought into something like an orderly arrangement all the enactments in the existing Acts relating to the income tax which concern the English income tax payer. I have made no attempt to bring in those which only concern the officials employed, or deal with the routine of the departments. The cases which have been decided upon the Income Tax Acts will be found shortly stated in connection with the enactments which they respectively elucidate. References to the Acts of Parliament quoted will be found

a 3

at the foot of each page; and I have added an index
which I hope will enable the reader to find readily any
enactment falling within the scope of the work to which
he may have occasion to refer. To make the work of
reference easier, I have added in the margins of the pages,
where the paragraphs are of some length, short analyses
of their contents. A list of cases cited, and a list of
statutes, will be found preceding the first chapter. The
work can make no claim to originality : I hope it may
make some to utility.

A. M. E.

February, 1885.

CONTENTS.

---

a 4

TABLE OF CASES.

a 5

TABLE OF STATUTES.

ERRATUM.

Page 219, note [3], *for* " 48 & 49 Vict. c. 35,"
read " 48 & 49 Vict. c. 51."

INCOME TAX ACTS.

CHAPTER I.

THE INCOME TAX AND THE OFFICIALS CONCERNED IN ASSESSING, CHARGING, AND COLLECTING IT.

The Income Tax an Annual Tax.—The income tax is levied year by year, under the authority of an Act of Parliament passed annually, which determines the amount of the tax for the current financial year—that is, for the year which [1] begins on the 6th April and ends on the 5th April following. The machinery by which the tax is charged and collected derives its force from each annual Act, which generally continues the existing machinery, with, perhaps, some changes made in certain particulars in which experience has suggested a possibility of improvement. The income tax, as we know it, was first established in 1842, and the Act of that year (5 & 6 Vict. c. 35) which imposed the tax constituted the machinery, which, in its main features, still remains. In describing the authorities concerned in the business of assessing, charging, and collecting, the income tax, the property, profits, and gains, which are the subject of the tax,

[1] 43 & 44 Vict. c. 19, s. 48.

E.   B

Chap. I. the mode of assessing, charging, and collecting, the tax, and the means to be employed in order to secure the various exemptions, allowances, and deductions, which may be claimed by persons who are assessed, we shall have to notice all the provisions, in whatever Act contained, by which at the present time these subjects are regulated ; but it must be remembered that all these provisions are, strictly, in force for one year only, and depend for their validity in any particular year upon the Act of that year which refers to, and continues, them, and without which they would expire. So much is this the case, that, to prevent the inconvenience which would otherwise arise from the passing of the annual Act being delayed until after the close of the financial year, it has now become the practice to insert in each annual Act a clause " to ensure the collection in due time of any duties of income tax which may be granted for the ensuing year," by which all provisions in any Act relating to the income tax which are in force on the 5th April, in the year current at the time the annual Act is passed (that is, on the last day of the then current financial year) are made to have full force and effect with regard to the duties of income tax which may be granted in the ensuing year.

Officials.—The persons concerned with the assessment and collection of the income tax are (1) The Commissioners of Her Majesty's Treasury, (2) The Commissioners of Inland Revenue, (3) The Commis-

sioners for Special Purposes, (4) The Commissioners
for General Purposes, (5) The Additional Commissioners, (6) The Clerks to the Commissioners, (7) The
[1]Surveyors, (8) The Assessors, and (9) The Collectors.

The Commissioners of Her Majesty's Treasury.—
[2]The Commissioners of Her Majesty's Treasury, or,
to give them their full title, the Commissioners of
Her Majesty's Treasury of the United Kingdom of
Great Britain and Ireland, are the persons appointed
by her Majesty's letters patent for executing the
offices of Lord High Treasurer of Great Britain and
Lord High Treasurer of Ireland. [3]The signatures
of any two of the Commissioners are sufficient to
validate any document which the Commissioners are
required to sign. In the [4]Taxes Management Act,
1880, these Commissioners are compendiously styled
"the Treasury," and we shall for the future in speaking of them adopt that term. The Treasury [5]has
chief control, and superintendence, as regards the
assessment, and collection, of income tax.

*The Commissioners of Inland Revenue.—*The Commissioners of Inland Revenue are [6]a consolidated

---

[1] To whom we should, perhaps, add Inspectors. See note[5]
p. 25, *post.*
[2] 56 Geo. III. c. 98, s. 2.
[3] 12 & 13 Vict. c. 89.
[4] 43 & 44 Vict. c. 19.
[5] 56 Geo. III. c. 98, s. 2; 43 & 44 Vict. c. 19, s. 12.
[6] 12 & 13 Vict. c. 1, s. 1.

Board of Commissioners representing the old Commissioners of Excise, and Commissioners of Stamps and Taxes, [1]whose powers and authorities they exercise. The Commissioners are appointed [2]by her Majesty under the Great Seal of the United Kingdom, and hold office during pleasure. [3]For income tax purposes any two of the Commissioners form a quorum. [4]Their chief office, which is called the "Chief Office of Inland Revenue," must be at such place, within the limits designated as the limits of the "Chief Office of Excise" by an Act passed in the eighth year of George IV., as the Treasury appoints. These limits are [5]the cities of London and Westminster, the borough of Southwark and the suburbs thereof, the parishes within the [6]weekly bills of mortality, and the parishes of St. Marylebone and St. Pancras in the County of Middlesex. The Commis-

---

[1] 12 & 13 Vict. c. 1, s. 3.
[2] 12 & 13 Vict. c. 1, s. 2.
[3] 43 & 44 Vict. c. 19, s. 5.
[4] 12 & 13 Vict. c. 1, s. 5.
[5] 7 & 8 Geo. IV. c. 53, s. 14.
[6] The weekly bills of mortality are accounts of the births and deaths within a certain district, which has varied from time to time, but may be said now to be comprised in the general description "the cities of London and Westminster, the borough of Southwark, and the suburbs thereof." The bills of mortality are said to date from 1592, but their regular publication from 1603, with some intermission during the Great Fire of London. The parishes of St. Marylebone and St. Pancras have never been included in the district.

sioners of Inland Revenue are styled in the [1]Taxes Chap. I.
Management Act, 1880, "the Board," and we shall
adopt that term. [2]The Board have the direction, and
management, under the Treasury, of the assessment
and collection of the income tax. We may conveniently describe here the offices of the Receiver-
General of Inland Revenue and the Collectors of
Inland Revenue, whom we shall by and by have occasion to mention. [3]The Receiver-General of Inland
Revenue is an officer who represents the old Receiver-
General of Excise, and Receiver-General of Stamps
and Taxes. His office was created by the same Act
which constituted the Board, and was a necessary consequence of the consolidation of the two old Commis-
sionerships of Excise and Stamps and Taxes. [4]The
Receiver-General of Inland Revenue holds office
during the pleasure of the Treasury. The [5]Collectors
of Inland Revenue are officers appointed by the
Board to be Collectors, or officers for receipt, either
of one, or of several, of the branches, or descriptions,
of revenue under the management of the Board, who
appoint the counties, or districts, or circuits, of receipt in which such Collectors respectively act.

The Commissioners for Special Purposes.—[6]The

[1] 43 & 44 Vict. c. 19.
[2] 16 & 17 Vict. c. 34, s. 4; 43 & 44 Vict. c. 19, s. 12.
[3] 12 & 13 Vict. c. 1, s. 6, and see sect. 17.
[4] 12 & 13 Vict. c. 1, s. 6.
[5] 12 & 13 Vict. c. 1, s. 15.
[6] 5 & 6 Vict. c. 35, s. 23, and 12 & 13 Vict. c. 1, s. 17.

Chap. I. Board, and such persons as the Treasury by warrant
under their hands and seals from time to time appoint
as they think expedient, are Commissioners for Special
Purposes, or, as we shall call them shortly, Special
Commissioners. No other qualification is required of
a Special Commissioner than the possession of his
office. The Special Commissioners are allowed such
salary for their trouble, and such incidental expenses,
as the Treasury may direct to be paid to them. The
Treasury cause an account of all appointments of
Special Commissioners with salaries to be laid before
each House of Parliament within twenty days after
appointment, if Parliament is then sitting, and if not,
within twenty days after the meeting of Parliament.
The following persons are also Special Commissioners for the purposes mentioned in connection
with such persons respectively in the following
list :—

Governor
and Direc-
tors of
Bank of
England.

[1] The Governor and Directors of the Company
of the Bank of England are Commissioners for
the purpose of assessing and charging the duties
of income tax in respect of all annuities payable to the said company at the receipt of the
exchequer, and the profits attached to the same
and divided amongst the several proprietors;
and in respect of all annuities, dividends, and
shares of annuities, payable out of the revenue
of the United Kingdom to any persons, cor-

---

[1] 5 & 6 Vict. c. 35, s. 24.

porations, or companies whatever, and entrusted to the said governor and company for such payment; and in respect of all profits and gains of the said company chargeable under Schedule D.; and in respect of all other dividends, annuities, pensions, and salaries payable by the said company; and in respect of all other profits chargeable with income tax and arising within any office or department under the management or control of the said governor and company.

[1] The Commissioners for the Reduction of the National Debt are Commissioners for the purpose of assessing and charging duties of income tax in respect of all annuities payable by them out of the revenue of the United Kingdom; and in respect of all salaries and pensions payable in any office or department under their management or control.

Commissioners for Reduction of National Debt.

[2] The Lord Chancellor, the judges, and the principal officer or officers of each Court or department of office under her Majesty throughout Great Britain, whether the same is civil, judicial, or criminal, ecclesiastical or commissary, military or naval, have authority to appoint Commissioners from amongst the officers of each Court or department of office respectively, and

Lord Chancellor, Judges, &c.

---

[1] 5 & 6 Vict. c. 35, s. 28.
[2] 5 & 6 Vict. c. 35, s. 30.

the persons so appointed, or any three or more of them, not in any case exceeding seven, are Commissioners for assessing and charging duties of income tax in relation to the offices in each such Court or department accordingly. But in relation to each department of office, not being one of her Majesty's Courts, civil, judicial, or criminal, or an ecclesiastical or commissary Court, the Treasury, whenever they think it expedient, settle and determine in what particular departments Commissioners shall not be appointed; and in such case they settle and determine in what other department of office the officers of that department in which Commissioners are not appointed shall be assessed. And whenever there is default in the officers of any department, or in any Court aforesaid, in appointing Commissioners, the Treasury appoint fit and proper persons to be Commissioners in the several Courts and departments of office aforesaid, for which they are appointed, from amongst the officers in the several departments respectively, uniting, in cases requiring the same, two or more offices under the same Commissioners, but nevertheless with distinct officers from each office so united for assessing the duties of income tax. The Treasury have authority to determine any dispute which may arise touching the department in which any office is executed.

[1] The Speaker and the principal clerk of either **Chap. I.** House of Parliament, the principal or other officers in the several Counties Palatine and the Duchy of Cornwall, or in any ecclesiastical Court, or in any inferior Court of Justice, whether of law or equity, or criminal or justiciary, or under any ecclesiastical body or corporation, whether aggregate or sole, throughout Great Britain, have authority to appoint Commissioners from amongst the persons executing offices in either House of Parliament, or in their respective departments of office, and the persons so appointed, or any three of them, not in any case exceeding seven, are Commissioners for assessing and charging the duties of income tax in relation to the places, offices, and employments of profit in each House of Parliament, and in each such department respectively. The names of the Commissioners appointed must be transmitted to the Board, and in default of appointment as aforesaid, the appointments are made by the Treasury.

The Speaker and Principal Clerk of either House of Parliament, Officers of Counties Palatine, &c.

[2] The Mayor, Aldermen, and Common Council, or the principal officers or members, by whatever name they are called, of every corporate city,

[1] 5 & 6 Vict. c. 35, s. 31.
[2] 5 & 6 Vict. c. 35, s. 32.   This section was repealed by s. 9 of the Customs and Inland Revenue Act, 1876 (39 & 40 Vict. c. 16), but was revived by sect. 7 of the Customs, Inland Revenue, and Savings Bank Act, 1877 (40 & 41 Vict. c. 13).

borough, town, or place, and of every cinque
port throughout Great Britain, or any three
or more of them, not exceeding seven, are
Commissioners for assessing and charging the
duties of income tax in relation to the public
offices, or employments of profit, in such city,
corporation, and cinque port, and in every guild,
fraternity, company, or society, whether corporate or not corporate, within such city, corporation, or cinque port.

[1] The appointment of Commissioners in relation to
the duties of income tax upon the offices, and employments of profit, mentioned in the foregoing list,
must be notified to the Board within one calendar
month after the 5th of April in every year, and in
default of notification the appointment devolves upon
the Treasury, to whom the Board notify the default.
If the appointment is not made by the Treasury
within a month after the default is notified to them,
the General Commissioners for the district act until
another appointment is made. [2] All persons appointed
Special Commissioners are required, before acting in
relation to [3] the duties in Schedule D., to take [4] the
prescribed oath, which may be administered by a
General or Special Commissioner, and any Special
Commissioner acting (except in administering the

[1] 5 & 6 Vict. c. 35, s. 33.
[2] 5 & 6 Vict. c. 35, s. 38.
[3] As to these duties, see *post*, pp. 102 *et seq.*
[4] 5 & 6 Vict. c. 35, s. 16.

oath) before he has taken the oath, is liable to a Chap. I. penalty of 100*l.*

The Commissioners for General Purposes.—The Commissioners for General Purposes, or, as we shall call them shortly, the General Commissioners, are selected from another body of Commissioners, called the Land Tax Commissioners. We must begin, therefore, by explaining who the Land Tax Commissioners are. In the first place, [1] all persons who act as justices of the peace for any county, shire, riding, division, or district, and who possess the estate qualification presently referred to, are Land Tax Commissioners within their respective counties, &c. In addition to these *ex officio* Commissioners, certain other persons holding good positions in the localities in which they reside are appointed from time to time by Act of Parliament to be Land Tax Commissioners for the several counties, divisions of counties, cities, boroughs, and other places, which form [2] separate districts for the purposes of the land tax.

Land Tax Commissioners.

[1] 7 & 8 Geo. IV. c. 75, s. 1.

[2] By "districts" we must be understood here to mean the "divisions of the country for which separate Commissioners act," not the "parishes and other districts for which separate Assessors act." The case of *Reg.* v. *Land Tax Commissioners for the Tower Division* (2 E. & B. 694) introduced the use of the word "division" for the Commissioners' district, and of the word "district" for the Assessors' district. The "divisions" may be found in 38 Geo. III. c. 5, s. 2. The enactment is concerned with the proportions in which the several "divisions" are to be assessed and taxed, and it proceeds

Chap. I. Formerly it was the custom to introduce their names and addresses and the localities in which they were empowered to act into the Act by which they were appointed; but in the year 1869 the practice seems to have commenced, which has since been continued, of including these particulars in a schedule, which is signed by, and deposited with, the clerk of the House of Commons, and afterwards published in the London Gazette. [1] The last Act appointing Land Tax Commissioners was passed on the 25th June, 1886, and, as it refers to no Act of the same kind earlier than the 7 & 8 Geo. IV. c. 75, we may infer that the names of all existing Land Tax Commissioners, who are not justices of the peace, may be found in that and the subsequent Acts which have been passed for the same purpose, or (since 1869) in the schedules referred to by these Acts, and published in the London Gazette. For the estate qualification required of a Land Tax Commissioner, and the oaths to be taken by him before exercising his office, we must refer to the enactments enumerated [2] below. The General Commissioners are

The General Commissioners.

upon the principle of stating the proportion in which some particular city, town, borough, liberty, or place in a county is to be assessed and taxed, and then the proportion in which the rest of the county is to be taxed. The land tax, which had before been an annual tax, was made perpetual by 38 Geo. III. c. 60.

[1] 49 & 50 Vict. c. 47.

[2] 38 Geo. III. c. 5, ss. 49, 50, 92—95; 38 Geo. III. c. 48, ss. 1, 3; 9 Geo. IV. c. 38, s. 3.

selected from the Land Tax Commissioners in the following manner :—[1]The Board, whenever they deem it necessary to do so, convene, by notice inserted in the London Gazette, meetings of the Land Tax Commissioners; and thereupon the Land Tax Commissioners for each county, riding, shire, or division of the same, and for each city, borough, cinque port, liberty, franchise, town, and place, for which separate Commissioners have been appointed with exclusive jurisdiction for putting in execution the [2]Land Tax Acts within the same, meet at the time and place appointed by the notice, within the district for which they act, and there choose such of the Land Tax Commissioners appointed for such district as possess the qualifications [3]presently mentioned, and are fit and proper persons to act as General Commissioners for the same district. The names of the persons chosen to be General Commissioners are set down in writing in the order in which the major part of the Land Tax Commissioners present think fit they should be appointed General Commissioners; and any seven, or any number less than seven not less than three, of the persons whose names are set down

[1] 5 & 6 Vict. c. 35, s. 4 ; 12 & 13 Vict. c. 1, s. 17.

[2] The phrase "Land Tax Acts" is used in the sense in which it is used in the Taxes Management Act, 1880 (43 & 44 Vict. c. 19), where it is defined (s. 5) as "any Act or part of any Act relating in any way to the assessment or redemption of the Land Tax."

[3] See *post*, pp. 18—20.

Chap. I. to act as General Commissioners, in the order in which their names are set down, are the General Commissioners for the district. Vacancies among the General Commissioners are supplied from a list made by the Land Tax Commissioners in the way we shall [1]presently mention. If the Land Tax Commissioners present at any meeting cannot find amongst the Land Tax Commissioners for the district seven persons to act as General Commissioners, and seven to supply vacancies, they may appoint any persons residing within the district and possessing the required qualification, who are in their judgment fit and proper persons, although not Land Tax Commissioners, to be General Commissioners, until the two numbers of seven and seven have been supplied; and if they cannot find amongst the Land Tax Commissioners of the district, and such other persons as have been referred to, the requisite number of fourteen, they may select so many persons as may be required to make up that number from the Land Tax Commissioners acting for any adjoining or neighbouring district. [2]In the case of a city, borough, town, or other place of the kind, if a sufficient number of persons capable of acting as General Commissioners are not chosen or appointed, any person qualified to act as General Commissioner for the county at large, or riding, or

If number of persons in district qualified to be General Commissioners is insufficient.

---

[1] See *post*, pp. 15, 16.
[2] 5 & 6 Vict. c. 35, s. 6.

shire, in, or adjoining to, which such city, &c. is Chap. I.
situate, may be chosen to act as General Commissioner for such city, &c. ; and in the case of a city, &c.,
as of a county, &c., a person otherwise duly qualified,
and resident within the city, &c., although not a
Land Tax Commissioner, may be appointed a
General Commissioner in case of need. [1]Where
seven persons duly qualified have been chosen to
act as General Commissioners for any district, no
other person may interfere. [2]In case any General In case any
General
Commissioner dies, or declines to act, or having Commissioner dies.
begun to act declines to act any further, the remaining General Commissioners choose one of the
persons whose names appear on the vacancy list,
who, if he has been chosen in the same manner as
the person in regard of whom the vacancy occurs, is
appointed to act in his place. [3]The vacancy list is The
"vacancy"
made thus:—[4]the Land Tax Commissioners at their list.
meeting, after choosing General Commissioners, go
on to set down the names of persons qualified to be
General Commissioners, and any seven, or any number less than seven not less than three, of these last-
named persons, whose names appear in the Land

[1] 5 & 6 Vict. c. 35, s. 4. Except, of course, when expressly
authorised to do so. That this is a necessary qualification
must be already evident; it is provided for by the words
contained in the section quoted, "except as hereinafter
mentioned," and its extent will appear as we proceed.
[2] 5 & 6 Vict. c. 35, s. 7.
[3] 5 & 6 Vict. c. 35, s. 6.
[4] 5 & 6 Vict. c. 35, ss. 4, 7.

Chap. I. Tax Commissioners' list next in order after the
names of those persons who have been chosen
General Commissioners are Commissioners to supply
vacancies in the body of General Commissioners.
If the Land Tax Commissioners cannot find within
their district seven persons to put upon the vacancy
list, they may fill up the number in the same manner
as in like case they may fill up the number of
General Commissioners. The vacancy list is made
up and renewed from time to time as need requires
by the Land Tax Commissioners at their meetings;
and if it happens at any time to be defective, so that
the due number of Commissioners cannot be supplied
from it, it is filled up and renewed by the acting

In certain
cities and
towns per-
sons may
be chosen
to act
with the
General
Commis-
sioners.

General Commissioners for the district. In certain
cities and towns persons may be chosen to act as
General Commissioners together with the General
Commissioners who have been chosen in the ordinary way. [1]Thus, in the City of London two Commissioners and two to supply their vacancies may be
named by the Mayor and Aldermen of London out
of eight persons, four of whom must be aldermen, to
be returned to them by the Common Council; two
other Commissioners and two to supply their vacancies may be named by the Governor and Directors of
the Bank of England; and one other Commissioner
and one to supply his vacancy may be named by
each of the following companies, viz.:—the Governor

---

[1] 5 & 6 Vict. c. 35, s. 5.

and Directors of the Royal Exchange Assurance
Company, the Governor and Directors of the London Assurance Company, the Directors for conducting and managing the affairs of the East and West
India Dock Company, and the Directors for conducting and managing the London Dock Company, and
the Saint Katharine Dock Company respectively for
the time being. In the City of Norwich, the magistrates and justices of the peace acting in, and for, the
city may choose eight persons to be Commissioners
and eight persons to supply their vacancies, not more
than four of the first eight, and four of the second
eight, to be chosen from among the magistrates and
justices, and the remainder to be chosen from among
the inhabitants of the city. In each of the following
cities and towns, viz. :—Bristol, Exeter, Kingston-
upon - Hull, Newcastle - upon - Tyne, Birmingham,
Liverpool, Leeds, Manchester, King's Lynn, and
Great Yarmouth, the magistrates and justices of the
peace acting in, and for, the city or town, together
with the justices of the peace acting in, and for, the
county, riding, or division, in which the same is situate, may choose eight persons to be Commissioners,
and eight to supply their vacancies. [1] The names of
all persons so chosen must be returned to the Board.
[2] If in any district there is neglect in appointing If in any
district
General Commissioners, or the General Commis- there is

---

[1] 5 & 6 Vict. c. 35, s. 5, and 12 & 13 Vict. c. 1, s. 17.
[2] 5 & 6 Vict. c. 35, s. 8, and 12 & 13 Vict. c. 1, s. 17.

Chap. I.

neglect in appointing General Commissioners, or the General Commissioners appointed decline to act. sioners appointed neglect, or refuse, to act, or having begun to act decline to act further, the Land Tax Commissioners for the district, on notice of the neglect to appoint, &c., being given to their Clerk by any Surveyor authorized by the Board to give such notice, being duly qualified to act as General Commissioners, or any of them not exceeding seven in number, must act as General Commissioners; and if there is in any district a want of General Commissioners, the Commissioners for any adjoining district in the same county, riding, division, or shire, if possessing the required qualification, must, on receiving like notice, act as General Commissioners, by themselves or in concurrence with any persons willing to act as General Commissioners in the district in which such want occurs. If the persons before mentioned, to whom notice as aforesaid has been given, do not, within ten days after receiving the notice, take upon themselves to act as General

In certain cases of default, Special Commissioners must act. Commissioners, the [1] Special Commissioners must act as General Commissioners within the district. [2] The

Estate qualification for General Commissioners in England, estate qualification required for any district, or division of any county in England, except the county of Monmouth, and for any of the ridings of the county of York, and for the cities or towns of London, Westminster, Bristol, Exeter, Kingston-upon-Hull, Newcastle-upon-Tyne, Norwich, Bir-

---

[1] See *ante*, pp. 5, 6.
[2] 5 & 6 Vict. c. 35, s. 10.

mingham, Liverpool, Leeds, Manchester, King's
Lynn, and Great Yarmouth, is the possession of except in
lands, tenements, or hereditaments, freehold, or mouth-
copyhold, or leasehold whereof not less than seven shire.
years are unexpired, in Great Britain, of the value of
200*l.* a year, or more, over and above all ground
rents, incumbrances, and reservations, payable out of
the same; or the possession of personal estate of the
value of 5,000*l.*, or of a personal estate, or an interest
therein, producing an annual income of 200*l.*; or the
possession of lands, tenements, or hereditaments, and
personal estate or an interest therein, which together
are of the annual value of 200*l.*; or being the eldest
son of some person who is possessed of an estate of
thrice the value required as the qualification of a
Commissioner in right of his own estate. One hundred pounds of personal estate is, for the purpose of
qualifying in right of the Commissioner's own estate,
reckoned as equivalent to 4*l.* a year; and an interest
from personal estate of 4*l.* a year as equivalent to
100*l.* of personal estate. [1]The estate qualification re- Estate
quired for the office of General Commissioner in qualification for
any district or division of the county of Mon- General
Commis-
mouth, or of any county in Wales, or in any city, sioners in
Mon-
borough, cinque port, liberty, franchise, town or mouthshire
or Wales.
place, in England or Wales, other than the cities
or towns before mentioned, is the possession of an
estate of the nature, and of four-fifths of the value,

[1] 5 & 6 Vict. c. 35, s. 11.

Chap. I. required for the estate of a Commissioner acting for a district, or division, of a county in England (other than the county of Monmouth), or being the eldest son of a person possessed of an estate of thrice the value required as the qualification of a General Commissioner for the same county, &c. [1] No estate consisting of lands or tenements for the qualification of a Commissioner need be situate in the county, riding, division, or shire, for which the person whose qualification it constitutes is a Commissioner.

Proof of qualification on person acting.

The proof of qualification lies on the person acting as Commissioner. [2] Every General Commissioner before he begins to act in relation to the [3] duties contained in Schedule D. must take the [4] prescribed oath,

Oath to be taken by General Commissioner.

which any one of the persons appointed General Commissioners may administer. The oath is subscribed by the person taking it, and any General Commissioner acting in relation to the duties in Schedule D. (except by administering the oath) is liable to a penalty of 100*l.*

The Additional Commissioners.—[5] The Additional Commissioners are appointed by the General Commissioners. The mode of appointment is as follows:—Whenever the General Commissioners for any district

[1] 5 & 6 Vict. c. 35, s. 14.
[2] 5 & 6 Vict. c. 35, s. 38.
[3] As to these duties, see *post*, pp. 102 *et seq.*
[4] The oath is given in Schedule F. of 5 & 6 Vict. c. 35.
[5] 5 & 6 Vict. c. 35, s. 16.

think it expedient that the powers given by the Income Tax Acts should be executed by Commissioners other than, and in addition to, General Commissioners appointed in the way we have described, and at the same time do not desire to exercise the power given them, as we shall [1] presently explain, to appoint a greater number of General Commissioners, they, at any meeting held for that purpose, set down in writing lists of the names of such persons residing within their respective districts as are in their opinion fit and proper persons to act as Additional Commissioners, and have the estate qualification required of an Additional Commissioner, that is, an estate of the nature, and of one-half the amount, required for the qualification of a General Commissioner in the same district. The General Commissioners may appoint so many Additional Commissioners as they in their discretion, after taking into consideration the size of the district, and the number of persons to be assessed therein, think requisite. The lists of the names of the persons appointed Additional Commissioners are, when signed by the General Commissioners, sufficient authority for the persons appointed Additional Commissioners to act in that capacity. [2] Notice in writing of their appointment is given by the General Commissioners to the Additional Commissioners, through the Assessors of the parishes or

[1] See *post*, pp. 22, 23.
[2] 5 & 6 Vict. c. 35, s. 19.

places in which the Additional Commissioners reside; and the notice requires them to assemble on a day, not more than ten days after the date of the notice, when the oath which they are required to take is administered to them by the General Commissioners. [1] The persons appointed to supply vacancies among the General Commissioners in any district may be appointed Additional Commissioners, until their services are required as General Commissioners. [2] The General Commissioners may, whenever they think proper, divide the Additional Commissioners into district committees, and allot to each committee distinct parishes, wards, or places, in which such committees may act separately. Not more than seven persons may act together as Additional Commissioners for the same district, if not formed into several divisions in the manner above mentioned ; and no more than seven persons may act as Additional Commissioners on any committee into which the Additional Commissioners for the district are divided. When more than seven Additional Commissioners attend any meeting, the seven first in order on the list then present act, and the rest withdraw. Two Additional Commissioners form a quorum at any meeting of

Acting General Commissioners

their body. [3] If the acting General Commissioners, whether they have been chosen, or act by virtue of

---

[1] 5 & 6 Vict. c. 35, s. 16.
[2] 5 & 6 Vict. c. 35, s. 20.
[3] 5 & 6 Vict. c. 35, s. 21.

their appointment as Land Tax Commissioners, think Chap. I.
it expedient that a greater number than seven General may appoint more
Commissioners, possessing the required estate quali- General
fication, should be appointed for any district, they Commissioners.
may appoint more General Commissioners, not
exceeding seven in number, instead of appointing
Additional Commissioners, observing with regard
to such appointment the same rules as in the
first appointment of General Commissioners, but
without adding any persons to supply their vacancies.
If the General Commissioners avail themselves of General
Commis-
this power to increase their number, they choose by sioners
acting as
lot not less than two, nor more than seven, of their Additional
Commis-
own body, to execute the office of Additional Com- sioners.
missioners, and the remaining members of their body
act as General Commissioners. If no Additional
Commissioners are appointed specially to execute
the powers vested in Additional Commissioners, the
Acting General Commissioners, whether chosen, or
acting by virtue of their appointment as Land Tax
Commissioners, divide themselves, so that two of them
at least are appointed to execute the powers vested in
Additional Commissioners. If, after such appointment as last mentioned, there are not two persons at
least remaining qualified to act as General Commissioners for the district, then the persons qualified to
act as General Commissioners for any adjoining district may act as General Commissioners in the district
in which the deficiency has occurred. All persons
appointed Additional Commissioners are required,

Chap. I. before acting in relation to the [1]duties in Schedule
D., to take the [2]prescribed oath, which may be administered by a General or Special Commissioner;
and [3]every person acting as Additional Commissioner
in relation to the duties in Schedule D. before he has
taken the oath, is liable to a penalty of 100*l.*

Clerks to Commissioners.—[4]The General Commissioners in each district, at their first meeting in every
year, which must be held before the 10th April, elect
a fit person to be their Clerk; and the person who is
elected Clerk becomes by virtue of such election sole
Clerk to the Commissioners for the year, and is not
removeable except for just cause, and at a meeting of
the Commissioners for that purpose duly summoned
by notice in writing, signed by the Commissioners,
and served on each of the Commissioners who have
qualified in, and for, the district, by the major part of
the Commissioners present. The Clerk is not to take
or receive any fees, gratuities, or perquisites, for anything done by him in his official character, except
from the person appointed by the Board to pay him
the allowances he is entitled to, which are set out in
the first schedule to the [5]Taxes Management Act,

[1] As to these duties, see *post*, pp. 102 *et seq.*
[2] The form of the oath is given in Schedule F. of 5 & 6
Vict. c. 35.
[3] 5 & 6 Vict. c. 35, s. 38.
[4] 5 & 6 Vict. c. 35, s. 9; 43 & 44 Vict. c. 19, s. 41.
[5] 43 & 44 Vict. c. 19.

1880. Any vacancy occurring in the course of the Chap. I. year by the death, dismissal, or resignation of any Clerk is filled up by the General Commissioners electing a person to be Clerk for the remainder of the year. Any Clerk or Clerk's assistant wilfully obstructing, or delaying, the execution of the Income Tax Acts, or negligently conducting, or wilfully misconducting, himself in the exercise of his office, renders himself liable to a penalty of 100*l.*, and dismissal from his office, and becomes incapable of again acting as Clerk or Clerk's assistant. [1] The Clerk to the General Commissioners for any district, or his assistant, acts also as Clerk to the Additional Commissioners for the same district. [2] Every person acting as Clerk, or Clerk's assistant, in relation to the [3] duties in Schedule D. is required to take the [4] prescribed oath, which may be administered by a General, or Special, or Additional Commissioner; and [2] any person acting as Clerk or Clerk's assistant in relation to the duties in Schedule D. before he has taken the oath is liable to a penalty of 100*l.*

Surveyors.—[5] The surveyors are officers appointed

[1] 5 & 6 Vict. c. 35, s. 19.
[2] 5 & 6 Vict. c. 35, s. 38.
[3] As to these duties, see *post*, pp. 102 *et seq.*
[4] The form of the oath is given in Schedule F. of 5 & 6 Vict. c. 35.
[5] 5 & 6 Vict. c. 35, s. 37 ; 43 & 44 Vict. c. 19, s. 17. The Inspectors, of whom frequent mention is made in the Acts relating to income tax, are chosen from the ranks of Sur-

from time to time by the Treasury for the survey and inspection of the duties of income tax. The Treasury appoint their allowances and salaries. [1]Every Surveyor is required, before he begins to act in relation to the [2]duties in Schedule D., to take the [3]prescribed oath, which any General, or Special, or Additional Commissioner may administer; and, if he acts in relation to the duties in Schedule D. before he has taken the oath, he is liable to a penalty of 100*l.* A Surveyor who [4]wilfully makes a false and vexatious charge of duty, or wilfully delivers or causes to be delivered to the General Commissioners a false and vexatious [5]certificate of charge of duty, or a false and vexatious [6]certificate of objection to any supplementary return, or is guilty of any fraudulent, corrupt, or illegal practices in the execution of his office, or knowingly or wilfully, through favour, undercharges or omits to charge, any person, incurs a penalty of 100*l.* for every such offence, and on conviction will be discharged from his office.

Assessors —appoint- *Assessors.*—The Assessors are appointed either by veyors of experience. As regards the public, their duties seem to be similar to those of Surveyors.

[1] 5 & 6 Vict. c. 35, s. 38.

[2] As to these duties, see *post*, pp. 102 *et seq.*

[3] The form of the oath is given in Schedule F. of 5 & 6 Vict. c. 35.

[4] 43 & 44 Vict. c. 19, s. 18.

[5] As to the certificate of charge, see *post*, p. 193.

[6] As to the certificate of objection to a supplementary return, see *post*, p. 194.

the General Commissioners, or, in certain cases, by Chap. I.
other persons. The mode of appointment by the ment by
General Commissioners is as follows :—[1] The General Commis-
Commissioners for the district, before the 10th April sioners.
in every year, direct their precept to such inhabitants
of each [2] parish within their district, and to such number of such inhabitants as they think most convenient,
to be Assessors for such parish, requiring the persons
to whom such precept is addressed to appear before
the General Commissioners of the district at such
place, and such time, not exceeding ten days after the
date of the precept, as the Commissioners appoint.
[3] Any person to whom such precept is addressed wilfully neglecting, or refusing, to appear before the
General Commissioners according to the tenour of the
precept, or appearing, but refusing to submit to be
appointed Assessor, incurs a penalty of 10l. When

[1] 43 & 44 Vict. c. 19, s. 42.
[2] By the Revenue Act, 1884 (47 & 48 Vict. c. 62), s. 6, the
parish for purposes of income tax is made coterminous with
the parish for purposes of poor law administration. And if,
in the opinion of the Board, any parish is so large that it
ought to be divided into districts, with separate Assessors
and Collectors, this may be done by the Board with the
sanction of the Treasury; and the Board may again, with
the like sanction, alter, or annul, such division. After any
such division, and whilst it continues, each district of the
divided parish is treated as a parish in itself for purposes of
income tax. The above-mentioned section is amended by
53 & 54 Vict. c. 8, s. 27, with regard to the Inner Temple,
Middle Temple, and Gray's Inn, and the parish of Lambeth.
[3] 43 & 44 Vict. c. 19, s. 46.

c 2

Chap. I. the inhabitants who have been summoned appear before the General Commissioners, the latter appoint such of them as they think proper to be Assessors for the parish, and give them instructions how they are to make their [1] certificates and assessments. [2] Any person appointed an Assessor by the General Commissioners who wilfully neglects, or refuses, to perform his duty as Assessor, or to charge and assess himself and all other persons chargeable, or to make his assessment according to law, incurs a penalty of 20*l.* [3] The appointment is for the year commencing on the 6th April in each year, and continues until other Assessors are appointed for the same parish. Where an Assessor is continued in office beyond the year for which he is appointed, notice thereof is given him by the General Commissioners, or by the Surveyor; and by such notice the Assessor may be required to attend on a day, and at a place, named in the notice, then and there to receive, and take charge of, all notices and papers to be delivered to him for the due execution of his office. In a parish where two able and sufficient inhabitants cannot be found, the General Commissioners for the district in which the parish is situate nominate and appoint fit persons, residing near such parish, to be Assessors for the parish. If a failure happens in the appointment of an Assessor

Period for which appointment made.

---

[1] As to certificates and assessments of Assessors, see *post*, Chap. III.

[2] 43 & 44 Vict. c. 19, s. 46.

[3] 43 & 44 Vict. c. 19, s. 42.

for any parish, whereby the assessment of the duties **Chap. I.** of income tax is likely to be delayed, the magistrates or justices of the peace having jurisdiction in or over such parish, or any two of them, on notice of such default given them by the Surveyor, appoint an Assessor, observing the rules and regulations prescribed for the appointment of Assessors by General Commissioners. [1]Any person appointed an Assessor **Penalty** by the magistrates or justices who wilfully neglects, or **cling** refuses, to take upon himself the office, or to perform **office.** his duty as Assessor, or to charge and assess himself and all other persons chargeable, or to make his assessment according to law, incurs a penalty of 50*l.* [2]In **Where in any parish** any parish where Assessors are not duly appointed, or **Assessors** being appointed do not take upon themselves the office **duly appointed, pointed,** within the time limited, or where the Assessors for any **or do not** former year upon whom the duty of Assessors devolves **office.** do not take upon themselves the office of Assessors at or before the time limited, the Surveyor of the district in which the parish is situate may execute the duty of Assessor of such parish until Assessors are appointed and take upon themselves the office. In the Metro- **Appointment of** polis, as defined by the [3]Valuation (Metropolis) Act, **Assessors**

[1] 43 & 44 Vict. c. 19, s. 46.
[2] 43 & 44 Vict. c. 19, s. 43.
[3] 32 & 33 Vict. c. 67. The term "Metropolis," as used in this Act, means (sects. 3 and 4) unions, and parishes not in union, which are for the time being either wholly, or for the greater part in value thereof, respectively situate within the jurisdiction of the Metropolitan Board of Works, appointed under the Metropolitan Management Act, 1855 (18 & 19

1869, the General Commissioners do not appoint Assessors, but the Surveyors acting therein are the Vict. c. 120). The jurisdiction of the Metropolitan Board of Works, which has now ceased to exist, having been abolished by the Local Government Act, 1888 (51 & 52 Vict. c. 41), extended over the Metropolis, as defined by sect. 250 of the last-mentioned Act; that is to say, the City of London and the following parishes and places:—

St. Marylebone.
St. Pancras.
Lambeth.
St. George, Hanover-square.
St. Mary, Islington.
St. Leonard, Shoreditch.
Paddington.
St. Matthew, Bethnal Green.
St. Mary, Newington, Surrey.
Camberwell.
St. James, Westminster.
St. James, } Clerkenwell.
St. John, }
Chelsea.
St. Mary Abbott, Kensington.
St. Luke, Middlesex.
St. George-the-Martyr, South-wark.
Bermondsey.
St. George-in-the-East.
St. Martin-in-the-Fields.
Mile End Old Town, Hamlet of.
Woolwich.
Rotherhithe.
St. John, Hampstead.
St. Mary, Whitechapel.
Christchurch, Spitalfields.
St. Botolph Without, Aldgate, Middlesex.
Holy Trinity, Minories.
St. Katherine, Precinct of.
Mile End New Town, Hamlet of.
Norton Folgate, Liberty of.
Old Artillery Ground.
Tower, District of.
St. Margaret, } Westminster.
St. John, }
St. Paul, Deptford (including Hatcham).

St. Nicholas, Deptford.
Greenwich.
Clapham.
Tooting Graveney.
Streatham.
*St. Mary, Battersea (excluding Penge).
Wandsworth.
Putney (including Roehampton).
Hackney.
St. Mary, Stoke Newington.
St. Giles-in-the-Fields.
St. George's, Bloomsbury.
St. Andrew, Holborn-above-Bars.
St. George-the-Martyr.
St. Sepulchre, Middlesex.
Saffron Hill, Hatton Garden, Ely-rents and Ely-place.
Glasshouse Yard, The Liberty of.
St. Anne, Soho.
St. Paul, Covent Garden.
St. John the Baptist.
Savoy, or Precinct of the Savoy.
St. Mary-le-Strand.
St. Clement Danes.
Liberty of the Rolls.
St. Peter and St. Paul, Hammersmith.
Fulham.
St. Anne, Limehouse.
St. John, Wapping.
St. Paul, Shadwell.
Ratcliff, Hamlet of.
All Saints', Poplar.
St. Mary, Stratford-le-Bow.
St. Leonard, Bromley.

Assessors, for the [1] duties of income tax under Sche- Chap. I.
dules A. and B., upon any property in the Metropolis.
[2] No person inhabiting any city, borough, or town No incorporate, can be compelled to be an Assessor for a of any
place outside the limits of such city, borough, or town. can be
[3] Every person appointed an Assessor is required on to be
his appointment, and before he acts, to make the pre- for a place
scribed declaration; and, [4] if he neglects, or refuses outside.
to do so, he incurs, if the neglect or refusal follows tion to be
upon a precept addressed to him by the General Com- Assessors.
missioners, a penalty of 10*l.*; if it occurs after appointment by the General Commissioners, a penalty of 20*l.*;
and if after appointment by the magistrates or justices, a penalty of 50*l.* [5] The remuneration of Asses- Remuner-
sors is prescribed in the first schedule to the [6] Taxes Assessors.
Management Act, 1880. The foregoing are the

Christchurch.	St. Thomas, Southwark.
St. Saviour's (including the Liberty of the Clink).	St. John, Horselydown.
Charlton-next-Woolwich.	The Close of the Collegiate Church of St. Peter.
Plumstead.	The Charterhouse.
Eltham.	Inner Temple.
Lee.	Middle Temple.
Kidbrooke.	Lincoln's Inn.
Lewisham (including Sydenham Chapelry).	Gray's Inn.
*Penge, Hamlet of.	Staple Inn.
St. Olave.	Furnival's Inn.

[1] As to these duties, see *post*, pp. 44, 45, 90, 91.

[2] 43 & 44 Vict. c. 19, s. 44.

[3] 43 & 44 Vict. c. 19, s. 45. The declaration is given in the section referred to.

[4] 43 & 44 Vict. c. 19, s. 46.

[5] 43 & 44 Vict. c. 19, s. 47. But see also 48 & 49 Vict. c. 51, s. 25.

[6] 43 & 44 Vict. c. 19.

Chap. I. general provisions relating to the appointment of

Special provisions for exercise of duties of Assessors may be made by the Income Tax Act for the year. Assessors, but special provision for the exercise of the duties of Assessor is sometimes made in the Act granting the duties of income tax for the year.

Collectors.—Collectors are appointed by the Land Tax, and General, Commissioners for each [1] parish or group of parishes. ([2] A group of parishes is formed by the Land Tax Commissioners for the district in which the group is situate, with the consent of the Board, for purposes of collection; and, when the group is formed, it is regarded as one parish for the purposes of collection, but for such purposes only. Where parishes have been grouped, and the grouping proves inconvenient, the Land Tax Commissioners may, with the consent of the Board, dissolve the grouping, either as regards all, or some, or one, of the

Appointment of Collectors. parishes so grouped.) The mode of appointment of Collectors by the Land Tax and General Commissioners is as follows. [3] The Land Tax Commissioners and the General Commissioners for a district, in the

Nomination. month of April in each year, nominate one or more

[1] As to the income tax parish being coterminous with the poor law parish, and as to the powers of dividing parishes into districts, with separate Assessors and Collectors, see p. 27, note [2], ante.

[2] 43 & 44 Vict. c. 19, s. 72. The powers of "grouping" given to the Board must now be exercised consistently with the provisions of s. 6 of the Revenue Act, 1884 (47 & 48 Vict. c. 62).

[3] 43 & 44 Vict. c. 19, s. 73.

able and sufficient person or persons, resident within **Chap. I.**
each parish, or group of parishes, within the district,
to the office of Collector of Taxes for such parish, or
group of parishes. The fact of the nomination of a
person to be Collector must be notified to him, personally, or by a registered letter sent through the
general post. Acceptance of the office is not com- *Accept-*
pulsory, but, if the person appointed is unwilling to *office not*
take the office upon himself, he must within fourteen *pulsory.*
days after the notification to him of his nomination, *Notice must be*
either personally or by registered letter addressed to *given if office de-*
the Clerk to the Commissioners, signify his refusal to *clined.*
accept the office. If he does not give such notice,
and fails, when required by the Commissioners, to
attend a meeting for the purpose of receiving his
appointment and warrant as a Collector, he incurs a *Collector's warrant.*
penalty of 20*l.* On the expiration of the time
limited for declining the office, viz., fourteen days
from the date of the notification to the person nominated of his nomination as Collector, the Commissioners proceed to appoint such person or persons as *Appoint-ment.*
they think fit, who has, or have, been nominated,
and not declined the appointment, to be Collector or
Collectors for the parish, or group of parishes, for
which he or they have been nominated. The fact of *Notifica-tion of*
the appointment of a person to be Collector must be *appoint-ment.*
notified to him, personally, or by registered letter
sent through the general post. In any case in which *Where a person*
a person nominated as Collector for any parish, or *nominated*
group of parishes, declines office, the Commissioners *declines office.*

c 5

may nominate some other able and sufficient person to the office. In the event of there being no able and sufficient person within any parish, or group of parishes, the Commissioners may nominate an able and sufficient person resident in a neighbouring parish, or group of parishes.

If the Collector for any parish has not been appointed by the 31st May in any year, the power of appointing a Collector for such parish for that and every subsequent year vests in the Board, and the Board must appoint a Collector accordingly.

If Collector for any parish has not been appointed by 31st May in any year.

In the event of the death of a Collector for any parish, or group of parishes, in the course of any year, or before his accounts for such year have been closed, the Board, or the Land Tax, and General, Commissioners, as the case may be, by whom such Collector was appointed, may appoint to the vacant office such person or persons willing to act, as they may think fit.

If a Collector dies in the course of the year.

If a vacancy occurring by the death of a Collector is not filled within forty days from the date of death by the Land Tax, and General, Commissioners, where the appointment has to be made by them, the power of filling such vacancy for such year vests in the Board.

If vacancy occurring by death not filled within forty days.

[1] The Board may, whenever they think fit, give notice to the Land Tax, and General, Commissioners that they require all, or any, of the persons nominated or appointed Collectors for any parish, or group of parishes, or division, specified in the notice to give security to

The Board may require security to be given by Collectors.

[1] 43 & 44 Vict. c. 19, s. 74.

the satisfaction of the Board for the due collecting, accounting for, and paying over, of the moneys collected, or to be collected, by such persons respectively, and for the due performance of their duties as Collectors; and the Board may also cause the like notice to be given to any person who has been appointed Collector. After such notice given by the Board to the Commissioners, they may not appoint any person to be Collector for any parish, group, or division, specified in the notice, unless he has previously given security to the satisfaction of the Board; and in case any person who has been appointed Collector, and to whom such notice is given by the Board fails to give security within the time limited by the notice for that purpose, his nomination, and appointment, and authority, as Collector, ceases at the end of that time. [1] If after such notice given by the Board there is neglect, or delay, in the appointment of Collectors, who previously have given security to the Crown, or a failure on the part of a person nominated, or appointed, Collector to give such security, the Board may appoint a Collector, or Collectors, for the parish or group of parishes, or division, in which such neglect, delay, or failure has occurred. The appointment by the Board of a Collector is made by warrant under their hands; and a person appointed Collector by the Board has like power and authority as a person appointed Collector by the Commissioners.

If after such notice there is neglect or delay in the appointment of Collectors.

Appointment of Collector by the Board— how made.

---

[1] 43 & 44 Vict. c. 19, s. 76.

Chap. I.

Security required by the Board— how given. Land Tax and General Commissioners may require security to be given by Collectors, and any two or more inhabitants of any parish.

The security given on the requirement of the Board is by bond to the Crown, entered into by the Collector with sureties to be approved by the Board, or as the Board determine, and in such sum as the Board require. [1]The Land Tax, and General, Commissioners may also require Collectors on their appointment to give security to their satisfaction; and any two or more inhabitants of a parish, or group, being respectively charged to the land tax, or income tax, in the assessment for the current year, may, by notice in writing to the respective Commissioners, served personally on, or by registered letter addressed to the Clerk to, the Commissioners, require, that the person whom the Commissioners propose to appoint Collector for the parish, or group, shall give security to the satisfaction of the Commissioners; and after receipt of such notice the Commissioners may not appoint a person who has not given such security.

Security given to Commissioners— how to be given.

The security to be given to the Commissioners may be by a joint and several bond, with two sureties at the least, to, and in the names of, any two or more Commissioners; and the penal sum in any such bond, must, if so required, be equal to the whole land tax, and moneys, assessed in the parish, or group of parishes, and to be collected by the person whom it is proposed to appoint Collector for such parish or group of parishes, and from whom security is required. [2]No bond or security given by a Collector

Bond given by

[1] 43 & 44 Vict. c. 19, s. 77.
[2] 43 & 44 Vict. c. 19, s. 78.

in respect of the collection, accounting for, or re- Chap. I.

mitting, of the land tax, or income tax, duties is Collector not liable

liable to stamp duty. [1]No parish is answerable for to stamp duty.

the acts, neglects, or defaults, of a Collector appointed No parish

by the Board, or who gives security to the Crown; answer-able for

nor is a parish liable to be re-assessed for an arrear, defaults of Collector

or deficiency, of the land tax, or income tax, arising appointed by the

from any default or failure of such Collector; but Board or having

where the Collector of a parish is not appointed by given security,

the Board, or does not give security to the Crown, but other-

the parish is answerable for the amount of the land wise is answer-

tax, and income tax, and for the same being duly able.

demanded of the persons charged therewith, and for

the Collector, or his executors, or administrators, duly

paying over the sums received by him to the Collector

of Inland Revenue. [2]Every Collector before he Oath to be taken by

begins to act in relation to [3]the duties in Schedule D. Collector.

must take the [4]prescribed oath, which may be ad-

ministered by a General, or Special, or Additional

Commissioner; and every Collector acting in relation

to the duties in Schedule D. before he has taken the

oath incurs a penalty of 100*l.* There are [5]other

penalties which Collectors incur by various breaches

of rule. [6]The remuneration of the Collectors is fixed Remune-ration of Collectors.

[1] 43 & 44 Vict. c. 19, s. 79.

[2] 5 & 6 Vict. c. 35, s. 38.

[3] As to these duties, see *post*, pp. 102 *et seq.*

[4] The form of the oath is given in Schedule F. of 5 & 6
Vict. c. 35.   [5] See 43 & 44 Vict. c. 19, s. 121.

[6] 43 & 44 Vict. c. 19, s. 80. But see also 48 & 49 Vict.
c. 51, s. 25.

Chap. I. by the first Schedule of the [1] Taxes Management Act, 1880.

Commissioners and other officers only liable to penalties inflicted by Income Tax Acts.

Actions against Commissioners and Officers.—We may mention here the following provisions. In the first place, [2] no Commissioner, Clerk, Surveyor, Assessor, or Collector, acting in the execution of the Acts relating to duties of income tax, is liable for any act done in execution thereof to any penalty other than such as is inflicted by those Acts respectively. In the second place, [3] actions or suits brought against a Commissioner, Surveyor, Collector, Assessor, or other person, for anything done in pursuance of the Acts relating to duties of income tax are subject to the following limitations; viz. :—

Limitation of right to sue Commissioners and other officers.

(1) Action must be commenced within six months.

(1) The action or suit must be commenced within six [4] months after the act committed, and

(2) Must be laid where cause of complaint arose.

(2) Must be laid in the county or place where the cause of complaint arose.

(3) Must not be commenced within one month after notice in writing.

(3) No writ, or process, can be sued out for the commencement of any such action or suit until the expiration of one month after notice in writing specifying (a) the cause of action, (b) the name and place of abode of the intended plaintiff, and of his attorney or agent, if any, has been delivered to, or left at the usual place of abode of, the intended

[1] 43 & 44 Vict. c. 19.
[2] 43 & 44 Vict. c. 19, s. 19.
[3] 43 & 44 Vict. c. 19, s. 20.
[4] Calendar months. 13 & 14 Vict. c. 21, s. 4.

defendant by the attorney or agent of the Chap. I.
intended plaintiff.

On the trial of any such action or suit no evidence On trial
evidence
may be given of any cause of action other than such confined
to cause
as is contained in the notice. The intended defen- of action
mentioned
dant to whom any such notice has been delivered in notice.
may at any time before the expiration of a month Defendant
may tender
after the notice has been delivered to him, or left at amends,
his usual place of abode, tender amends to the intended plaintiff, or his attorney or agent; and, if the and plead
tender if
amends tendered are not accepted, may plead the not accepted.
tender in bar to any action or suit brought against
him founded upon such notice. Every action or suit Actions
brought
brought against any Collector must be defended by against
Collectors
the respective Land Tax Commissioners, or General appointed
by Gene-
Commissioners, for the parish, when the Collector has ral, or
Land Tax,
been appointed by them, or has acted under their Commissioners
warrant, or directions; and the costs and charges must be
defended
attending any such action or suit, or any action or by them.
suit brought by, or against, the Commissioners, or any
Collector appointed by them, for any act done in pursuance of the Acts relating to duties of income tax,
are defrayed by an assessment made in a just proportion on the several persons, lands, tenements, and
hereditaments liable to be assessed in the parish in,
or relating to, which the alleged cause of action has
arisen, or for which such Collector has been appointed.
[1] All penalties exceeding 20l. imposed by virtue of the Recovery
of penal-

---

[1] 43 & 44 Vict. c. 19, s. 21.

Chap. I.

ties exceeding 20*l.* imposed by Income Tax Acts by action.

Recovery of penalties directed to be added to assessments, and penalties not exceeding 20*l.*

Acts relating to duties of income tax, excepting[1] such as are directed to be added to the assessments, are recoverable in the High Court, with full costs of suit, and are sued for (except in Scotland and Ireland) by information in the name of the Attorney-General for England, and, in default of prosecution within twelve months of the penalty being incurred, no penalty is afterwards recoverable in any other manner. Subject to the above restriction as to time, all pecuniary penalties not exceeding 20*l.*, and also such of the penalties exceeding 20*l.* as are directed to be added to the assessments, are recoverable before the Land Tax Commissioners, and General Commissioners, respectively, who must take cognizance of the offence in respect of which a penalty may be imposed by them upon information in writing made to them, and upon a summons to the party assessed to appear before them at such time and place as they fix. The Commissioners examine into the matter of fact, and [2]hear,

[1] Sect. 185 of 5 & 6 Vict. c. 35, enacts as follows:—
"Wherever by this Act any increased rate of duty is imposed as a penalty, or as part of, or in addition to, any penalty, every such penalty and all such increased rate of duty may be added to the assessment, and be collected and levied in like manner as any duties included in such assessments may be collected and levied."

[2] The provisions of the Taxes Management Act, 1880 (43 & 44 Vict. c. 19), s. 57, that no barrister, solicitor, or person practising the law, shall be allowed to plead before the General Commissioners on an appeal (see *post*, pp. 275, 276), does not apply to proceedings for penalties under the Acts relating to income tax before the General Commissioners. Bourdin's Land Tax, 3rd ed. by Bunbury, p. 41, note (*f*).

and determine, the same in a summary way; and on Chap. I.
proof made thereof, either by voluntary confession of
the party assessed, or by the oath, or solemn affirmation, of one or more credible witness or witnesses, or
otherwise as the case may require, give judgment for
the penalty, or for such part thereof as they think
proper to mitigate the same to, and assess the penalty
on the party by way of supplementary assessment.
The penalty so assessed is levied in like [1]manner as
the duties. The adjudication of the Commissioners
is final and conclusive, and there is no appeal from
it. The Board, however, may at their discretion
mitigate, or stay, or compound, proceedings for any
penalty recoverable in the High Court; and may
reward any informer who may assist in the recovery
of any such penalty. [2]All constables, and other
peace officers, are required to aid in the execution
of the Acts relating to duties of income tax, and
to obey and execute such precepts, and warrants, as
are directed to them in that behalf by the respective
Commissioners. [3]If any person wilfully obstructs a Penalty
Surveyor, Assessor, or Collector in the execution of structing
his office, he incurs a penalty of 50*l*.   a Sur-
                                                        veyor, &c.

Exemption from Stamp Duty.—[4]Receipts, certificates of payment, affidavits, appraisements, and

[1] As to the manner of levying the duties, see *post*,
Chap. III.
[2] 43 & 44 Vict. c. 19, s. 22.
[3] 43 & 44 Vict. c. 19, s. 23.
[4] 5 & 6 Vict. c. 35, s. 179.

Chap. I. valuations, made, or given, in pursuance of, and for
the purposes of the Income Tax Act, 1842 (5 & 6 Vict.
c. 35), are exempt from stamp duty, as are also [1]all
affidavits and declarations made upon a requisition of
the Commissioners of any public Board of Revenue,
or of any of the officers acting under any such Board,
and all affidavits, and declarations, required by law,
and made before any justice of the peace, and all
receipts given for, or upon the payment of, any parliamentary taxes or duties.

[1] 33 & 34 Vict. c. 97, Sched. 1.

CHAPTER II.

WHAT IS SUBJECT TO INCOME TAX—THE SCHEDULES.

Upon what the Duty is charged.—Speaking generally, we may say, that [1] everything in the nature of
property, which produces, or is capable of producing,
or itself consists in, an annual income or revenue, is
the subject of the taxation we are considering, if
either the property is situate, or the income enjoyed,
in the United Kingdom. The titles of the [2] Income
Tax Acts, 1842 and 1853, as well as of the various
Acts which have from time to time continued, and
modified, their provisions, speak of duties on *profits,*
arising from property, professions, trades, and offices.
It is not, however, as we shall see, in all cases necessary that a profit shall actually be made out of property in order that its owner may become liable to
the duty.

[1] In the case of *Attorney-General* v. *Black* (*post*, pp. 120, 121),
Martin, B., speaking of the five schedules, and of sect. 100
of the Income Tax Act, 1842, as a net large enough to include
every description of property, said, "In fact, the care dis-
played in embracing every possible source of profit is, I may
say, carried to an almost ludicrous extent; it is practically
impossible to escape the operation of the Act."
[2] 5 & 6 Vict. c. 35, and 16 & 17 Vict. c. 34.

The Schedules.—For purposes of classification and distinction, and of applying the provisions of the various Acts relating to the income tax, the several kinds of property, in respect of which the duty is granted, are arranged in "schedules;" each schedule being marked by one of the five letters of the alphabet, A., B., C., D., and E., and each containing a description of one kind, or class, of property. Rules are given for ascertaining, charging, and levying, the duties with reference to each kind, or class, of property; but, [1]so far as they are applicable, and not inconsistent with special provisions, they are applicable to the duties in all the schedules.

Section I. Schedule A.

Property in Land, &c.—[2]Under Schedule A. the duty is charged "for and in respect of the property in all lands, tenements, hereditaments, and heritages in the United Kingdom, for every [3]twenty shillings of the annual value thereof." The word "property," we may remark, is used in two senses in the [4]Income Tax Acts, of 1842 and 1853. Sometimes it is used as it is colloquially, and as we have used it above; for instance, after enumerating the subjects of the duties,

---

[1] 5 & 6 Vict. c. 35, s. 188.

[2] 16 & 17 Vict. c. 34, s. 2.

[3] Fractional parts of 20*s.* are also charged with duty by sect. 3 of the Act, 16 & 17 Vict. c. 34; but no duty is to be charged of a lower denomination than 1*d.*

[4] 5 & 6 Vict. c. 35, and 16 and 17 Vict. c. 34.

the Act of 1853 goes on to say, that they are granted " in respect of the annual profits or gains arising from any kind of *property* whatever ; " but in Schedule A. the word is used to designate the interest in land of the *owner*, as distinguished from that of the *occupier*. The duty charged under Schedule A. is, therefore, a duty which is imposed upon, and has ultimately to be paid by, the owner, and not the occupier, of land. We say " ultimately " because, as will be seen [1] by-and-bye, it is generally paid in the first instance by the occupier, who deducts what he has so paid from the rent he pays to his landlord. A very common name for this duty is " Landlord's Property Tax."

The generality of the words used in describing the extent of the application of the general rule by which the annual value of property chargeable under Schedule A. is determined (see *post*, p. 49, " *Extent of application,* &c.") is not sufficient to destroy the prerogative of the Crown which exempts from taxation property occupied for it. A Scotch case, *Clerk v. Commissioners of Supply for Dumfries* (17 Sco. L. R. 774), had decided that police stations, acquired for the purpose of local government, owned and occupied by the county authorities, were chargeable with income tax. But in *Coomber* v. *Justices of Berks* (L. R. 9 App. 34; 53 L. J. Q. B.

Cases of Coomber v. Justices of Berks : Clerk v. Commissioners of Supply for Dumfries.

---

[1] See *post*, pp. 181, 182, 197, 198.

239; 50 L. T. 405; 32 W. R. 525), the House of Lords decided that buildings containing Assize Courts, the necessary rooms and offices, and a police station, erected by the justices of a county acting under statutory powers, the buildings in question being erected out of the county rate, and used for purposes of police, that is, for the discharge of functions which of common right belong to the Crown, were exempted from income tax by virtue of the prerogative of property occupied by the Crown. The case of *Clerk* v. *Commissioners of Supply for Dumfries*, was cited, and disapproved of. It is to be observed that the special case which came before the House of Lords showed that as a matter of fact no profit whatever had been made out of the buildings: whether a surplus revenue could be, or ought to have been, raised by letting the Assize Courts and rooms in the buildings when not in use, was a question of fact not raised by the case, which the House of Lords, having only to decide questions of law raised by the case, expressly abstained from considering.

Case of
Adam v.
Maughan

In the Scotch case of *Adam* v. *Maughan* (27 Sco. L. R. 64) it was held that a Burgh Court, being a Court for the administration of public justice, the building or rooms in the municipal buildings which were occupied for the administration of justice in that Court were part of the Queen's establishment for the administration of justice, and were not taxable. But it was held that neither municipal offices nor corporation baths could be exempted on the ground that they yielded no profit, and could be used only for public purposes.

But in the case of a county lunatic asylum, established under 16 & 17 Vict. c. 97, and provided for the reception and relief of pauper lunatics, where the medical superintendent, medical officers, and steward, occupied apartments situate in the asylum building, and the chaplain a house within the asylum grounds; each of these officers being assessed to income tax in amounts exceeding 150*l.* per annum; the medical superintendent, medical officers, and steward, being bound to be resident in the asylum, and liable at any time to be transferred from one set of rooms to another; neither the apartments, nor the house, being rated or charged in the poor rate assessment in accordance with sect. 35 of 16 & 17 Vict. c. 97; it was held that the apartments and the house were not in the occupation of the Crown, or of persons using them exclusively in and for the service of the Crown, and that they were taxable. In this case the county justices had been assessed in respect of the apartments and the house. A question was raised whether the justices were the proper persons to be assessed, but this question, which Bowen, L. J., charac-

Case of Bray v. Justices of Lancashire.

terised as ridiculously technical, not having been raised before the Commissioners, the Court held that it had no power to entertain it. (*Bray* v. *Justices of Lancashire*, 22 Q. B. D. 484; 37 W. R. 392; 58 L. J. M. C. 54.)

Annual Value under Schedule A.—It will have been observed, that the duty under Schedule A. is charged "for every twenty shillings of the *annual value.*" Rules are given for ascertaining the annual value of the lands, tenements, hereditaments, and heritages mentioned in Schedule A.

General Rule for ascertaining Annual Value under Schedule A.—First of all, we have a general rule which meets the common case of lands, &c. in the occupation of the owner, or of some one to whom he has let them. We have said already, that the duty under Schedule A. is payable in the first instance by the occupier, whether he be owner or tenant, and this general rule, therefore, meets all cases in which the lands, &c. are "in the occupation of the party to be charged," except those [1] presently enumerated, for which special rules are given. The general rule is as follows:—[2] "The annual value of lands, tenements, hereditaments, or heritages, charged under Schedule A. shall be understood to be the rent by the year at which the same are let at rack-rent, if the amount of

[1] See *post*, pp. 51 *et seq.*
[2] 5 & 6 Vict. c. 35, s. 60, No. 1.

such rent shall have been fixed by agreement commencing within the period of seven years preceding
the fifth day of April next before the time of making
the assessment: but if the same are not so let at rack-
rent, then the rack-rent at which the same are worth
to be let by the year."

Extent of Application of the foregoing General Rule.
—The foregoing general rule extends to [1] " all lands,
tenements, and hereditaments or heritages, capable of
actual occupation, of whatever nature, and for whatever purpose occupied or enjoyed, and of whatever
value," except those [2] presently enumerated. But it
is in some degree qualified by the following provisions:—

1.[3] If an owner of land, &c., whether he is also Case of
the occupier or not, pays rates and taxes, which are tenant's rates and
by law a charge upon the occupier, or any composi- taxes paid by land-
tion for tithes, the annual value is to be estimated lord.
exclusively of the amount of such rates and taxes, or
composition.

2.[4] But if a tenant pays rates and taxes which are Case of landlord's
by law a charge upon the owner, then the annual rates and
value is to be the rent, either actually paid or that taxes paid by tenant.
might be obtained, as the case may be, *plus* the
amount of such rates and taxes.

[1] 5 & 6 Vict. c. 35, s. 60, No. 1.
[2] See *post*, pp. 51 *et seq.*
[3] 5 & 6 Vict. c. 35, s. 63, No. 10, r. 1.
[4] *Ibid.*, No. 10, r. 2.

E.   D

Chap. II.

Case of rent depending on price of corn, &c.

3.[1] If the rent reserved depends in whole or in part upon the price of corn or grain, the estimate shall, if possible, be made on the amount payable according to the average prices fixed in the year preceding the year appointed for the payment of the duty, and in the manner by which such rent has usually been ascertained between landlord and tenant.

Case of rent reserved in corn, &c.

4.[1] If the whole, or a part, of the rent is reserved in corn or grain, the estimate shall, if possible, be made on the average price computed on the quantity of corn or grain to be delivered in the year appointed for payment of the duty. Where such computation cannot be made, the estimate may be made on the annual value ascertained according to the General Rule.

Case of rent depending on actual produce.

5.[2] If the amount of rent depends on the actual produce, either in respect of the price, or the quantity, thereof, the estimate shall be made on the amount, or value, of such produce in the year preceding the year appointed for payment of the duty, according to the price fixed, and the quantity produced, for that year, and in the manner by which such rent has usually been ascertained between landlord and tenant. If the price, or the quantity, of produce varies in the two years, the assessment may be rectified upon [3] appeal or surcharge.

---

[1] 5 & 6 Vict. c. 35, s. 63, No. 10, r. 3.

[2] *Ibid.*, No. 10, r. 4.

[3] As to appeals, see *post*, pp. 274, 275; as to surcharges, see *post*, p. 192.

Exceptions to the foregoing Rule.—The six cases of exceptions to the foregoing general rule which follow agree in this particular, that the profits charged arise from lands, &c., which are not "in the occupation of the party to be charged." They are governed by the six special rules which follow :—

1.[1] Tithes taken in kind.—The annual value is the average amount for one year of the profits received within the three preceding years. First case of exception: Tithes in kind.

2.[2] Ecclesiastical dues : that is, "all dues and money payments in right of the Church, or by endowment, or in lieu of tithes (not being tithes arising from lands)." The annual value is estimated by the same rule as is employed in the case of tithes taken in kind. Second case of exception: Ecclesiastical dues.

3.[3] Compositions, rents, and money payments, in lieu of tithes, [4] other than rent-charges comprised under the Act passed for the commutation of tithes. The annual value is the amount of such composition, Third case of exception: Compositions for tithes.

---

[1] 5 & 6 Vict. c. 35, s. 60, No. 2, r. 1. But the duty upon tithes may be charged upon the occupier of the lands out of which the tithes arise. See No. 4, r. 4.

[2] *Ibid.*, No. 2, r. 2.

[3] *Ibid.*, No. 2, r. 3.

[4] "Why this exception was made from this rule we do not know, nor could the Solicitor-General or Mr. Davey enlighten us on the subject." *Stevens* v. *Bishop*, 35 W. R. 839. The "annual value" of the rent-charge is not the gross value, but the gross value less such outgoings as are necessary to realize the rent-charge, or, in other words, the "net value or profits." From the net value or profits the deductions allowed may afterwards be made. *S. C.*

Chap. II. rent, or payment, for one year preceding.[1] Where the owner pays any parochial rates or taxes charged on any such composition, rent, or money payment, the amount so paid by him is to be deducted from the annual value.

Case of *Stevens* v. *Bishop*.

An owner of tithe rent-charge is entitled to deduct from the gross rent-charge what he necessarily and properly expends, and is compelled to spend, in order to realize his tithe. No reason can be given for the distinction made between tithes in kind, tithes compounded for, and tithes commuted under the Act, 6 & 7 Will. 4, c. 71. Annual value as regards tithes means net, not gross, value. *Stevens* v. *Bishop*, 19 Q. B. 442; 35 W. R. 839; on appeal, 20 Q. B. D. 442; 36 W. R. 421; 57 L. J., Q. B. 283; 58 L. T. 669; see *post*, p. 184.

Fourth case of exception: Manors and other royalties.

4.[2] Manors and other royalties.—The annual value is the average amount for one year of the profits received within the seven preceding years. The profits referred to in this rule include all dues, and services, and other casual profits, but not rents, or other annual payments.

[1] 5 & 6 Vict. c. 35, s. 60, No. 10, r. 1. A deduction in respect of parochial rates and taxes may also be made in the case of a rent-charge comprised under the Act passed for the commutation of tithes. See *post*, p. 73.

[2] 5 & 6 Vict. c. 35, s. 60, No. 2, r. 4. Costs of collection may not be deducted. *Duke of Norfolk* v. *Lamarque*, 24 Q. B. D. 548; 38 W. R. 382; 59 L. J., Q. B. 119; 62 L. T. 153.

5.[1] Fines upon demise of lands or tenements.— **Chap. II.** The annual value is the amount received within the Fifth case year preceding. If the person chargeable proves to ception : the satisfaction of the General Commissioners of the Fines. district that such fines, or any part thereof, have been applied as productive capital, on which a profit has arisen, or will arise, otherwise chargeable to income tax for the year in which the assessment is made, the General Commissioners may discharge the amount so applied from the profits liable to assessment under this rule.

6.[2] Other profits of the same kind : that is, profits Sixth case of exception : that arise from lands, &c., not in the occupation of ception : the party to be charged, and not before enumerated. profits of The annual value is the average amount for one year same kind. of the profits received within such a number of years preceding as the Commissioners judge proper.

[3] In all cases to which the special rules above stated apply, if the possession, or interest, of the party to be charged has commenced within the time for which the average by which the annual value is to be estimated is directed to be taken, then the profits of one year are to be estimated in proportion to the profits received within the time which has elapsed since the commencement of the possession, or interest, of the party to be charged.

[1] 5 & 6 Vict. c. 35, s. 60, No. 2, r. 5.
[2] *Ibid.*, No. 2, r. 6.
[3] *Ibid.*, No. 4, r. 6.

Chap. II.   *Further Exceptions to the foregoing General Rule.—*
In the cases of the "lands, tenements, hereditaments,
or heritages," enumerated below, the foregoing general
rule is replaced by the special rules which follow,[1]
and by the [2]rules prescribed by Schedule D., which
apply so far as they are not inconsistent with these
special rules :—

First
special
rule :
Quarries.

1.[3] Quarries of stone, slate, limestone, or chalk.
The annual value is the average amount for one year
of the profits received in the preceding year.

Case of
Jones v.
*Cwmorthen
Slate Co.*

The statute is imposing a tax upon that which
is worked, not upon the mode of working it.
Works for getting slate, although carried on un-
derground, and so that they would ordinarily be
described as a mine, rather than as a quarry, are,
nevertheless, within the expression "quarries,"
as it is here used.   *Jones* v. *Cwmorthen Slate Co.*,
L. R., 5 Ex. D. 93 ; 49 L. J., Ex. 210 ; 41 L. T.
575 ; 28 W. R. 237.   As to the intention with

[1] 5 & 6 Vict. c. 35, s. 60, No. 3 ; 29 & 30 Vict. c. 36, s. 8.
The effect of this latter enactment is not to transfer cases in
Schedule A. (No. 3) to Schedule D., so as to change the respective times for which the profits are to be assessed.   But
mines, for instance, are, by this enactment to be charged
and assessed according to the rules prescribed by Schedule D.
so far as those rules are consistent with No. 3 of Schedule A.
Coltness Iron Co. v. *Black*, L. R., 6 App. 315 ; 51 L. J., Q. B.
626 ; 45 L. T. 145 ; 29 W. R. 717.   Railway Companies,
however, now pay income tax under Schedule D., *post*, p. 60,
note[1].

[2] As to these rules, see *post*, Chap. II., sect. 4.

[3] 5 & 6 Vict. c. 35, s. 60, No. 3, r. 1.

which the words "quarries" and "mines" (see Chap. II. below) are used in the Act, and the reason for the difference of treatment established between the two concerns, Brett, L. J., in this case said : "I apprehend, that the true intent of using the words 'quarries' and 'mines' is only to fix the place at which the tax is to be imposed, or, in other words, the persons upon whom the tax is to be imposed ; that is to say, those who are obtaining the profits of certain produce are to be taxed in one way, and those who are obtaining the profits of certain other produce are to be taxed in another way; and I should think myself that the reason of the difference of average is on account of the mercantile difference between the sales of the different kinds of produce. It is to be noticed that the tax is upon profits. That implies a sale, and deduction of expenses ; and the difference of average probably is to be accounted for in this way, that it is well known that the profits on those matters which are in the *first class* are tolerably uniform; whereas it is equally well known that the profits in the *second class* are exceedingly varying from year to year."

Reason for difference of treatment between "quarries" and "mines."

2.[1] Mines of coal, tin, lead, copper, mundic, iron and other mines, except [2] alum mines. The annual value is the average amount for one year of the

Second special rule: Mines (except alum mines)

[1] 5 & 6 Vict. c. 35, s. 60, No. 3, r. 2.
[2] As to alum mines, see below.

Chap. II. profits received in the five preceding years. But, [1] if any mine has decreased, or is decreasing in annual value, so that the average of five years will not give a fair estimate of its annual value, the Commissioners may take the actual amount of the profits in the preceding year to be the annual value.

Case of Jones v. Cwmorthen Slate Co. The expression "other mines" means mines *ejusdem generis* with those before mentioned. It clearly does not mean *all* other mines, because there is special mention afterwards of "alum mines." *Jones* v. *Cwmorthen Slate Co.*, L. R., 5 Ex. D. 93; 49 L. J., Ex. 210; 41 L. T. 575; 28 W. R. 237.

Case of Addie & Sons v. Solicitor of Inland Revenue. Addie and Sons, who were coal and iron masters, claimed to deduct from the sum in which they had been assessed a percentage for pit sinking, on the ground that the expenditure which such percentage would represent was part of the annual expenditure necessarily incurred in realising the profits of their trade. It was held

Pit sinking, expenditure for. that expenditure for pit sinking was an expenditure of capital, and that the deduction claimed could not be allowed. *Addie and Sons* v. *Solicitor*

Case of Coltness Iron Co. v. Black. *of Inland Revenue,* 12 Sco. L. R. 274. In *Coltness Iron Co.* v. *Black* (L. R., 6 App. 315; 51 L. J., Q. B. 626; 45 L. T. 145; 29 W. R. 717), however, Blackburn, L. J., commenting upon the foregoing case of *Addie and Sons* v. *Solicitor of*

[1] 5 & 6 Vict. c. 35, s. 60, No. 4, r. 5.

Inland Revenue, said, "I see that in *Addie and* *Sons* v. *Solicitor of Inland Revenue*, reliance is placed on the judgment of the Lord President, on the third rule as to concerns under the first case of Schedule D., that no deduction is to be made ' for any sum intended to be employed as capital.' But I do not think reliance can be placed on this. If, from the nature of the concerns in No. 3, an allowance ought to be made for capital, then this rule should be rejected as inconsistent with No. 3. If no such deduction should be made, the rule is not required." In *Coltness Iron Co.* v. *Black*, it was decided, not [1] that a mine owner will not in any case be entitled to an allowance in respect of the cost of sinking a pit, by means of which pit the minerals Pit sink-are gotten, which are the source of profit for the penditure year in which the pit is sunk—a point which was for. not involved—but that a mine owner cannot write off, and deduct, from the gross earnings of his mine in a particular year, a sum to represent that year's depreciation of all his pits wherever sunk.

The Broughton and Plas Power Coal Com- Case of *Broughton* pany were lessees of certain collieries which they & *Plas.*

---

[1] See, however, what was said by Grove, J., in the case of *Gillatt and Watts* v. *Colquhoun, post*, p. 125, note [3]. The case of *Coltness Iron Company* v. *Black* overruled the case of *Knowles* v. *M'Adam*, L. R., 3 Ex. D. 23; 47 L. J., Ex. 139; 37 L. T. 795; 26 W. R. 114.

commenced working in October, 1880. By the
agreement under which they held the collieries
the lease was to commence from the 25th March,
1874, and to continue for forty-two years. The
dead rent was to be 1,000*l.* a year for the first
three years, 2,000*l.* a year for the next seven
years, and 3,000*l.* a year for the residue of the
term, to be repayable out of royalties during the
first sixteen years, and afterwards the deficiency
in any year was to be recouped out of the excess
of any of the next five years. The dead rent
and the royalty were actually one and the same
payment, and were merged together, the dead
rent being a device to secure the lessor against
the fluctuations of mining, whereby the lessor
received, on account of his share of the profits of
the company, not less than a certain annual sum ;
so that, when the lessor's share of the royalties
did not amount to that sum, he received that
sum, but, when his share of the royalties exceeded the fixed annual sum, the fixed sum only
was paid to him until the company had been
reimbursed the excess previously paid to the
lessor when his share of the profits did not
amount to the fixed sum. For the years 1878,
1879, and 1880, 2,000*l.* each year was assessed
to the income tax, as the mine was not working.
For the year 1881-1882 the royalties amounted
to 3,477*l.* The company claimed that a sum of
1,477*l.* in the assessment for 1881-1882 should

be allowed from that assessment, on the ground Chap. II.
that it had already borne income tax when it
was previously paid to the lessor. It was held
that income tax must be paid upon the 1,477*l*.
[1] Income tax had been paid upon that sum, but
by the landlord, *not* by the tenant, the company.
The company had paid no income tax, making
no profits. When the mine began to be a profit-
able concern, the company could not deduct past
losses, and the fact that they had made a bar-
gain with a third party made no difference.
The case of the *Coltness Iron Company* v. *Black*
(*ubi sup.*) was held to be in point, and the present case was distinguished from the case of *Last*
v. *London Assurance Corporation*, [2] as it had then
been decided by the Court of Appeal (*post*,
pp. 137—142). *Broughton and Plas Power Coal
Company* v. *Kirkpatrick*, 14 Q. B. D. 491; 54
L. J., Q. B. 268; 33 W. R. 278.

3. [3]Iron works, [4]gasworks, salt springs, alum Third special rule:

[1] That income tax has been already paid upon a particular
sum is, therefore, of itself no reason why such sum should not
be charged, unless the previous payment of income tax was
made by the person whom it is sought to charge.

[2] The appeal to the House of Lords, which resulted in the
reversal of the judgment of the Court of Appeal, had not
then been carried through.

[3] 5 & 6 Vict. c. 35, s. 60, No. 3, r. 3.

[4] The gasworks intended are gasworks in England. Profits
derived from gasworks on the Continent of Europe or in
the Colonies are chargeable under Schedule D. *The Imperial
Continental Gas Association* v. *Nicholson*, 37 L. T., N. S. 717.

Chap. II.

Iron works, &c.; alum mines, water works, &c.; fishings, rights of market, &c.; railways, &c.; bridges, &c.

Deduction for wear and tear of machinery.

Case of Mersey

mines or works, waterworks, streams of water, canals, inland navigations, docks, drains, and levels, fishings, rights of markets and fairs, tolls, [1]railways and other ways, bridges, ferries and other concerns of the like nature. The annual value of these concerns is the profits of the year preceding.

In making the assessment upon any of the above-mentioned concerns chargeable by reference to the rules of Schedule D., the Commissioners [2]must allow such deduction as they may think just and reasonable, as representing the diminished value by reason of wear and tear during the year of any machinery or plant, used for the purposes of the concern, and belonging to the person or company by whom the concern is carried on ; and where machinery or plant is let to the person or company by whom the concern is carried on, upon such terms, that the person or company is bound to maintain the machinery or plant, and to deliver over the same in good condition at the end of the term of the lease, the machinery or plant is deemed to belong to such person or company.

The Mersey Docks and Harbour Board were

---

[1] The annual value, profits, or gains of any railway, are charged and assessed by the Special Commissioners. 29 & 30 Vict. c. 36, s. 8, *post*, p. 172. And by sect. 95 of the Taxes Management Act, 1880 (43 & 44 Vict. c. 19), railway companies are to pay income tax under Schedule D.

[2] 41 & 42 Vict. c. 15, s. 12. As to claims for repayment of part of the sum assessed by the lessor where the burden of maintaining machinery falls upon him, see *post*, p. 75.

constituted by Act of Parliament a corporation *Chap. II.* for the management of the Mersey Dock Estate. *Docks and Harbour* Under the Act the surplus revenue of the Board *Board v.* was to be applied in a particular manner for the *Lucas.* reduction of debt, and not otherwise. It was held that this surplus was liable to income tax. *Mersey Docks and Harbour Board* v. *Lucas*, 8 App. 891 ; 53 L. J., Q. B. 4 ; 49 L. T. 781 ; 32 W. R. 34. *See further, as to concerns of the kinds above enumerated, post*, Chap. II., sect. 4.

The Glasgow Corporation Water Commis- *Case of Glasgow* sioners were empowered by Act of Parliament *Corporation Water-* to obtain a supply of water for the city of *works.* Glasgow and its suburbs. They were authorized to acquire, and had acquired, by purchase, the works of certain previously-existing water companies. They were required by compulsory clauses in their Act to supply water within the municipal boundaries of the city of Glasgow, and outside those boundaries to the suburbs within a prescribed area. They were authorized to borrow money by annuities, mortgage, and otherwise, which was to be applied in defraying the expense of purchasing and acquiring lands and other property, and in executing the authorized works. Householders within the municipal boundaries were rated compulsorily under the authority of the Act for the water supply, whether they took the water supplied or not; outside those boundaries only those who took the water paid for it. The rates compulsorily levied, and the voluntary payments for the water supplied were fixed, within certain prescribed limits of charge, at values sufficient to provide a sum to cover all annual expenses, and in addition a sum not less than one per cent. on the money borrowed, to be applied as a sinking fund applicable to the redemption of mortgages and annuities. Any surplus there might be in any one year went to reduce the domestic water rate in the next year. It was held that the sum applied towards the formation of the sinking fund, and the balance carried forward to the reduction of the water rate, was not assessable for income tax. *In re Glasgow Corporation Waterworks*, 12 Sco. L. R. 466. The difference between this case and the case of the Brighton Corporation (see *post, Attorney-General* v. *Black*, pp. 120, 121) was that in this case the citizens of Glasgow, through the Water Corporation as their representatives, assessed themselves for the purpose of obtaining a water supply, not with a view of making any profit by the undertaking; while the Brighton Corporation made a profit out of a tax levied upon the lieges generally, and applied the proceeds of that tax for the benefit of the community which they represented. It should be observed that no attempt was made in the case of the Glasgow Corporation to discriminate between that portion of the

revenue which arose from the rates levied within *Chap. II.*
the municipal boundaries—the limits of compulsory supply—and that portion of the revenue
which was raised beyond those limits.

But when the Water Commissioners were *Case of*
assessed upon the principle of taking the total *Glasgow Corpora-*
amount of the receipts, and deducting from that *tion Water Commis-*
amount all expenses necessarily incurred in *sioners v. Miller.*
carrying on the concern, and maintaining and
repairing the property, but not the annuities or
interest payable upon the debt, except [1] such
proportion thereof as was payable out of the
compulsory rates levied from occupiers of dwelling-houses and owners of property within the
limits of compulsory supply, a clear distinction
being thus drawn between revenue derived from
the compulsory rates levied within the municipal boundaries, and that derived from the sale
of water for trading purposes, and non-compul-
sory rates levied from persons and properties
beyond those boundaries, and the sum charged
thus representing the surplus revenue derived
from the supply of water outside the limits of
compulsory supply, and from the supply of
water within those limits [2] for purposes of trade,

---

[1] This proportion, however, being chargeable under sect.
102 of 5 & 6 Vict. c. 102. See *post*, pp. 157, 158, 249.

[2] The water supplied within the "limits of compulsory
supply," for purposes of trade, manufacture, &c., was paid
for at such rates and upon such terms as the Water Commissioners might fix, not by compulsory rates.

Case of
Allan v.
*Hamilton
Water-
works
Commis-
sioners.*

manufacture, &c., exclusive of the compulsory rates levied within the limits of compulsory supply, the assessment was upheld. *Glasgow Corporation Water Commissioners* v. *Miller*, 23 Sco. L. R. 285. And where the Hamilton Waterworks Commissioners, who had powers somewhat similar to those of the Glasgow Corporation Water Commissioners, supplied Hamilton Barracks, belonging to the Government, situated within the boundaries of the burgh, under a section of the local Act which enabled the Waterworks Commissioners to supply any corporation, or company, or person, with water for other than domestic use, at such rates, and upon such terms and conditions as should be agreed upon, it was held that, whether or not the Crown, or whoever represented Hamilton Barracks, were entitled to demand a supply of water, and to be assessed only at the domestic rate, inasmuch as the barracks were in fact supplied upon other terms and conditions, fixed by agreement, the profit made by so supplying the barracks with water was chargeable with income tax. *Allan* v. *Hamilton Waterworks Commissioners*, 24 Sco. L. R. 360.

By a private Act, the Corporation of Dublin had power to construct waterworks for the borough, and for certain extra-municipal districts, and, for the purposes of the Act, to borrow money on security of the rates, and to levy water rates on owners and occupiers within *Chap. II.* the borough, and to contract with owners and occupiers in extra-municipal districts for the supply of water. By a later Act, the income from the supply of the extra-municipal districts was to form a consolidated fund, available for paying loans and interest, and for all the purposes of the Act. It was held that the excess of income over expenditure in respect of the extra-municipal districts was chargeable with income tax. *Mayor, &c. of Dublin* v. *M'Adam,* 20 L. R., Ir. 497.

The Glasgow Gas Commissioners were em- *Case of* powered by Act of Parliament to purchase the *Glasgow* *Gas Com-* undertakings of two gas companies previously *missioners.* authorized by Act of Parliament to supply Glasgow with gas. The price was to be paid by way of annuity to the shareholders in the previously-existing gas companies. The Gas Commissioners were empowered to manufacture and sell gas to the inhabitants of Glasgow and suburbs, and it was provided that a sinking fund should be formed to pay off the expenses incurred in erecting works and setting the concern going. It was held that the Commissioners were liable to assessment in respect of the profits of their gasworks ; and that their case differed from that of the Waterworks Corporation, inasmuch as they had no authority to levy a rate, and were not bound to apply any profits they might make in reduction of the charge for gas, but might apply it for their own purposes and uses. They had all the attributes of a trading corporation; and it is not necessary that profits should be for the benefit of individuals in order that they may become liable to assessment for income tax. Case of *Glasgow Gas Commissioners*, 13 Sco. L. R. 556.

Case of
Dillon v.
*Corpora-
tion of
Haver-
fordwest.*

So the Corporation of Haverfordwest, who, by their private Act of Parliament, acquired the power to light the streets of the town with gas, the charges of which were defrayed by a rate levied annually upon the occupiers of all dwelling-houses and other buildings within the district, not exceeding one shilling in the pound, and, after sufficiently lighting the streets, to supply any persons who were willing to buy their gas, and to receive payment for it, provided that all money to arise therefrom should be, in the first instance, applied towards defraying the expenses of the gas apparatus and other things connected therewith, and that, if there should be any overplus, the same should be applied generally for the purposes of the Act, were held to be chargeable upon the profit made upon the gas which they sold to customers on the private account. They claimed to be allowed to deduct the expense incurred in lighting the public lamps, on the ground that, though it was an expense

incurred by the Corporation in the discharge of
their public duties, yet it was wholly and exclusively laid out for the purposes of the trade
of the Corporation, for by sect. 56 of the private
Act a private customer could not be supplied
unless this expense was incurred, inasmuch as it
was only after they had sufficiently lighted the
streets that the Corporation might sell gas to
private customers. But it was held that they
were not entitled to the deduction, because the
expenditure was not an expenditure for the purposes of the trade, which was a trade for supplying private customers only, but was for the
purpose of enabling the Corporation to enter
upon that trade, and the deduction allowed for
money wholly and exclusively expended for the
purposes of a trade ([1] 5 & 6 Vict. c. 35, s. 100,
first rule applying to first and second cases) does
not include initial expenditure incurred by a
person to enable him to enter a particular trade.
Dillon v. *Corporation of Haverfordwest*, [1891] 1
Q. B. 575; 39 W. R. 478; 60 L. J., Q. B. 477;
64 L. T. 202.

The Edinburgh Southern Cemetery Co. were *Case of Edinburgh*
in the habit of selling the use in perpetuity of *Southern*
grave spaces in their cemetery, to be used for *Cemetery Co. v.*
burial purposes only. A certain portion of the *Kinmont.*
sum realised during each year by the sale of

---

[1] See *post*, p. 127.

these grave spaces was set apart to form a fund for the replacement of the money expended in the purchase of the land occupied by the cemetery. It was held that the yearly receipts for the sale of grave spaces constituted income, and that no deduction could be allowed for so much of those receipts as was paid to the fund for replacing capital. The Company had been assessed under [1] Schedule A., No. II., Rule 6, of the [2] Income Tax Act, 1842, and the rules applicable to the [3] first and second cases of Schedule D., applied under authority of [4] section 188 of the Income Tax Act, 1842, but it was held that this was a mistake, and that the Company, being in occupation of the cemetery, could not be assessed under a rule applicable only [5] where the land which is the subject of charge is not in the occupation of the party to be charged, but that they should be assessed under [6] No. 3 of Schedule A., Rule 3, their business falling very fairly within the words " other concerns of a like nature." *Edinburgh Southern Cemetery Co.* v. *Kinmont,* 17 Sess. Cas., 4th series, 154.

---

[1] See *ante,* p. 53.
[2] 5 & 6 Vict. c. 35.
[3] See *post,* pp. 124 *et seq.*
[4] 5 & 6 Vict. c. 35, s. 188, see *ante,* p. 44.
[5] See *ante,* p. 53.
[6] See *ante,* pp. 59, 60.

The Portobello Town Council were required Chap. II. by Act of Parliament to provide a burial ground. Case of *Portobello* They were empowered to assess the ratepayers *Town Council* and to mortgage the assessment, and in this v. *Sulley*. way they borrowed the money with which they acquired and constructed the cemetery. The receipts from the cemetery exceeded the working expenses, but the borrowed money had to be repaid by instalments, and interest had to be paid on the undischarged capital debt. It was contended that the case differed from that of the Edinburgh Southern Cemetery (*ubi sup.*), inasmuch as that was a commercial company trading for profit to the shareholders, while the Town Council were acting without regard to profit, under compulsion of an Act of Parliament, which required them to provide a public burial ground, and to assess the ratepayers for that purpose, and until they attained the position of not requiring to assess there could be no pecuniary benefit. It was also contended that the case differed from that of the Paddington Burial Board (*post*, pp. 121, 122), inasmuch as in that case the money borrowed for the purchase of the ground had been repaid, so that, it was held, the cemetery was carried on for the benefit of the ratepayers. But it was held that the whole of the profit, without deducting the interest paid upon the borrowed capital, was liable to income

Case of
Highland
Railway
Company
v. Special
Commis-
sioners of
Income
Tax.

Profits of
a business
in the year
preceding
the year of
assessment
may form
the basis
of assess-
ment,
though a
part of the
business
has been
discon-
tinued in
the year
of assess-
ment.

tax. *Portobello Town Council* v. *Sulley*, 27 Sco. L. R. 863.

The Highland Railway Company were empowered to provide and use steam and other vessels. Finding that they had been running certain lines of steamships at a loss, they discontinued them. The traffic of one of these lines of steamships was undertaken by an owner of steamships under an agreement with the company; the traffic of the other line was undertaken by a shipping company entirely on their own account, and without any agreement with the Railway Company. The Railway Company made up their account for income tax of the profits of the year preceding that of assessment. During the year of assessment and the preceding year the agreement made by the Railway Company, which provided for the traffic formerly carried on by one of their lines of steamers, was in force. During a part of the year preceding the year of assessment the Railway Company had run the other of their lines of steamers, but in the latter part of the year they had abandoned this line, the traffic of which was undertaken, as has been said, by an independent shipping company. The Railway Company claimed to deduct the loss sustained by them in the year preceding the year of assessment upon the line of steamers which they had con-

tinued to run during a part of that year. It **Chap. II.**
was objected that they were not entitled to do
this, because during the year of assessment the
running of steamers had in fact formed no part
of the undertaking of the railway company, and
the basis of assessment must be determined by
the character of the undertaking during the
year of assessment. But it was held that the
Railway Company had not, by discontinuing a
part of their business, changed the character of
their undertaking, and that, the assessment
having to be made upon the profits of the year
preceding the year of assessment, the profits of
that year must be taken as they actually stood,
and that the Railway Company were entitled to
the deduction which they claimed. Had they
changed the character of their undertaking, the
undertaking would not have been the same in
the year of assessment that it was in the preceding year, but a different undertaking, and
then the profits of the preceding year would not
have formed the basis of assessment. *Highland
Railway Company* v. *Special Commissioners of
Income Tax*, 23 Sco. L. R. 116.

[1] In all cases to which the special rules above stated
apply, if the possession, or interest, of the party to
be charged has commenced within the time for which
the average by which the annual value is to be

---

[1] 5 & 6 Vict. c. 35, s. 60, No. 4, r. 6.

Chap. II. estimated is directed to be taken, then the profits of one year are to be estimated in proportion to the profits received within the time which has elapsed since the commencement of the possession, or interest, of the party to be charged.

Deductions and Allowances.—It is further necessary, in order to arrive at the annual value of any property chargeable to the duty under Schedule A., to have regard to the deductions and allowances which it is permitted to make. [1]No deductions, except such as are specified, are allowed; and those, only if claimed in [2]the prescribed manner. [3]The deduction or allowance (the two names seem to be used interchangeably) is of a sum equal to the duty at the rate per 20s. in force for the time being upon the sums paid in respect of which the deduction or allowance is granted; and it is not granted if such sums are paid by a tenant. The following are the deductions or allowances which may be granted if claimed:—

1. Deduction allowed for tenths, &c.

1. [4]Tenths, &c. The amount of the tenths and first-fruits, duties and fees, on presentations, paid by any ecclesiastical person within the year preceding that in which the assessment is made.

---

[1] 5 & 6 Vict. c. 35, s. 159. See *post*, p. 155, as to the deduction allowed to a clergyman, or minister of any religious denomination, for expenses incurred in the performance of his duty or function.

[2] As to the mode of claiming the deduction or allowance, see *post*, Chap. IV., sect. 1.

[3] 5 & 6 Vict. c. 35, s. 60, No. 5.

Ibid, No. 5, first deduction.

2. [1]Procurations,&c. For procurations and synodals Chap II.
paid by ecclesiastical persons, on an average of seven 2. De-
years preceding that in which the assessment is made. duction allowed

3. [2]Repairs of chancels, &c. The amount expended for pro-curations,
in repairs of collegiate churches and chapels, and &c.
chancels of churches, or of any college or hall in any 3. De-duction allowed
of the universities of Great Britain, by any person for repairs
bound to repair the same, in the year preceding that of chancels, &c.
in which the assessment is made.

4. [3]Parochial rates on tithe rent-charge. The 4. De-duction
amount of parochial rates, taxes, and assessments, allowed for paro-
upon any rent-charge confirmed under the Act passed chial rates
for the commutation of tithes, paid in the year in on tithe rent-
which the assessment is made. charge, &c.

5. [4]Land tax. The amount of land tax unre- 5. De-duction
deemed charged upon any lands, &c. allowed for land
6. Drainage rates, &c. [5]The amount charged on tax.
lands, &c., by a public rate or assessment in respect 6. De-duction
of draining, fencing, or embanking, the same. [6]A allowed for drain-
deduction is allowed in respect of the amount expended age, &c., sea walls,
by the owner on an average of the twenty-one preced- &c.
ing years in making or repairing sea walls, or other

[1] 5 & 6 Vict. c. 35, s. 60, No. 5, second deduction; 16 & 17 Vict. c. 34, s. 34.
[2] Ibid., No. 5, third deduction.
[3] Ibid., No. 5, fourth deduction.
[4] Ibid., No. 5, fifth deduction.
[5] Ibid., No. 5, sixth deduction. This would appear not to allow a deduction in case of a private drainage act.
[6] 16 & 17 Vict. c. 34, s. 37.

E.   E

embankments necessary for the [1]protection of land against the encroachment or overflowing of the sea, or any tidal river, although the sums expended have not been charged upon such land by any public rate or assessment.

Case of
Hesketh
v. *Bray*.

Where land, open to a tidal river, and liable to be more or less flooded at every tide, but covered with short herbage, and worth as pasturage 5s. to 10s. an acre, and so assessed to poor rate and income tax, was reclaimed by the construction of an embankment, with provision of drainage, and for access by roads, so as to be worth from 3l. to 3l. 10s. an acre, it was held that no allowance or deduction could be made or allowed for the amount expended in making the embankment. The object of the works was not protection, but the increase of the capital value of the land, by a change of the character of the land. If, in the course of time, a further expenditure should be incurred for the purpose of preserving and protecting the land in its new condition, an exemption claimed on that further expenditure would in all probability be allowed. *Hesketh* v. *Bray*, 20 Q. B. D. 589; 35 W. R. 622; 57 L. J., Q. B. 184; 58 L. T. 313. The

---

[1] "Protection," not "reclamation," see *Hesketh* v. *Bray*, 20 Q. B. D. 589; 36 W. R. 622; 57 L. J., Q. B. 184; 58 L. T. 313. Affirmed on appeal, 21 Q. B. D. 445; 37 W. R. 22; 57 L. J., Q. B. 633.

judgment was affirmed on appeal, 21 Q. B. D. **Chap. II.**
445; 37 W. R. 22; 57 L. J., Q. B. 633.

7. Wear and tear of machinery. We have [1] already **7. Deduction** mentioned the deduction allowed for wear and tear of **allowed** machinery to the person or company by whom the **for wear and tear of** concern in which the machinery is used is carried on. **machinery.** [2] If the machinery or plant is let upon such terms that the burden of maintaining and restoring the same falls upon the lessor, he may claim repayment of so much of the duty charged in respect of the machinery or plant, and deducted by the lessee on payment of rent, as represents the income tax upon such an amount as the Commissioners think just and reasonable as representing the diminished value of the machinery by wear and tear. The mode in which the claim is made will be explained [3] later on.

Allowances for certain Public and Charitable Institutions.—The following allowances [4] are also directed to be made:—

1. Colleges and halls in universities. For the **1. Allow-** duties charged on any college, or hall, in any of the **ance for** **colleges** universities of Great Britain, in respect of the public **and halls** buildings, and offices, belonging to such college or **in univer-** hall and not occupied by any individual member **sities.** thereof, or by any person paying rent for the same;

[1] *Ante*, p. 60.
[2] 41 & 42 Vict. c. 15, s. 12.
[3] See *post*, pp. 295, 296.
[4] 5 & 6 Vict. c. 35, s. 61, No. 6.

E 2

and for the repairs of the public buildings, and offices, of such college or hall; and of the gardens, walks, and grounds for recreation, repaired and maintained by the funds of such college or hall.

2. Allowance for hospitals, &c.

2. Hospitals, &c. For the duties charged on any hospital, public school, or almshouse, in respect of its public buildings, offices, and premises, not occupied by any officer thereof whose income amounts to, or exceeds, 150*l.*, or by any person paying rent for the same; and for the repairs of such hospital, public school, or almshouse, and offices; and of the gardens, walks, and grounds, repaired and maintained by its funds.

Case of
Blake v.
*Lord
Mayer, &c.
of London.*

The exemption is not limited to charitable institutions. A hospital would not be the less entitled to the benefit of this rule because it had taken certain fees from its patients (*per* Denman, J., in *Blake* v. *Lord Mayor, &c. of London, infra*). The City of London School is a school maintained by the Corporation of the City of London. Certain payments are made by the scholars, but no profit is made by the Corporation, but on the contrary a yearly deficiency of income to meet expenditure is made up by the Corporation out of their own moneys. It was contended that the term "public school" was limited by prior statutes, *i. e.*, 43 Geo. 3, c. 122; 46 Geo. 3, c. 65; and 48 Geo. 3, c. 55, to schools which are supported by charity funds or endowments, and that if the scholars paid anything the school ceased to be a "public school." Mr. Justice Denman said that the words "public schools" were not to be construed as words of art, but meant "schools which are in their nature public." He added that the school in question was in some sense a charitable institution, but that it was not necessary to show that it was a charitable institution in order to establish its claim to exemption. On appeal the decision of the Court below was upheld. But all the judges in the Court of Appeal took note of the charitable element in the school. Lord Esher, M. R., founded his judgment on the facts that (1) the school was partially maintained by a donation in its origin voluntary and charitable; (2) the object of the foundation was a public object, and therefore the school was of the same nature as one of the colleges or halls in the universities, which were also subjects of exemption; and - said that the mere fact that some money was paid by those who were interested in the education of the boys did not prevent the school being a public school within the meaning of the Act where those circumstances existed. Fry, L. J., said that all the exemptions must be construed in the light of each other, and that "public school" must be read not only with hospitals or almshouses, but also with "colleges or halls of any of the universities." He said that it would be unwise to attempt to lay down any definition of a public school, but that there were certain notes of a public school which the school in question had. (1) It was a public foundation; (2) a portion of its income was charitable; (3) it was managed by a public body; (4) no private person had any interest in the school; and (5) no profit was in contemplation in carrying it on. Lopes, L. J., said that the legislature did not intend by the words "public school" only a pure charity school. It intended to relieve from taxation schools where a sufficiently large number of the public received their education gratis, or mainly gratis. That was not an exhaustive definition of the term "public school," but the City of London School came within it. *Blake* v. *Lord Mayor, &c. of London*, 18 Q. B. D. 437; 35 W. R. 212; on appeal, 19 Q. B. D. 79; 35 W. R. 791; 56 L. J., Q. B. 424.

Where a hospital for the treatment of persons suffering from mental diseases was conducted on the principle of the richer patients paying sums above what their treatment and maintenance cost, to enable poor patients to be also treated, so that from the payments so made by the richer patients there was an excess of 7,000*l.* over the ordinary expenditure, which was applied in extending and improving the hospital, so as to make it more fit for the purpose for which it was intended, it was held that the excess was profit, and assessable to income tax.

St. Andrew's Hospital v. *Shearsmith*, L. R. 19
Q. B. D. 624; 35 W. R. 811.

And where a hospital of a similar kind was *Case of Needham* conducted on similar principles, with the result *v. Bowers.* that there was an annual surplus which was expended in enlarging, improving, and other-wise better adapting the institution for its work, it was held not entitled to exemption from the duties charged on profits by the Income Tax Acts. *Needham* v. *Bowers*, 21 Q. B. D. 436; 37 W. R. 125.

But the question in these cases is not whether *Case of Cawse v.* an institution may flourish for a few years by *Committee* reason of taking fees, nor whether in any par- *of the Lunatic* ticular year it receives payments which enable *Hospital, Notting-* it to pay its way, but, What is the character *ham.* of the institution itself? Is its eleemosynary character blotted out, or does it still exist? The Lunatic Hospital, Nottingham, was a building provided for the reception and relief of lunatics who were not paupers, for whose maintenance and medical attendance sums vary-ing from 10s. to 40s. a week were paid (except that about five patients paid an extra 1l. a week for extra room accommodation); it was founded and built with charitable donations, it was an institution for the relief of persons suffering from a distressing disease, and it was managed by charitable persons not deriving any pecuniary benefit therefrom, but, on the contrary, assisting it by their subscriptions. The real property on which the institution was carried on was vested in trustees upon trust to be used as a lunatic hospital, and for the benefit of the inmates thereof, and for no other purpose, and in such manner as the rules of the institution should direct, and there was no power of sale; the endowment funds were also vested in trustees for the benefit of the hospital and the inmates, as a majority of the voluntary donors and subscribers should direct, and the hospital and its inmates could alone derive benefit from the real or personal estate connected with it. An assessment had been made upon an alleged profit of 580*l.* The committee of the hospital submitted that "profits," as defined by the Income Tax Acts, meant what remained after deducting the value of the occupation of the premises where the profit was made, and that, if this was allowed, a loss of 420*l.* would appear instead of the alleged profit of 580*l.* They also alleged that the income of the hospital was exempt as being applied to charitable purposes only. There had been a change in the amount of support and in the class of patients received by the hospital, so that for three years at least there had been an occasional balance in favour of the trustees. It was held that the institution, being endowed with a substantial charitable endowment, was exempt from income tax as a "hospital." It was pointed out that if the profits were assessed apart from the buildings as upon a going concern from which profit was derived, a very different question would arise. But the assessment appealed against was not an assessment under Schedule D., and the appeal must be allowed. (*Cause* v. *Nottingham Lunatic Asylum*, [1891] 1 Q. B. 585; 39 W. R. 461; 60 L. J., Q. B. 485; 65 L. T. 155.)

The Whittingham Asylum was a county lunatic asylum established under 16 & 17 Vict. c. 97, and was provided for the reception and relief of pauper lunatics. The medical superintendent, medical officers, and steward occupied apartments situate in the asylum building; the chaplain occupied a house within the asylum grounds. The apartments and house were not rated or charged in the poor rate assessment, in accordance with sect. 35 of 16 & 17 Vict. c. 97. The medical superintendent, medical officers, and steward, were bound to be resident in the asylum, and might at any time be transferred from one set of rooms to another. The county justices, being assessed in respect of the apartments and house, appealed, contending that, as they were bound by 16 & 17 Vict. c. 97 to provide an asylum for the reception of pauper lunatics, and as there was no beneficial occupation on the part of these officers, who were acting as their servants, they were not liable to

Case of Bray v. *Justices of Lancashire.*

E 5

assessment. It was held that the assessment had been rightly made. (*Bray* v. *Justices of Lancashire*, 22 Q. B. D. 484; 37 W. R. 392; 58 L. J., M. C. 54.)

3. Allowance for literary or scientific institutions.

3. Literary or scientific institutions. For the duties charged on any building the property of any literary or scientific institution, used solely for the purposes of such institution, in which no payment is made for any instruction there afforded; provided that the building is not occupied by any officer of such institution, nor by any person paying rent for the same.

4. Allowance for charity lands, &c.

4. Charity lands, &c. For the duties charged on the rents and profits of lands, &c., belonging to any hospital, public school, or almshouse, or vested in trustees for charitable purposes, so far as the same are applied to charitable purposes.

Cases of *Regina* v. *Commissioners of Income Tax*: *Commissioners for Special Purposes* v. *Pemsel*.

The meaning of the words " charitable purposes " was considered in the case of *Regina* v. *Commissioners of Income Tax* (22 Q. B. D. 296; 37 W. R. 294; 58 L. J., Q. B. 196; 60 L. T. 446). Lands had been conveyed to trustees upon trust to apply the rents and profits in part to the maintenance of the missionary establishments of the United Brethren, in part to the maintenance of educational establishments of the same religious body, such educational establishments being for the maintenance, support, and education of the children of their ministers and missionaries, and special regard was to be

had to the children of such ministers as were Chap. II.
least able to support the expense of their children's education; in part to establishments of
the same religious body called choir houses,
which were used for the residence and support
of single or unmarried persons belonging to the
United Brethren, selected either as deserving in
themselves of the benefit of the endowment, or
as likely to advance the religious interests of the
community. Other lands had been conveyed to
the same trustees, upon trust to apply the rents
and profits for the benefit and general purposes
of the establishment of the Protestant Episcopal
Church of the United Brethren at Gracehill,
Ballymena, in the county of Antrim, in Ireland.
The question was whether the purposes to which
the income of the estates were applied were
"charitable purposes" within the meaning of
the Income Tax Act, 1842. In the Queen's
Bench Division (England), the judges (Lord
Coleridge, C. J., and Grantham, J.) differed,
but, the junior judge withdrawing his judgment, judgment was given for the Crown. In
the Court of Appeal, the judgment of the Court
below was reversed. Lord Esher, M. R., said
that he agreed with all the reasoning of the
Lord Chief Justice, but not with his conclusions.
He agreed with the decision in a case in Scotland which had been cited in argument (*Baird's
Trustees* v. *Inland Revenue*, 25 Sc. L. R. 533),

that the phrase must be construed in its popular sense, as it would be understood by all the educated people in the United Kingdom, not in a technical sense in which it would be understood by a part only of such people. It must not be construed in the large sense which had been given to it by the English Court of Chancery in using the Statute of Elizabeth (43 Eliz. c. 4) as a means of formulating and extending its jurisdiction, in which sense it would include many things which no educated person would think of considering charities. The term might be paraphrased thus :—"Rents and profits are given for charitable purposes, when lands are given in trust that the income shall be expended in assisting people to something considered by the donor to be for their benefit, and the donor intends that such assistance shall be given to people who, in his opinion, cannot, in consequence of their poverty, obtain the benefit without his assistance, and where the donor's intention to assist such poverty is the substantial cause of his gift." The missions to the heathen, which were one of the objects of the trust, were missions to poor heathen, who had not the means of getting religious instruction for themselves, and therefore the assistance to these missions was a charitable purpose. The education of the children of missionaries and ministers, which was another object of the trust,

was intended for the assistance of persons who **Chap. II.**
without such assistance could not get the education given ; that assistance was, therefore, a
charitable purpose.   The choir houses, which
were the third object of the trust, were also a
charitable purpose, the object being to benefit
persons whom the donor considered to require
assistance on account of their poverty.   Fry,
L. J., was of opinion that the words "charitable
purposes " were technical words, to be understood in their technical meaning, but held that
the statute 43 Eliz. c. 4 had determined that
technical meaning, and amounted to a declaration by the legislature of the sense in which the
word " charitable " was then understood.   From
that time forward "charity " meant, in all the
Courts which had to do with it, all the uses and
intents mentioned in the preamble to the statute,
and analogous uses and intents.   There was no
question but that that technical meaning would
include the case before the Court.   If he was
wrong in his principle of construction, he agreed
with the Master of the Rolls that, according to
the popular meaning of the words, the three
objects to which the money was dedicated were
charitable purposes.   Lopes, L. J., arrived at
the same conclusion, but by the mode of reasoning of the Master of the Rolls.   On appeal to
the House of Lords, the decision of the Court of
Appeal was affirmed, the case of *Baird's Trustees*

Chap. II.   ·   v. *Lord Advocate* (*ante*, p. 84) being disapproved. *Commissioners for Special Purposes of Income Tax* v. *Pemsel*, [1891] A. C. 531; 61 L. J., Q. B. 265.

5. Exemption of trades unions' "provident benefits" fund.   5.[1] Trade unions duly registered under the [2] Trade Union Acts, 1871 and 1876, and the rules of which limit the amount assured to any member, or person nominated by or claiming under him, to a sum not exceeding in the total 200*l.*, and the amount of any annuity granted to any member, or person nominated by him, to a yearly sum not exceeding 30*l.*, are exempt from income tax under schedule A. in respect of interest and dividends applicable to and applied solely for the purpose of "provident benefits." The

Meaning of "provident benefits."   phrase "provident benefits" is defined to mean payment to a member during sickness, or incapacity from personal injury, or while out of work, or to an aged member by way of superannuation, or to a member who has met with an accident, or has lost his tools by fire or theft, or a payment in discharge, or aid of, funeral expenses on the death of a member or a wife of a member, or as provision for the children of a deceased member; where the payment in respect of which exemption is claimed is a payment expressly authorized by the rules of the trade union claiming the exemption.

 · The mode in which the allowances are claimed and

---

[1] "The Trade Union (Provident Funds) Act," 1893 (56 Vict. c. 2), ss. 1, 3.

[2] 34 & 35 Vict. c. 31; 39 & 40 Vict. c. 22.

made, will be described [1] later on. [2] Like allowances Chap. II.
are made to the trustees of the British Museum. It
must be understood that the properties are assessed,
and the duties levied, in the usual way, notwithstanding the allowances made afterwards.

*Allowance to Owner of Land when Profits are found
to fall short of Assessment.*—[3] If, at the end of any
year of assessment, an owner of land, being also the
occupier thereof, and occupying the land for purposes
of husbandry only, whether he obtains his living
principally from husbandry or not, finds, and satisfies
the Commissioners by whom he has been assessed in
respect of such land, that his profits and gains arising
from the occupation of such land during the said year
fall short of the sum upon which the assessment was
made, the Commissioners may cause an abatement to
be made from the amount of the assessment. If the
applicant for relief satisfies the Commissioners that
his income from every source for the year of assessment was under 150*l*., he is entitled to relief as [4] a
person whose yearly income is less than 150*l*.

*Allowance on account of Life Insurance or Purchase
of Deferred Annuity.*—[5] Any person who has made

---

[1] See *post*, pp. 272 *et seq.*
[2] 5 & 6 Vict. c. 35, s. 149.
[3] 14 & 15 Vict. c. 12, s. 3; 16 & 17 Vict. c. 34, s. 46;
43 & 44 Vict. c. 20, s. 52. As to the mode in which the
allowance is to be claimed, see *post*, pp. 278, 279.
[4] As to this relief, see *post*, p. 96.
[5] 16 & 17 Vict. c. 34, s. 54; 16 & 17 Vict. c. 91, s. 1;

Chap. II. insurance on his own life, or on the life of his wife, or who has contracted for any deferred annuity on his own life, or on the life of his wife, in or with any insurance company existing on the 1st November, 1844, or registered pursuant to the Act 7 & 8 Vict. c. 110, or [1]under any Act passed in the Session of Parliament of the 16th and 17th years of her Majesty, or [2]in or with any friendly society legally established under any Act of Parliament relating to friendly societies, and [3]any person who has contracted for any deferred annuity on his own life, or on the life of his wife, with the Commissioners for the Reduction of the National Debt, and [1]any person who under any Act of Parliament is liable to the payment of an annual sum, or to have an annual sum deducted from his salary or stipend in order to secure a deferred annuity to his widow, or a provision to his children after his death, may, if he has been

22 & 23 Vict. c. 18, s. 6. The provision does not apply to insurance with a foreign insurance company. It is doubtful whether it applies to insurance with a Scotch company, Scotch insurance companies being expressly excepted from the operation of 7 & 8 Vict. c. 110. *Colquhoun* v. *Haddon*, 24 Q. B. D. 491; 38 W. R. 366; 59 L. J., Q. B. 142; and on appeal, 25 Q. B. D. 129; 38 W. R. 545; 59 L. J., Q. B. 465; 62 L. T. 853.

[1] 16 & 17 Vict. c. 34, s. 54. No Act for the registration of insurance societies was in fact passed during this session.

[2] 18 & 19 Vict. c. 35, s. 1. The premiums payable in respect of such insurances must not be made for shorter periods than three months.

[3] 22 & 23 Vict. c. 18, s. 6.

assessed to the duty under Schedule A., and has paid the duty assessed upon him, or if he has been charged with duty by way of deduction, [1] claim repayment of such a proportion of the duty paid by him as the amount of such annual premium, &c., bears to the whole amount of his profits or gains on which he is chargeable under all or any of the schedules. [2] But no such allowance may be made in respect of such annual premium beyond one-sixth part of the whole amount of the profits and gains of the claimant.

Exemption in Case of Annual Income being less than 150l., and Allowance in Case of Annual Income being less than 400l.—[3] A person whose income is less than. 150l. a year is exempted from payment of income tax; and a person whose income, though exceeding 150l. a year, is less than 400l. a year, is entitled to an abatement in respect of 120l. of his income. The mode in which the exemption and abatement respectively are claimed and allowed will be described [4] later on. [5] For the purpose of claiming such exemption, the annual value of lands, &c. belonging to, or in the occupation of, any person claiming the exemption is estimated, for the purpose of ascertaining

---

[1] As to the mode in which the claim is made, see *post*, pp. 271, 272.

[2] 5 & 6 Vict. c. 35, s. 54.

[3] 39 & 40 Vict. c. 16, s. 8.

[4] See *post*, pp. 265—271.

[5] 5 & 6 Vict. c. 35, s. 167.

Chap. II. his title to the exemption, according to the rules
and directions contained in the Schedules A. and B.
respectively ; and the income arising from the *occupation* by the claimant of lands, &c. chargeable
under Schedule B. is deemed, for the purpose aforesaid, to be equal in England to one-half of the full
annual value thereof, estimated according to the said
rules and directions ; and where the claimant is the
proprietor, as well as the occupier, of any such lands,
&c. the amount deemed as aforesaid to be the income
arising from the occupation of such lands, &c. is
added to the amount of the full annual value thereof ;
and the aggregate amount is deemed, for the purpose aforesaid, to be the income of the claimant
arising from the lands, &c. of which he is the proprietor and occupier as aforesaid. The income
arising from any lease of, or composition for, tithes,
is deemed, for the purpose aforesaid, to be equal to
one-fourth of the full annual value of such tithes
estimated in manner aforesaid.

SECTION II.—SCHEDULE B.

Occupation of Land, &c.—Under Schedule B. the
duty is charged " for [1] and in respect of the *occupation*

[1] 16 & 17 Vict. c. 34, s. 2. As to the duty charged in
respect of land occupied by a dealer in cattle, or by a dealer
in, or seller of milk, see *post*, pp. 156, 157. Farmers may
now elect to be charged under Schedule D. This option was
first given in 1887, by the Customs and Inland Revenue Act
of that year (50 & 51 Vict. c. 15), the provisions of the 18th
section of which are as follows: " It shall be lawful for any

of all such lands, tenements, hereditaments, and Chap. II.
heritages as aforesaid" (that is, as are comprised in
Schedule A.), [2] except dwelling-houses, with their
offices, not occupied with farms of lands, or tithes, for
farming purposes, and except warehouses, or other
buildings, occupied for the purpose of carrying on a
trade or profession, "for every [3] twenty shillings of
the annual value thereof." The duty charged under
Schedule B. is a duty which is imposed upon, and
has to be paid by, the *occupier*, and not the *owner* of
land.

A police-officer, compelled by the duties of Case of
his office, and the circumstances in which he Roberts.
holds that office, to occupy a house, separate

person occupying land for the purposes of husbandry only to
elect to be assessed to the duties of income tax under
Schedule D., and in accordance with the rules of that'
schedule, in lieu of assessment to the duties under Schedule B.
The election of such person shall be signified by notice in
writing, delivered personally, or sent by post in a registered
letter, to the Surveyor of Taxes for the district, within two
calendar months after the commencement of the year of
assessment; and from and after the receipt of such notice
the charge upon him to the duties of income tax for such
year shall be under Schedule D., and the profits or gains
arising to him from the occupation of the lands shall for all
purposes be deemed to be profits or gains of a trade chargeable
under that schedule." Each "year of assessment" begins on
the 6th April; any such election must therefore be made
between the 6th April and the 6th June in any year, and is
operative for "the current year of assessment."

[2] 5 & 6 Vict. c. 35, s. 63, No. 7.
[3] 16 & 17 Vict. c. 34, s. 2. See p. 44, note [3].

Chap. II.

from the police-station, but communicating with the prison yard; the house being liable to be used for purposes connected with the police force as the chief constable of the county may direct; and the police-officer being liable to be removed at any time, is not an "occupier," although the house is for the time being wholly occupied by him, and furnished with his own furniture, and a sum is deducted from his salary by way of rent. *Burt* v. *Roberts*, L. R., 3 Ex. D. 66.

Annual Value under Schedule B.—The rules for determining the annual value under Schedule B. are generally [1] the same as those employed for determining the annual value under Schedule A.; but the following modifications of those rules, so far as concerns assessments under Schedule B., must be noticed:—

1. Lands subject to tithe rent-charge or tithe free.

1. [2] Lands subject to tithe rent-charge and lands tithe free. In all cases where lands are subject to a rent-charge in lieu of tithes under the [3] Act passed for the commutation of tithes, and in all other cases where lands in England are not subject to tithe, or to any modus or composition real in lieu thereof, there shall be deducted out of the duties contained in Schedule B. a sum not exceeding one-eighth part thereof.

[1] 5 & 6 Vict. c. 35, s. 63, Nos. 9, 10, 11.
[2] *Ibid.*, No. 7.
[3] 6 & 7 Will. IV. c. 71.

2. [1] In all cases where lands in England are sub- ject to a modus or composition real, and not subject to any tithe, there shall be deducted out of the duties contained in Schedule B. so much thereof as, together with the like rate on such modus or composition real, shall not exceed one-eighth part of such duties.

3. [1] In all cases in which lands in England are subject to a modus or composition real in lieu of certain specific tithes, and also are subject to certain other specific tithes; or where such lands are free of certain specific tithes, and are subject to certain other specific tithes, the annual value of such lands shall, for the purpose of charging the duties under Schedule B., be estimated at the rack-rent at which the same would let by the year if wholly free from tithes, and there shall be deducted therefrom the amount or value of one-eighth of the said duties, chargeable on the said estimate.

The occupier of a deer forest in Scotland claimed to be assessed under Schedule B. upon the ordinary value of the land, part of the rent actually paid, which exceeded this ordinary value, being paid for the privilege of shooting deer, which, it was argued, was not "a property capable of actual occupation" as required by the Act, and the duty under Schedule B. being, it was said, really chargeable in respect of

[1] 5 & 6 Vict. c. 35, s. 63, No. 7.

profits only. But it was held that the claim was not maintainable; that in the case of lands no estimate of profits is required as in the case of trades and professions, but a statutory mode of proving what the profits are is established—

A deer forest is within s. 60 of 5 & 6 Vict. c. 35. A right of shooting is part of a right of property.

i. e., by taking the annual value; that a deer forest is within the meaning of sect. 60; and that the privilege of shooting game let to a tenant is part of a right of property. Case of *Sir George Nathaniel Broke Middleton, Bart.,* 13 Sco. L. R. 378.

Exceptions—Lands occupied as Nurseries or Gardens for the Sale of Produce.—[1] The profits arising from lands so occupied are estimated according to the rules contained in Schedule D., which we shall state [2] presently, and the duty thereon charged at the rate contained in that schedule; and, when the duty has been so ascertained, it is charged under Schedule B., as upon profits arising from the occupation of lands. [3] But lands occupied for the growth of hops are charged wholly under Schedule B.

Deductions and Allowances under Schedule B.—The rules for determining the annual value under Schedule B. being, as we have said, generally the

---

[1] 5 & 6 Vict. c. 35, s. 63, No. 8. This enactment includes lands occupied for the growth of hops; but by 16 & 17 Vict. c. 34, s. 39, such lands are to be assessed under Schedule B.

[2] See *post*, Chap. II., sect. 4.

[3] 16 & 17 Vict. c. 34, s. 39.

same as those employed for determining the annual. **Chap. II.**
value under Schedule A., the deductions and allowances made under that schedule will also be made,
so far as they may be applicable, in cases of duties
chargeable under Schedule B. The following allowance in the case of duty payable under Schedule B.
is, it will be seen, very similar to that allowed in the
case of duty chargeable under Schedule A. [1]If at
the end of any year of assessment any occupier of
land, occupying the same for the purposes of husbandry only, not being the owner thereof, who has
been assessed in that year under Schedule B. in
respect of such land, finds, and satisfies the Commissioners by whom the assessment was made, that his
profits and gains arising from the occupation of such
land during the said year fell short of the sum upon
which the assessment was made, the said Commissioners may [2]cause an abatement to be made from
the amount of the assessment. [3]In cases where an
abatement from the amount of the assessment would
afford inadequate relief, the occupier of lands for the
purposes of husbandry only may obtain an adjustment of his liability by reference to the loss, and to
the aggregate amount of his income for that year.

[1] 14 & 15 Vict. c. 12, s. 3; 16 & 17 Vict. c. 34, s. 46;
43 & 44 Vict. c. 20, s. 52.

[2] As to the mode in which the abatement is made, see
post, pp. 278, 279, 287.

[3] 53 & 54 Vict. c. 8, s. 23. As to the mode in which the
relief is claimed, and the time within which the claim must
be made, see *post*, p. 287.

Chap. II. But, if he avails himself of this relief, he will not be
entitled to claim, or be allowed, a deduction on the
assessment for a subsequent year by reference to the
amount of loss in respect of which he has obtained
relief. [1]If the applicant for relief satisfies the Commissioners that his income from every source for the
year of assessment was under 150*l.*, he is entitled to
relief as a [2]person whose yearly income is under
150*l.*

*Abatement on account of Life Insurance or Purchase
of Deferred Annuity.*—What [3]we have said with
reference to this abatement, when dealing with the
duty under Schedule A., will apply equally to the
duty under Schedule B.

*Exemption in Case of Annual Income being less than
150l., and Allowance in Case of Annual Income being less
than 400l.*—The exemptions and abatement we [4]have
mentioned in dealing with the duty under Schedule
A. may also be claimed in case of the duty under
Schedule B. We have [5]already incidentally referred
to the mode in which, for the purpose of this exemption and abatement, the annual value of the occupation of lands, &c. is estimated. The mode in which

[1] 16 & 17 Vict. c. 34, s. 30; 39 & 40 Vict. c. 16, s. 8.
[2] See below. As to the mode in which the relief is
claimed, see *post*, pp. 265—271, 287.
[3] *Ante*, pp. 87—89.
[4] See *ante*, pp. 89, 90.
[5] *Ibid.*

the exemption or abatement is claimed and allowed Chap. II.
will be described [1] later on.

SECTION III.—SCHEDULE C.

Interest and Annuities payable out of Public Revenue.
—Under Schedule C. the duty is charged " [2] for and
in respect of all profits arising from interest, annuities,
dividends, and shares of annuities, payable to any
person, body politic or corporate, company or society,
whether corporate or not corporate, out of any public
revenue," for " [3] every twenty shillings of the annual
amount thereof." The duty extends to " [4] all public
annuities whatever payable in Great Britain out of
any public revenue in Great Britain or elsewhere ;
and to all dividends, and shares of such annuities,
respectively ;" [5] and also to interest payable out of
the public revenue, or securities, issued at the ex-

[1] See *post*, pp. 265—271, 286, 287.

[2] 16 & 17 Vict. c. 34, s. 2. See p. 155, *post*, as to the
deduction allowed to a clergyman, or minister of any religious denomination, for expenses incurred in the performance of his duty or function.

[3] Fractional parts of 20s. are also charged with duty by
sect. 3 of the Act, 16 & 17 Vict. c. 34; but no duty is
charged of a lower denomination than 1d.

[4] 5 & 6 Vict. c. 35, s. 88. Annuities or dividends payable
out of the revenue of a foreign state are chargeable. 5 & 6
Vict. c. 80, s. 2. And, of course, annuities and dividends
payable out of any colonial revenue. See 5 & 6 Vict. c. 35,
s. 96.

[5] 5 & 6 Vict. c. 35, s. 97.

E.   F

Chap. II. chequer or other public office, by whatever names such securities are called, except in the following cases of exemption, viz. :—

First case of exemption: Stock of friendly societies. 1. [1]Stock, &c., of friendly societies. The stock, dividends, or interest, of any friendly society legally established under any Act relating to friendly societies, not assuring to any individual more than 200*l.*, and not granting any annuity exceeding 30*l.*

Second case of exemption: Stock of savings banks. 2. [2]Stock, &c., of savings banks. The stock, or dividends, of any savings bank established under the provisions of the Act 9 Geo. 4, c. 92 ("An Act to consolidate and amend the laws relating to savings banks"), arising from investments with the Commissioners for the Reduction of the National Debt; and also the dividends, or interest, payable by the trustees of any savings bank upon any funds therein invested belonging to any depositor, or to any charitable institution.

Case of *In re the Yorkshire Penny Bank.* The Yorkshire Penny Bank had been originally constituted as a Savings Bank under 9 Geo. 4, c. 92. It was subsequently incorporated as a company limited by guarantee for the promotion of [3]objects within sect. 23 of the Companies Act, 1867. There were no profits. With the money received from depositors the

---

[1] 5 & 6 Vict. c. 35, s. 88, first exemption.

[2] *Ibid.*, second exemption.

[3] These objects are such as serve to promote commerce, art, science, charity, or any other useful object unconnected with the making of profit.

Bank made investments, and income tax was Chap. II.
deducted in the usual course from the interest
paid on such investments. For many years the
Bank obtained repayment from the Special
Commissioners of the duty deducted from the
interest, but, attention having been drawn to the
fact that the operations of the Bank were no
longer confined to the receipt of small deposits,
the Special Commissioners declined to repay any
larger sum than the duty on so much of the
interest received as had been paid, or credited,
to depositors whose annual interest did not
amount to 3*l.* The Bank obtained a rule *nisi,*
requiring the Special Commissioners to show
cause why a mandamus should not issue direct-
ing them to allow the Bank an exemption from
income tax. They contended that they were
entitled to the allowance under the second exemption of sect. 88 of 5 & 6 Vict. c. 35, or under
[1] the third exemption of the same section, either
as a savings bank, or as a charitable institution,
or under sections 98 and 105 of 5 & 6 Vict.
c. 35. The Board of Inland Revenue offered
to entertain a claim for repayment of income
tax in respect of the interest paid to those depositors whose annual interest in any year did
not amount to 3*l.*, and ultimately, the offer being

[1] See *post,* p. 100.

accepted, the rule *nisi* was discharged by agreement, with costs. *In re The Yorkshire Penny Bank*, unreported.

Third case of exemption: Stock of charitable institutions;

3 [1]Stock, &c., of charitable institutions. The stock or dividends of any corporation, fraternity, or society of persons, or of any trust, established for charitable purposes only, so far as the same are applied to charitable purposes only; and the stock, or dividends, in the names of any trustees applicable solely to the repairs of any cathedral, college, church, or chapel, or any building used solely for the purposes of divine worship, so far as the same are applied to such purposes. [2]Stock and dividends, vested in

including British Museum.

the Trustees of the British Museum, are also exempt from duty; and no salary or payment made out of her Majesty's Exchequer to such trustees is to be charged. But the duties on all salaries of officers or persons employed under the said trustees, are to be charged on the said officers respectively. [3]And a trade union duly registered under the [4]Trade Union Acts, 1871 and 1876, by the rules of which the amount assured to any member, or person nominated by, or claiming under, him, is limited to a sum not exceeding 200*l.*, and the amount of any annuity granted to any member or person nominated by him is limited to a

---

[1] 5 & 6 Vict. c. 35, s. 88, third exemption.

[2] 16 & 17 Vict. c. 34, s. 149.

[3] "The Trade Union (Provident Funds) Act, 1893" (56 Vict. c. 2), s. 1.

[4] 34 & 35 Vict. c. 31 ; 39 & 40 Vict. c. 22.

yearly sum not exceeding 30*l*., is entitled to exemption from income tax chargeable under Schedule C., in respect of the interest and dividends of the trade union applicable and applied solely for the purpose of [1]provident benefits.

4. [2]Stock in the name of the Treasury or of the Commissioners for the Reduction of the National Debt. The stock, or dividends, standing in the names aforesaid.

5. [3]Stock belonging to her Majesty, or to accredited ministers. The stock, or dividends, belonging to her Majesty; and the stock, or dividends, of any accredited minister of any foreign state resident in Great Britain.

Fourth case of exemption: Stock in name of Treasury or Commissioners for Reduction of National Debt.

Fifth case of exemption: Stock of her Majesty, or accredited ministers of foreign states.

Allowance on Account of Life Insurance and Purchase of Deferred Annuities.—What we [4]have said with reference to this abatement when dealing with the duty under Schedule A. will apply equally to the duty under Schedule C.

Exemption in Case of Annual Income being less than 150*l.* ; *and Allowance in Case of Annual Income being less than* 400*l.*—The exemption and abatement we [5]have mentioned in dealing with the duty under Schedule A. may also be claimed in case of the duty

---

[1] As to what are "provident benefits," see *ante*, p. 86.
[2] 5 & 6 Vict. c. 35, s. 88, fourth exemption.
[3] *Ibid.*, fifth exemption.
[4] See *ante*, pp. 87, 89.
[5] See *ante*, pp. 89, 90.

Chap. II. under Schedule C. The mode in which the exemption or abatement is claimed and allowed, will be described [1] later on.

Small Dividends to be charged under Schedule D.—
[2] When the half-yearly payment on any annuities, dividends, and shares of annuities, otherwise chargeable under Schedule C., does not amount to fifty shillings, the same is to be accounted for, and charged under Schedule D. ; [3] except in the case of dividends attached to stock certificates issued under the National Debt Act, 1870, from which the duty is deducted, although the dividend does not amount to fifty shillings.

Section IV.—Schedule D.

Annual Profits and Gains from Property and Professions.—Under Schedule D. the duty is charged [4] " for and in respect of the annual profits, or gains, arising, or accruing, to any person residing in the United Kingdom, from any kind of property whatever, whether situate in the United Kingdom or elsewhere; and for and in respect of the annual profits, or gains, arising, or accruing, to any person residing in the United Kingdom, from any profession, trade, employment, or vocation, whether the same shall be

---

[1] See *post*, p. 290.
[2] 5 & 6 Vict. c. 35, s. 95.
[3] 33 & 34 Vict. c. 71, s. 36.
[4] 16 & 17 Vict. c. 34, s. 2.

carried on in the United Kingdom or elsewhere; ... Chap. II. and for and in respect of the annual profits, or gains, arising, or accruing, to any person whatever, whether a subject of her Majesty or not, although not resident within the United Kingdom, from any property whatever in the United Kingdom, or any profession, trade, employment, or vocation exercised within the United Kingdom" for every [1]twenty shillings of the annual amount of such profits and gains; and "for and in respect of all interest of money, annuities, and other annual profits, and gains, not charged by virtue of any of the other schedules" for every [1]twenty shillings of the annual amount thereof.[2]

A man "resides" in Great Britain if he has his ordinary residence there, although he is absent from that residence for a greater or shorter period of each year (Case of *Captain H. Young, Master Mariner*, 16 Sco. L. R. 682), even although he is not in Great Britain for six months of the year (Case of *Captain H. Young, ubi sup.*), or even although he is absent from Great Britain the whole year. (*Rogers* v. *Inland Revenue*, 16 Sco. L. R. 682.) A merchant having a permanent residence, and carrying on

Case of Young.

Case of Rogers v. Inland Revenue.

Case of Lloyd v. Sully.

---

[1] Fractional parts of 20s. are charged with duty by sect. 3 of the Act, 16 & 17 Vict. c. 34; but no duty is charged of a lower denomination than 1d.

[2] Farmers may elect to be assessed under this schedule and in accordance with its rules, rather than under Schedule B., 50 & 51 Vict. c. 15 ("Customs and Inland Revenue Act, 1887"). See *ante*, p. 90, note [1].

business, at Leghorn, but having also a residence in Scotland which he visited in the summer months, always returning to his permanent abode in Italy, was held liable to be assessed on the profits of his foreign trade brought into Great Britain to meet his expenditure in Scotland, and elsewhere in Great Britain, although the period of his residence in Great Britain had been less than six months in the year. (*Lloyd* v. *Sully*, unreported.) A joint stock company is charged as a "person." (5 & 6 Vict. c. 35, s. 40.) It "resides" in the place in which it carries on its real trade and business. (*Calcutta Jute Mills Company* v. *Nicholson*, L. R., 1 Ex. D. 437; 45 L. J., Ex. 821; 35 L. T. 275; 25 W. R. 71.) The place of registration of the

Place of residence of a company.

company is not conclusive as to its place of "residence," although it is a fact to be taken notice of in connection with all other circumstances in order to determine the place of "residence" of the company. The "Calcutta Jute

Case of *Calcutta Jute Mills Co.* v. *Nicholson*.

Mills Company, Limited," was a company registered in England, having its registered office in England, managed by a Board of not less than five directors in England, who appointed a resident director and manager in Calcutta. There were Indian and English shareholders of the company. The whole of the business of the company, the realising, and disposing of, its funds, and the division among the Indian shareholders of the part of the profits due to them, Chap. II. was transacted in India. The company made no profits in England. The company was held liable to assessment upon the whole of its profits, not upon so much only as was divided between the shareholders in England. [1] The case of *The* Cesena *Cesena Sulphur Company, Limited* (L. R., 1 Ex. *Sulphur Co.* D. 428 : 45 L. J., Ex. 821 ; 35 L. T. 275 ; 25 W. R. 74) was similar.

The Imperial Ottoman Bank was a body in- Case of *A.-G. v.* corporated according to the law of Turkey by a *Alexander.* firman of the Sultan, established as a state bank for the Ottoman Empire, and having its seat in Constantinople. It had an agency in London London by which the usual business of bankers was carried foreign on, managed by the London members of a com- company. mittee, appointed to administer the affairs of the

---

[1] In the case of *Colquhoun* v. *Brooks* (see *post*, p. 118), where the question was whether a partner in a business carried on in Australia, residing in England, was liable to pay income tax upon the profits of the business in Australia not brought into this country, the question was finally decided in the negative by the House of Lords. Lord Herschell in his judgment expressly abstained from considering whether the facts in the case of the *Cesena Sulphur Company* raised the same question as was raised in the case before him, but said that, inasmuch as the important considerations which had been pressed in argument in the House of Lords were not present to the minds of the learned judges who took part in the decision in the *Cesena Sulphur Company's Case*, it could not be considered as an authority determining the question.

F 5

bank by the shareholders. The bank was held to be not resident in the United Kingdom. *Attorney-General* v. *Alexander and others*, L. R., 10 Ex. 20; 44 L. J., Ex. 3; 31 L. T. 694; 23 W. R. 255.

Case of Tischler & Co. v. Apthorpe.

Messrs. Tischler & Co. were wine growers and wine merchants, carrying on business as Tischler & Co. at Bordeaux, where they resided. Mr. Tischler, the senior partner, was in the habit of spending about four months in every year in England at different times, and dwelt during that period chiefly in London, and then always at the Royal Hotel, Blackfriars. He had no other place of residence in England. When in England he saw customers, and took orders for wine, which was shipped from Bordeaux by his firm, who sent invoices, sometimes to the purchaser direct, and sometimes to Messrs. Feuerheerd & Co., who acted as general agents for Tischler & Co. Feuerheerd & Co. were paid by commission upon the amount of all wines sold either through them or by Mr. Tischler when in London. The commission included a guarantee of all debts for wine sold in England. A room was provided for Mr. Tischler in Feuerheerd & Co.'s office, the rent of which was paid by Tischler & Co., who had their own clerk there, and their name painted on the door. Payment for wines ordered was made to Feuerheerd & Co. for Tischler & Co., and Feuerheerd & Co. received invoices, or

copies of invoices, of all wines sent by Tischler Chap. II.
& Co. from Bordeaux to England. It was held
that Tischler & Co. did not "reside" in the
United Kingdom, but were liable to income tax
as carrying on a trade there. *Tischler & Co.* v.
Apthorpe, 52 L. T. 814; 33 W. R. 548.

The Great Northern Telegraph Company Case of *Erichsen* v. *Last.*
of Copenhagen was a company "resident" at
Copenhagen. It had submarine cables in connection with the United Kingdom, and other
submarine cables and foreign telegraph lines not
in connection with the United Kingdom. It
had also, under an agreement with the Post-
master-General, separate wires between Aberdeen, Newcastle, and London, worked by its own
staff in workrooms in Aberdeen, Newcastle, and
London. No profits were made by the company
from the land lines in the United Kingdom
used by them, except so far as the use of these
lines enabled the company to make profits by the
transmission of messages abroad. It was held
that the company must be assessed on what they
received in the United Kingdom for transmission
of messages abroad, after deducting sums paid
by them for the use of foreign lines. *Erichsen*
v. *Last,* L. R., 8 Q. B. D. 414; 51 L. J., Q. B.
86; 45 L. T. 703; 30 W. R. 301.

Messrs. Pommery and Greno were wine mer- Case of *Pommery* v. *Ap-thorpe.*
chants and shippers, having their chief office for
business at Rheims, in France, where they re-

sided.　They were in the habit of shipping champagne to England for the purpose of sale. They had an agent in England, one Hubinet, who acted as their representative in England in the sale of their wine and the transaction of their business.　He had a place of business in Mark Lane, in the City of London, the premises being taken in his own name. He, on behalf of Messrs. Pommery and Greno, employed travellers, and appointed sub-agents who sought for orders for Messrs. Pommery and Greno's wines.　All orders obtained were sent by Hubinet direct to Messrs. Pommery and Greno at Rheims; in the case of small orders the wine was supplied from a stock of wine kept in London; in the case of larger orders the wine was shipped by Messrs. Pommery and Greno direct to the customers.　The amounts due were collected by Hubinet on behalf of Messrs. Pommery and Greno, who kept a banking account in London.　Drafts given in payment were sent to Messrs. Pommery and Greno for indorsement.　In case of default in payment proceedings were taken in English Courts.　The agent received a commission on all wines sold in England, as an equivalent for his expenses in rent, clerks' salaries, and otherwise, and as remuneration for his services.　The name of Pommery and Greno was inserted among the London wine merchants in the "London Directory," coupled with that of Hubinet as agent.　Hubinet

was duly assessed to income tax on all profits Chap. II.
made by him in respect of his agency, and paid
income tax thereon. Messrs. Pommery and
Greno were assessed on their profits in the name
of their agent Hubinet, and appealed on the
ground that the profits were made in France
and not in England. It was attempted to distin-
guish the case from that of *Tischler and Co.* v.
Apthorpe, on the ground that in the latter case one
of the appellants' firm spent four months in the
year in this country, and personally took orders,
and the English agent received all the moneys;
and from the case of *Erichsen* v. *Last*, on the
ground that in that case the whole business was
certainly done in this country. But it was held
that no serious distinction could be drawn between the cases, and that Messrs. Pommery and
Greno were rightly assessed. *Pommery* v. *Apthorpe*, 35 W. R. 307; 56 L. J., Q. B. 155; 56
L. T. 24.

The facts were not so strong in the case of Case of
Werle &
Messrs. Werle and Co., who were wine mer- *Co.* v. *Col-*
chants, resident at Rheims, in France. They *quhoun.*
employed a London firm of wine merchants as
their sole agents in the United Kingdom. The
agents' office was taken in their own name, and
on their own account, and they carried on their
own business there. The agents, with the
authority of Messrs. Werle and Co., issued advertisements and circulars in England for the

purpose of securing contracts. The name of "Werle and Co." was exhibited on the inside window of the agents' office in London, and was entered in the "London Directory." Contracts for wine were made by the agents in England, and transmitted to Rheims. No stock of wine was kept in England by Messrs. Werle and Co., nor had they any banking account in England. The purchasers either paid the agents, who remitted the amount to Messrs. Werle and Co., or paid Messrs. Werle and Co. direct. Messrs. Werle and Co. sent receipts to the purchasers for all payments. The agents were paid by a commission (upon which they paid income tax) on all wines sold by Messrs. Werle and Co. in the United Kingdom, and paid all expenses. It was held that there was a trade carried on in England, and that the profits were assessable to income tax. Lord Esher, M. R., said that it was not essential that the profits should be received in England, nor that there should be an establishment in England. It was not necessary that anyone should be found to be assessed in England under [1] sect. 41 of 5 & 6 Vict. c. 35. If the Crown can find such an agent as is mentioned in that section it can assess him; but if it cannot, that does not derogate from the right of the Crown, if there is a person assessable. The Crown must by some means or other get at

[1] See *post*, p. 179, note [3].

that person. Fry, L. J., agreed with the Master Chap. II.
of the Rolls upon the construction to be placed
on sect. 41 of 5 & 6 Vict. c. 35, but thought
that Messrs. Werle and Co. had an agent within
the United Kingdom in receipt of the profits and
gains, as part of the gross sum which was paid
him by the purchaser. *Werle and Co.* v. *Colquhoun*, 20 Q. B. D. 753 ; 36 W. R. 613 ; 57 L.
J., Q. B. 323 ; 58 L. T. 756.

In the case of the Imperial Ottoman Bank, Case of
Gilbertson
mentioned above, it was held that English profits v. *Fergusson.*
made by the London agency of the bank were London
agency of
liable to assessment. *Gilbertson* v. *Fergusson,* foreign
banking
L. R., 7 Q. B. D. 562 ; 46 L. T. 10. company.

It was also held, in the case of the Imperial
Ottoman Bank (*ubi sup.*), that the English share- English
share-
holders' share of the profits made in Turkey holders'
share of
was liable to assessment : *e. g.*, if the shares had profits of
foreign
been equally held in England and in Turkey, banking
company.
and the profits made in England and in Turkey
had been equal, three-fourths of the profits would
have been assessable.

Mr. Brooks resided in England, but was Case of
Colquhoun
partner in a firm which carried on business v. *Brooks.*
exclusively in Australia. The question was
whether he was only liable to be assessed in
respect of his interest in the Australian firm on
the sums from time to time received by him in
England in respect of that interest, or whether
he was liable to be assessed on the whole of his

share in the profits of the Australian firm, whether received in England or not. In the Queen's Bench Division, the judges, Wills, J., and Stephen, J., differed. Wills, J., held that the generality of the words in the first portion of Schedule D. was cut down by the provisions of 5 & 6 Vict. c. 35, applicable to Schedule D., more especially sects. 100, 106, and 108; that the method of construction summarized in the maxim *expressio unius exclusio alterius*, from which it had been argued that, from the very fact that such limitations are imposed in the case of profits derived from foreign or colonial securities or possessions, it is to be inferred that no such limitation is to be imposed in the case of profits derived from a trade carried on abroad, did not help him to arrive at what was meant; that there was authority for saying that there is a general rule as to the extent to which English Acts of Parliament dealing with property in general are to be treated as applying to foreign property (using the word " foreign " as including colonial property), that is, property which, whether situate in England or elsewhere, is not, at the time to which the discussion relates, English property, and that, in the words of Lord Westbury in *Attorney-General* v. *Campbell* (L. R., 5 H. L. 524—530; 21 W. R. 34, n.), " You cannot apply an English Act of Parliament to foreign property while it remains

foreign property "; that the question in every
instance was one of fact, "Is the property
sought to be affected British property or not?"
and that there was absolutely nothing to give a
British character to the unremitted portion of
the profits made in Melbourne by a business
carried on in the colony of Victoria only; that
the principle of the decision in *Sulley* v. *Attorney-General* (8 W. R. 472; 5 H. & N. 711;
reversing *Attorney-General* v. *Sulley*, 7 W. R.
666; 4 II. & N. 769) was that the profits of a
business carried on abroad, and not in the
United Kingdom—profits made abroad, and
never remitted here—are not taxable; that it
was far easier to suppose that the omission of
any special mention of the case of a person
resident here and not receiving the whole of the
profits of a business carried on abroad by a
firm of which he is a partner was an accident, than that there should be, in respect
of an isolated case of this kind, a departure,
without express words, from a well-understood
principle regulating the application of Acts of
Parliament in general; and that the provisions relating to the profits of foreign securities
pointed out what, for the purposes of the Income
Tax Acts, effected the conversion of foreign into
British property, viz., the receipt of the profits,
whether of foreign securities or of foreign trade,
in this country. Stephen, J., differed. He

thought the language of Schedule D. concluded the question. It could not be limited in the way suggested. He pointed out that the words of Lord Westbury, quoted by Wills, J., were used with reference to statutes imposing duties on property when, by the death of its owner, it changes hands. The Income Tax Acts were directed to taxation of persons, not to distribution or management of things; and he saw no reason why an Act which in terms taxed residents in England for the profits of trade carried on abroad should be cut down by implication, so as to apply to those parts only of the profits which were brought home. Wills, J., as junior judge, withdrew his judgment, in accordance with the old practice in the [1] Court of Exchequer, and judgment was given for the Crown. But in the Court of Appeal, the judgment was reversed by Lord Esher, M. R., and Lopes, L. J., Fry, L. J., dissenting. Lord Esher, M. R., said that it was impossible to have words larger than those used in Schedule D. of the [2] Income Tax Act, 1853 ; if taken in their largest sense, they would apply to a foreigner just as much as to a servant of the Queen, so that any foreigner residing in this country for a time sufficient to make his stay a residence would have to pay income tax for any kind

---

[1] The old Court of Exchequer had jurisdiction in revenue cases.   [2] 16 & 17 Vict. c. 34.

of property whatever, whether situate in the Chap. II.
United Kingdom or elsewhere; that such an
enactment would amount to a tyrannical and
abnormal interference in regard to matters with
which this country has nothing to do; and that,
unless it was perfectly clear (which it was not)
that Parliament had intended to commit an
outrage on the law and comity of nations, it
could not be supposed that any such conse-
quences were intended to result from the general words used. He adopted all the arguments
which Wills, J., had given in his judgment.
Lopes, L. J., concurred, but Fry, L. J., found
himself, unable to place any limitation upon the
words used in Schedule D. He thought that
the obvious and express language of the legislature did create a charge upon persons resident
in this country in respect of any profits,
wherever they had been earned. The argument
that such legislation would have amounted to
an outrage upon the law of nations, he dis-
missed as one for the legislator, not for the
judge; he quoted with approval the language
of Lord Cairns in *Parlington* v. *The Attorney-
General* (L. R., 4 H. L. 100) : " The principle
of all fiscal legislation is this. If the person sought to be taxed comes within the
letter of the law, he must be taxed, however
great the hardship may appear to the judicial
mind to be "; he did not dissent from the pro-

position of Lord Westbury, but held that it had
no application to the case before him; he said
that the income tax was not like the succession
duty, or the legacy duty, a charge upon a thing,
but was a charge upon a person in respect of a
thing, and he knew of no principle of law which
prohibited the Legislature from using foreign
property, or anything in the world they liked,
as the standard by which the person resident
within this country was to be charged; he
thought the rules in [1] cases 4, 5, and 6 furnished
no general guide for the interpretation of the
statute. The judgment of the Queen's Bench
Division was reversed in accordance with the
opinion of the majority of the Court of Appeal.
The case was carried to the House of Lords,
where the decision of the Court of Appeal was
affirmed, but for different reasons. Lord Fitzgerald thought that there would be no hardship
in charging Mr. Brooks on his share of the
profits of the Australian firm, actually ascertained, but held that there was no sufficient
finding to warrant him in coming to the conclusion that such profits had been so ascertained
as to be legitimately the subject of taxation
here. He also held that profits derived from
trade carried on entirely elsewhere than in the
United Kingdom are not accessible for income
tax until received here by the person entitled to

[1] See *post*, pp. 158, 159, 162, 163.

them, being a resident in the United Kingdom. Lord Herschell did not attach weight
to the argument that the result of allowing
the contention of the Crown to prevail, which
must be extended to the case of a foreigner,
would involve a violation of international law,
nor did he consider that the decisions under the
Legacy and Succession Duty Acts, which imposed a limit upon the broad language of the
enactments subjecting legacies and successions to
taxation, supplied a rule applicable to questions of
income tax. But he pointed out the anomalies
in the incidence of the tax which would result
from adopting the view put forward on the
part of the Crown; that none of the elaborate
machinery provided for carrying out the taxing
purposes of the Income Tax Acts was applicable
to the assessment of the profits of a trade carried
on entirely outside the United Kingdom, no
part of which is received here; and that the
shares of the Australian partners of the Australian firm clearly could not be taxed, and that
there was no provision for a separate statement
and assessment of the profits of the English
partner such as the Crown contended for. And
referring to the rule styled the [1] fifth case of
Schedule D., dealing with the duty to be
charged in respect of possessions in any of her

[1] See *post*, p. 162.

Majesty's dominions out of Great Britain, and foreign possessions, he expressed himself unable to see why the word "possessions" might not be fitly interpreted as relating to all that is possessed in her Majesty's dominions out of the United Kingdom, or in foreign countries, and so as including the interest which a person in this country possessed in a business carried on elsewhere. This construction would have the advantage of removing the glaring anomaly which would inevitably flow from the rival construction, and of taxing alike such portion only of the profits arising abroad, whether from property or trade, as is received in the United Kingdom. In the case of the *Cesena Sulphur Co.* v. *Nicholson* (see *ante*, p. 105), the head office, and therefore the principal place of business, of the companies whose income was under consideration, was in England, and the argument turned principally upon where those companies resided. Without stopping to inquire whether the facts in that case raised the same question as was then to be decided, it was certain that the important considerations which had been pressed in argument were not present to the minds of the learned judges who took part in the decision upon that case, which could not, therefore, be regarded as an authority determining the question. Lord Macnaghten, after saying that he did not think that any light was

thrown upon the question by considering the Chap. II.
Legacy Duty Acts, or the Succession Duty Act,
or the decisions on those statutes; or that there
was any room for the argument that "arising
or accruing to any person" in the first sentence
of Schedule D., meant "received by any person
in the United Kingdom"; or that there was
sufficient force in the argument founded upon
the comity of nations; entered into an elaborate
examination of the language of the earlier
Income Tax Acts, from which the existing Acts
were more or less copied, and, comparing the
language of the existing Income Tax Acts, and
noting the inadequacy of the provisions for
stating and assessing the profits of a partnership
business wholly carried on abroad, he came to
the conclusion that the profits and gains arising
from Mr. Brooks' Melbourne business fell under
the [1] fifth case of Schedule D., and were chargeable accordingly on the actual sums received in
the United Kingdom. · *Colquhoun* v. *Brooks*, 19
Q. B. D. 400 ; 57 L. J. Q. B. 70; 57 L. T. 448.
On appeal, 21 Q. B. D. 52; 36 W. R. 657; 57 L. J.
Q. B. 439 ; on appeal to the House of Lords, 14
App. Cas. 493 ; 38 W. R. 289 ; 59 L. T. 850.

The ground of the decision in *Colquhoun* v. Case of
Brooks (*ubi sup.*) was that a person who carries on Bank of
a business solely abroad, was not liable to pay South
income tax in England upon the profits of that Apthorpe.

London
Mexico and
America v.

[1] See *post*, p. 162.

business unless the profits are received in England. If a person carries on one business in England, and another distinct business abroad, the two businesses must be looked at as separate businesses, and the person can only be assessed upon the profits of the business carried on abroad which he receives in this country. But where there is no business carried on solely abroad, but one business carried on in England, although a portion of the profits of that business is earned abroad by transactions carried out there, there is no rule that in such a case the profits must be received in this country before they can be assessed. *London Bank of Mexico and South America* v. *Apthorpe*, [1891] 1 Q. B. 383; 60 L. J., Q. B. 196; 64 L. T. 416; on appeal, [1891] 2 Q. B. 378; 39 W. R. 564.

Under the authority of certain Acts of Parliament a rate was levied on coals landed on the beach of, or in any other way brought or delivered within the limits of the town of, Brighton. The proceeds of the rate were applied to the purchase of land, the extension of the market, the enlargement of streets, the erection of a town hall, and to parochial purposes. The incidence of the tax was upon the importer of the coal, which was sold indiscriminately to persons not inhabitants of Brighton, and to non-rateable inhabitants of Brighton. It was not therefore a tax upon the inhabitants of Brighton,

or on those among them who were otherwise Chap. II.
rateable. It was held that the rate was a
"profit" within Schedule D. *Attorney-General*
v. *Black*, L. R., 6 Exch. 78, 308; 40 L. J. 89,
194; 24 L. T. 370; 25 L. T. 207; 19 W. R.
416, 1114.

The Corporation of the City of London derived Case of
A.-G. v.
a large annual income from profits of markets, *Scott.*
corn and fruit metages, brokers' rents, mayor's
court and other fees, and from other sources.
The receipts were carried to a general account,
from which was deducted the whole expenditure
of the Corporation for the civil government of the
city, and the balance was returned as the profits
of the Corporation chargeable under Schedule D.
It was held that the profits derived by the Corporation from the sources above mentioned were
liable to income tax under Schedule D. without
reference to the purposes for which they were
applied, and that the proper principle upon
which the assessment should be made was to take
each item, or head, of income separately, and to
assess the net produce of such item after deducting from the gross receipts the expenses incurred
in earning and collecting the same. *Attorney-
General* v. *Scott, Chamberlain of the City of
London*, 28 L. T. 302; 21 W. R. 265.

The Paddington Burial Board, formed in Case of
Paddington
1853 under the provisions of 15 & 16 Vict. c. 85, *Burial*
Board v.
derived their sole income from payments made *Inland*
Revenue.

E.   G

in accordance with a scale of charges fixed under sect. 34 of that Act. By sect. 22 of the Act any surplus income in any year, after satis-fying all liabilities, and providing such a balance as should be deemed by the Board sufficient to meet their probable liabilities during the then next year, was to be paid to the overseers in aid of the poor rate. It was held that the surplus income was profit chargeable with income tax, and that the case differed from that of the Glasgow Corporation Water Commissioners (*ante*, pp. 63, 64), inasmuch as in that case the inhabitants of Glasgow were not carrying on any business at all, and there was no profit made, the ratepayers paying only as much as it cost to supply them with water, neither more nor less; while in this case the burial board carried on the business of undertakers for the benefit of the ratepayers. *Paddington Burial Board* v. *Inland Revenue Commissioners*, 13 Q. B. D. 9; 53 L. J., Q. B. 224; 50 L. T. 211; 32 W. R. 551.

Case of
Partridge
v. *Mallan-
daine.*

Professional bookmakers, who attend races, and carry on the business of betting, and make profits thereby, must pay income tax on such profits. *Partridge* v. *Mallandaine*, 18 Q. B. D. 276; 35 W. R. 276; 56 L. J. Q. B. 251; 56 L. T. 203. It was argued that the Legislature intended that income tax should be paid under Schedule D. only where some business recognized by the law was carried on, and that this was not a lawful business. But Hawkins, J., said the calling was an honest one, and Denman, J., said that, in his opinion, if a man carried on a systematic business of receiving stolen goods, and made a profit of 2,000l. a year by it, the Income Tax Commissioners would be right in assessing him on it.

In the case of *Turner* v. *Cuxson* (22 Q. B. D. 151; 37 W. R. 254; 58 L. J., Q. B. 131; 60 L. T. 335) the question was raised whether a sum of 50l. paid to a curate of the Church of England, by way of an allowance from the Society of the Curates' Augmentation Fund, and which was not renewable save at the discretion of that Society, was assessable to income tax. It was held that it was not so assessable, inasmuch as the sum in question was a voluntary gift or gratuity, not derived from the employment or profession of the curate. It differed from payment made to a clergyman by parishioners in return for services rendered, which was the case in *The Board of Inland Revenue* v. *Strong* (15 Sco. L. R. 704; see *post*, p. 158), for it was not a payment made by parishioners, nor was it made in respect of his services in a particular parish, but it was given to him as being a poor and deserving clergyman.

G 2

Classification of Sources from which Annual Profits or Gains chargeable under Schedule D. arise.[1]—The sources from which annual profits or gains chargeable under Schedule D. arise are divided into six classes; and for the case of each of those six classes there are provided special rules for ascertaining the duties payable; some of the rules being common to more than one of the classes. The classification, and the rules applicable to each class, are as follows :—

First Source.—The first source is [2]every "art, mystery, adventure, or concern," carried on by any "person, body politic or corporate, fraternity, fellowship, company, or society," except "such adventures or concerns on or about lands, tenements, hereditaments, or heritages, as are mentioned in Schedule A." The duty to be charged on annual profits or gains arising from this source is to be computed [3]exclusively of the "profits or gains arising from lands, tenements, or hereditaments, occupied for the purpose of any trade, manufacture, adventure, or concern"; and [4]on a sum not less than the full amount of the balance of such profits or gains, upon a fair and just average of three years ending on the day of the year immediately preceding the year of assessment on which the

---

[1] Where profits or gains may be charged under either of two or more sources or classes, the Crown may make the charge as may be most to its advantage. (*Scottish Mortgage Co. of New Mexico* v. *McKelvie*, see *post*, p. 160.)

[2] 5 & 6 Vict. c. 35, s. 100, second rule of first case.

[3] *Ibid.*, second of rules applying to first and second cases.

[4] *Ibid.*, first rule of first case.

accounts of the trade, &c., have been usually made up, or on the 5th day of April preceding the year of assessment. If the trade, &c., has been commenced within such period of three years, the duty is computed on the average of the balance of the profits and gains from the commencement of the trade, &c.; while, if it has been commenced within the year of assessment, the duty is computed according to the rule applicable in [1] the case of the sixth class. In ascertaining the profits [2] the value of all doubtful debts due or owing to the person charged may be estimated; and in the case of the bankruptcy or insolvency of a debtor, the amount of the dividend which may reasonably be expected to be received on the debt due from him is to be deemed to be the value thereof.

First Source—Deductions allowed.—The deductions allowed in estimating the balance of profits and gains upon which duty is charged under Schedule D., and which arise from the first source, are for the most part indicated only by an enumeration of the deductions *not* allowed, which are as follows:—

1. [3] No sum is to be deducted for repairs of premises, or for supply, repairs, or alterations of imple-

1. No deduction to be allowed for repairs of premises, supply or

[1] See *post*, pp. 162, 163.

[2] 16 & 17 Vict. c. 34, s. 50.

[3] 5 & 6 Vict. c. 35, s. 100, third rule of first case. Here nothing is contemplated in the way of outlays of money in the shape of expenditure of capital for the future benefit of the estate, but only what may be called current expenditure. Per Grove, J., in *Gillatt and Watts* v. *Colquhoun*, 33 W. R. 258.

repairs of implements, beyond a three years' average;

ments, beyond the sum usually expended for such purposes according to an average of three years preceding the year of assessment.

2. Or on account of loss unconnected with the trade, &c.;

2. [1]No sum is to be deducted on account of loss not connected with, or arising out of, the trade, &c., the profits or gains arising from which are the subject of charge.

3. Or on account of capital withdrawn from the trade, &c.;

3. [2]No sum is to be deducted on account of any capital withdrawn from such trade, &c.

4. Or for capital employed in the trade, &c.;

4. [2]No sum is to be deducted for any sum employed as capital in such trade, &c.

5. Or for capital employed in improvement of premises;

5. [2]No sum is to be deducted on account of any capital employed in improvement of premises occupied for the purposes of such trade, &c.

6. Or for interest which might have been made;

6. [2]No sum is to be deducted on account of any interest which might have been made on such sum.

7. Or for debts, except bad debts;

7. [2]No sum is to be deducted for any debts, except bad debts, which must be proved to be such to the satisfaction of the Commissioners.

8. Or for average loss, beyond actual amount;

8. [2]No sum is to be deducted for any average loss, beyond the actual amount of loss after adjustment.

[1] See *ante*, p. 125, note [3].

[2] 5 & 6 Vict. c. 35, s. 100, third rule of first case.

9. [1] No sum is to be deducted on account of any Chap. II.
annual interest, or any annuity or other annual pay- 9. Or for
ment, payable out of profits or gains. interest, &c. ;

10. No sum is to be deducted for any sum re- 10. Or for
coverable under an insurance or contract of indem- recover-
nity. able under insurance, &c. ;

11. [2] No sum is to be deducted for any disburse- 11. Or for
expenses
ments or expenses whatever, not being money wholly not being
money
and exclusively expended for the purposes of such wholly
employed
trade, &c. for the
purposes
of the
12. [2] No sum is to be deducted for any expenses of trade, &c. ;
maintenance of the parties, their families, or esta- 12. Or for
expenses
blishments. of main-
tenance
of the
13. [2] No sum is to be deducted for the rent or parties ;
13. Or for
value of any dwelling-house, or domestic offices, or the rent
or value
any part thereof respectively, [3] except such part of any
dwelling-
thereof as may be used for the purposes of such house not
used for
trade, &c. purposes
of the
trade, &c. ;
14. [2] No sum is to be deducted for any expendi- 14. Or for
expendi-
ture on any other domestic or private purposes ture on
private
distinct from the purposes of such trade, &c. purposes.

[1] 5 & 6 Vict. c. 35, s. 100, fourth rule of first case.
[2] 5 & 6 Vict. c. 35, s. 100, first rule applying to first and
second cases. The deduction allowed does not include initial
expenditure incurred by a person to enable him to enter a
particular trade. *Dillon* v. *Corporation of Haverfordwest*,
ante, pp. 66, 67.
[3] See *post*, p. 130.

Chap. II.

Deduction allowed for—

1. Wear and tear of machinery;

2. Life assurance, &c.

3. Deferred annuity.

But [1]the deduction which is allowed in the case of a concern chargeable under Schedule A. with reference to the rules of Schedule D. for the diminished value by reason of wear and tear of machinery or plant used for the purposes of the concern [2]is allowed also in the case of any trade, &c., chargeable under Schedule D. And any person who has made insurance on his own life, or on the life of his wife, or who has contracted for any deferred annuity on his own life, or on the life of his wife, [3]in or with any insurance company existing on the 1st November, 1844, or registered pursuant to the Act 7 & 8 Vict. c. 110, or [4]under any Act passed in the session of Parliament of the 16th and 17th years of her Majesty, or [5]in or with any friendly society legally established under any Act of Parliament relating to friendly societies; [6]and any person who has contracted for any deferred annuity on his own life, or on the life of his wife, with the Commissioners for the Reduction of the National Debt; [7]and any person who under any Act of Parliament is liable to the payment of an annual sum, or to have an annual sum deducted from his salary or stipend, in order to

[1] See *ante*, pp. 60, 75.
[2] 41 & 42 Vict. c. 15, s. 12. See the case of *The Caledonian Railway Co.* v. *Banks, post*, pp. 131, 132.
[3] 16 & 17 Vict. c. 91.
[4] 16 & 17 Vict. c. 34, s. 54.
[5] 18 & 19 Vict. c. 35, s. 1.
[6] 22 & 23 Vict. c. 18, s. 6.
[7] 16 & 17 Vict. c. 34, s. 54.

secure a deferred annuity to his widow, or a provi- Chap. II.
sion to his children after his death, may deduct the
amount of the annual premium paid by him for such
insurance or contract, or the annual sum paid by
him or deducted from his salary or stipend as aforesaid, from any profits or gains in respect of which he
is liable to be assessed under Schedule D.; and if he
has been assessed, and has paid the duty, he may
[1] claim repayment. But [2] the amount deducted, or Amount
deducted
repaid, is not to exceed one-sixth part of the whole not to ex-
ceed one-
profits and gains of the person claiming the allow- sixth of
profits.
ance, and no such deduction entitles any person to No de-
claim exemption from duty on [3] the ground that his duction
entitles to
annual profits and gains are thereby reduced below claim for
deduction
150*l.* [4] And any person carrying on, either solely or on account
of income
in partnership, two or more distinct trades, manufac- being less
than 150*l.*
tures, adventures, or concerns in the nature of trade, a year.
the profits of which are [5] chargeable under the rules Persons
carrying
of Schedule D., may deduct from, or set against, the on more
than one

[1] As to the mode of claiming and obtaining repayment, see
post, pp. 271, 272, 294, 295.

[2] 16 & 17 Vict. c. 34, s. 54.

[3] As to this ground of exemption, see *post*, pp. 170, 171.

[4] 5 & 6 Vict. c. 35, s. 101.

[5] The trades, &c. must be chargeable under the same
schedule, so that where, before the passing of the "Customs
and Inland Revenue Act, 1887" (*ante*, p. 90, note [1]), a seed
merchant, who had taken a farm and worked it in connection
with his seed business, claimed an allowance from the assessment on his profits as seed merchant in respect of losses on
the farm, it was held that the claim could not be sustained.
Brown v. *Watts*, 23 Sco. L. R. 403.

Chap. II.

trade may set losses in one against profits in another.

profits acquired in one or more of the said concerns the excess of the loss sustained in any other of the said concerns over and above the profits thereof, in the same manner as a loss may be deducted from the profits of the same concern. And in such a case the person or persons carrying on the several concerns may make separate statements in respect of each.

And persons renting dwelling-houses partly occupied for purposes of trade, &c., may deduct a sum not exceeding two-thirds of rent.

And any such person renting a dwelling-house, of which part is used by him for the purposes of any trade or concern, or any profession, the profits of which are chargeable with duty, may deduct from, or set off against, the profits of such trade, concern, or profession, such a sum not exceeding two-thirds of the rent *bonâ fide* paid by him for such dwelling-house as the Commissioners may on due consideration allow.

Case of the *Birmingham Corporation*.

The Corporation of Birmingham were assessed in respect of their market hall, fish market, vaults, and meat market, in sums amounting in the aggregate to 6,250*l.* They did not dispute this assessment, but alleged that they suffered losses in respect of the following concerns, viz. : utilisation and disposition of sewage, industrial schools, baths and parks, and that they were entitled, as persons carrying on more concerns than one, to set these losses against the profits arising from the market hall, fish market, vaults, and meat market. The Court, however, decided in favour of the surveyor of taxes, who con-

Corporation of

tended on behalf of the Crown that the Corpora-

tion could not be considered to be persons Chap. II.
carrying on trades or adventures, and that the Birming-
concerns from which they derived no profits ham not to be con-
were part of the authorized and legitimate sidered persons
expenditure of the borough, provided for the carrying on trades.
benefit of the inhabitants, and that the losses
incurred in connection with these last-mentioned
concerns could not be set against the profits
derived from the market hall, fish market, vaults,
and meat market, which were applied in aid of
the rates which the burgesses were called upon
to pay. *In re Corporation of Birmingham* (unreported).

The Caledonian Railway Company having Case of *Caledonian*
been allowed deduction of all sums actually *Rail. Co.*
expended by them during the year in repairs v. *Banks.*
and renewals of stock, claimed to deduct a sum
of $4\frac{1}{2}$ per cent. on stock added during the
preceding five and a-half years, such added
stock not having been repaired (because until it
had depreciated to the extent of 25 per cent.
it would need no repairs, and it would not
have depreciated to that extent until it had
been in use five and a-half years), but depre-
ciating in value at the rate of $4\frac{1}{2}$ per cent. a
year. It was held that they were not entitled
to make the deduction; that "diminished "Diminished
value" means value for the purpose for which value,"
meaning
the article was intended in a going concern, not of.
for purpose of sale; and that the Commissioners

had decided as a question of fact—from which decision there was no appeal—that there had been no such diminution of value; that the plant in question required no repairs to enable it to produce the same amount of income that it did at first; and that, in allowing a deduction of sums actually expended in repairs and renewals, the Commissioners had allowed the sum expended in maintaining the whole of the company's plant in good working order, which sum might fairly be regarded as making up the whole deterioration which the wear and tear of the year had occasioned. *Caledonian Railway Company* v. *Banks*, 18 Sco. L. R. 85.

The Highland Railway Company, in making their return under the Income Tax Acts, claimed to deduct sums expended in improving a section of their line so as to bring it up to the standard of their main line, and in substituting heavy rails and chairs for lighter ones, on the ground that, although these sums had been charged against capital in the books of the company, they were properly chargeable against income. But it was held that the expenditure was not an expenditure for the maintenance of the line, but for altering the character of the line, and so a charge against capital, properly entered as such in the books of the company, and that the deduction could not be allowed. *Highland Rail. Co.* v. *Balderston*, 26 Sco. L. R. 657.

The Corporation of Newcastle-under-Lyme, under Parliamentary powers, purchased gas-works from a private company, understanding that the structural condition of the works was imperfect and defective, and that in the course of a few years a large outlay would have to be made to restore certain parts of the plant and apparatus. To meet this contingency the Corporation had set aside 500*l.* a year for five years. It was expected that the expenditure must of necessity take place within the next two or three years. A deduction had been made from the assessment upon the Corporation for the actual cost of all renewals, repairs, and maintenance of works for the year. The Corporation claimed a deduction in respect of the 500*l.* appropriated yearly to the special depreciation fund. It was held that they were not entitled to such deduction. *Clayton* v. *Newcastle-under-Lyme Corporation* (unreported).

Chap. II.

Case of *Clayton* v. *Newcastle-under-Lyme Corporation.* Special depreciation fund to meet expenditure on property purchased in defective state. No deduction allowed.

A company undertook to construct a railway in Brazil under a guarantee by the Government of Brazil of interest at the rate of 7 per cent. upon the money expended. The money was raised by debentures, upon which interest at the rate of 5½ per cent. was paid, and the balance of the 7 per cent. interest paid by the Brazilian Government was applied to the formation of a sinking fund. It was argued that the transaction amounted to a contribution by the

Case of *Blake* v. *Imperial Brazilian Rail. Co.* Excess of guaranteed interest paid to a company over interest payable by the company to its debenture holders

being
applied to
a sinking
fund,
cannot be
considered
as a con-
tribution
of capital
by instal-
ments.

Brazilian Government of capital in a number of annual payments, instead of in a lump sum, that the interest paid by the Brazilian Government was not, therefore, a profit or gain within the meaning of the Income Tax Acts, and that, although no question could arise as to the 5½ per cent. interest payable to the debenture holders, from which income tax would be deducted by the company, a deduction should be made from the amount upon which the company should pay income tax of the difference between the 5½ per cent. interest paid by the company to the debenture holders, and the 7 per cent. interest paid by the Brazilian Government to the company. But it was held that no such deduction could be allowed. *Blake* v. *Imperial Brazilian Rail. Co.* (unreported).

Case of
*Nizam's
Guaran-
teed State
Rail. Co.*
v. *Wyatt.*

And in the case of *Nizam's Guaranteed State Rail. Co.* v. *Wyatt* (L. R., 2 Q. B. 548), the Nizam of Hyderabad guaranteed to the company for twenty years an annuity of 5 per cent. on their issued share and debenture capital, which annuity was to be applied in paying interest on such capital, and in forming a sinking fund for the redemption of the debentures, subject to provisions for repayment of the sum paid under the guarantee, with interest, out of profits earned. In the case of *Blake* v. *Imperial Brazilian Rail. Co.* (*ubi sup.*), the formation of the sinking fund had not been provided for by

agreement, but in the present case it was part Chap. II.
of the agreement with the Nizam that the
sinking fund for the redemption of the debenture capital should be formed in the manner
stated. It was held that the whole of the
annuity, including the sums applied to the
sinking fund, was chargeable with income tax.

The Alexandria Water Company claimed a Case of
Alexandria
deduction in respect of interest payable to *Water Co.*
v. *Mus-*
foreign debenture holders. It was held that the *grave.*
deduction claimed could not be allowed, whether
the income tax paid could be recovered from the
foreign bondholders or not, being prohibited by
sect. 100, rule 4. *Alexandria Water Company*
v. *Musgrave*, 11 Q. B. D. 174 ; 52 L. J., Q. B.
349 ; 49 L. T. 287 ; 32 W. R. 146.

The directors of a fire insurance company Case of
Imperial
claimed to make a deduction for " unearned *Fire As-*
surance Co.
premiums," or premiums the period of accruing v. *Wilson.*
of which was unexpired. They argued that, " Unearned
inasmuch as insurances were effected at all premiums "
periods of the year, and the company's liabilities of fire
insurance
under the policies upon which those premiums company.
were paid did not expire with the expiration of
each year, the gross amount of premiums paid
to the company in any one year ought not to be
credited to them as profits actually realized in
that year ; that, in estimating their annual
profits, the company were entitled to deduct
from the gross amount of the premiums paid to

them within the year, 33 per cent., in order to make fair allowance for the premiums so unearned at the expiration of the year, and to enter such percentage amongst the profits realized in the succeeding year; that, in estimating their annual profits, the company were entitled to deduct from the gross amount of premiums paid to them within the year, such a sum as it would cost to re-insure the premiums which had not been exhausted during the year.[1] It was held that the company were not entitled to make the deduction claimed. The Court recognized the impossibility of doing complete justice between the Crown and the company; but said the injustice upon the company was in fact confined to the first year, when they commenced business; for, as they went on year by year, the charge upon them, under the mode of assessment appealed against, would, taking the average, be right; and in the last year of the business sect. 134 of 5 & 6 Vict. c. 35 (see *post*, p. 164) afforded a means of remedying any overcharge. The 33 per cent. was an arbitrary figure. Huddleston, B., suggested that the company might have adopted another mode of keeping their accounts, viz.: by ascertaining what amount of each premium was applicable to the year

---

[1] See cases of *Scottish Union, &c. Company* v. *Smiles*, and *Northern Assurance Company* v. *Russell, post*, pp. 146, 147.

current at the time of payment, and what to the succeeding year, and then have carried out a figure which would really represent the amount applicable to the risks of the last-named year. *Imperial Fire Assurance Company* v. *Wilson*, 35 L. T. 271.

An insurance company carried on the business of marine, fire, and life insurance. Its profits were derived from the following sources :— Case of *Last* v. *London Assurance Corporation.*

(1) Interest on paid up capital and reserve fund; (2) profit on marine business; (3) profit on fire business; (4) profit on life business. As regarded the profits derived from the first source no question arose, inasmuch as income tax was levied and paid by deduction from the interest, and dividends, of the investments of the funds. These profits were, therefore, not included in the return made by the company. As regarded the other three sources of profit, the company contended that the results of the three branches of their business should be thrown into one general account, and that if, and so far as, the total sum on which they paid income tax in respect of their investments exceeded the sum total of the profits they made, they were not liable to be assessed under Schedule D. The Surveyor contended that, assuming the company to be right in their contention, that the three branches of their business should be brought into one account, the assessable profit of the life branch was not to be

determined merely by the amount of profit available for division among the shareholders, but must be found by the third rule of the first case of Schedule D., and that, over and above the profit so appropriated to the shareholders, the accounts of the company showed (1) sums paid to policy-holders in the shape of bonuses, which was a distribution of assessable income or revenue; (2) additions made to the life fund, which was a transfer of income to capital. That, to arrive at the net balance of profit chargeable for the life branch under the above rule, account must be taken, on the one hand, of the life premiums received during the last three years, and on the other nothing must be allowed in the way of deduction beyond the claims actually paid under policies becoming payable in the same period, together with the expenses of managing the business; that the balance remaining would be the profit chargeable to the income tax for the life branch; and that this profit, added to the untaxed profit of the marine and fire branches, would represent the total liability of the company under Schedule D. In answer to the contention of the Surveyor, the company explained that in the life branch of their business there were three classes of policies, called respectively the "old," the "1831," and the "1846" series. The three classes were worked independently. As regarded the "old" series, any surplus which remained

after payment of policies belonged to the company for payment of expenses and profit. As
regarded the "1831" and the "1846" series,
by the terms of the contracts with the assured,
the surplus which remained after payment of
policies was dealt with as follows :—Two-thirds
of the surplus were returned to the assured, who
received payment, either by way of bonus, or by
abatement of premium ; and the remaining third
of the surplus went to the company, the balance
of which, after payment of expenses, constituted
the only profit of the company available for
division among the shareholders. The question
for the opinion of the Court was, whether or not,
for the purposes of assessment to income tax, the
contention of the company, that the results of
the three branches of their business should be
thrown into one account, was sound ; and upon
what principle the profits of the life business
should be calculated. It was held that the business of the company must be dealt with as a
whole, and not as three separate businesses,
although the accounts were naturally, as well
as by compulsion of law, kept separate; and
that the amounts yearly transferred from income to the life fund were not part of the
profits of the company, and were not, therefore,
subject to income tax. As regarded the question whether the amount set aside for distribution among the bonus policy holders was part

of the expenses of the business, or profits, the judges (Day and A. L. Smith, JJ.) differed. Day, J., holding that it was part of the expenses of the business and not profits, while A. L. Smith, J., held that it was profits. It was held that the case of the *Imperial Fire Assurance Co.* v. *Wilson* (*ubi sup.*) had no bearing upon the first question, inasmuch as [1]there was a radical difference between fire and life insurance; fire insurance premiums running out in all their incidents in one year, while in life insurance each premium has relation to the whole duration of the life or risk, and every year's premium has to be set aside and capitalised for payment of the future debt. *Last* v. *London Assurance Corporation*, 12 Q. B. D. 389; 53 L. J., Q. B. 325; 50 L. T. 534; 32 W. R. 702. On appeal, the judges were again divided upon the question whether the amount distributed amongst the bonus policy holders was expenses or profits, which was, in fact, the only question remaining to be decided. Brett, M. R., held that two sets of persons must be considered—the company, or, in other words, the shareholders, who carried on the business, and the customers, who were the assured. The taxable profits were, therefore, what the share-

Difference between premiums on fire and life insurance.

---

[1] See *Scottish Union, &c. Co.* v. *Smiles*, and *Northern Assurance Co.* v. *Russell*, *post*, pp. 146, 147.

holders received, while what was distributed
amongst the bonus policy holders was expenditure by which the profits were earned.
Cotton, L. J., agreed with the Master of the
Rolls, but Lindley, L. J., dissented, agreeing
with A. L. Smith, J., in the Court below. The
result was that the Court of Appeal affirmed
the judgment of the Court below. (14 Q. B. D.
245; 54 L. J., Q. B. 4; 52 L. T. 604; 33 W. R.
207.) The case was carried to the House of
Lords, where there was again a difference of
opinion. Lord Blackburn, with whom Lord
Fitzgerald agreed, held that the amount distributed amongst the bonus policy holders was
not expenditure by which the shareholders
earned the dividends payable to them, which
alone were taxable profits, but that the bonus
policy holders had in fact contracted for a share
in the profits, and that the taxable profits included the amount divided amongst the bonus
policy holders, as well as the amount paid in
dividends to the shareholders. The case of the
Mersey Docks v. *Lucas* (*ante*, pp. 60, 61) had decided
that income tax was payable on profits, whatever
the corporation earning the profits might be
bound to do with them, and not only so, but
the question was concluded by 5 & 6 Vict. c. 35,
s. 54, which enacted that the estimate of the
profits of a corporation should be made " before
any dividend shall have been made thereof to

any other person having any share, right, or title in, or to, such profits." Lord Bramwell, however, dissented, and in the course of his judgment pointed out that, if the contention of the Crown was right, all that insurance offices would have to do would be to alter their language, but that income tax would be payable in all cases in which employers had agreed with employed that, besides fixed wages, the employed should receive what is called a share of profits. The income tax would apply to co-operative societies strictly so called, and be payable on a sum falsely called profits, with no deduction of the wages contingently payable to workmen if gross profits enabled them to be paid. In the result, the judgment of the Court of Appeal (which had affirmed that of the Court below) was reversed. (L. R., 10 App. 438.)

Employers contracting to pay employed a share of profits— Lord Bramwell's opinion.

Co-operative societies— Lord Bramwell's opinion.

In the case of *Last* v. *London Assurance Corporation* (*supra*), it was assumed that the corporation was entitled to credit for income tax paid at the source on interest on investments, and, in the form of return after the final judgment in the House of Lords agreed upon between the Board of Inland Revenue and the corporation, the corporation were credited with taxed interest accordingly. But, although the account was adjusted on this basis, the case did not expressly decide whether, where interest on the investments of a life insurance society has not been

Case of Clerical, Medical, and General Life Assurance Society v. Carter.

taxed at the source, but paid in full, the Crown is entitled to charge income tax upon it, although the taxed interest paid at the source exceeds the sum which would be payable on trade profits. This latter question was raised in the case of the *Clerical, Medical, and General Life Assurance Society* v. *Carter* (21 Q. B. D. 339; 37 W. R. 124; 57 L. J., Q. B. 614; 59 L. T. 827), and was decided by the Queen's Bench Division in the affirmative, and the decision was affirmed on appeal. 21 Q. B. D. 444; 37 W. R. 346; 58 L. J., Q. B. 224.)

The Gresham Life Assurance Society sold annuities, the consideration being a lump sum paid down in the case of an immediate annuity, and either a lump sum, or a series of periodical premiums, in the case of a contingent, or deferred, annuity. The annuity obligations of the Society were in many instances dischargeable abroad. The Society claimed to deduct from its gross income the sums paid in discharge of its annuity obligations. The Queen's Bench Division held that the Society was not entitled to make the deduction, that the annuities were payable out of profits and gains—profits and gains meaning not strictly net profits, but such sums received as a merchant would bring into his account, and it having been the intention of the Legislature to give to the revenue the benefit of taxing, upon the first possible occasion of

Case of Gresham Life Assurance Society v. Styles.

taxation, any moneys which were taxable. The Court held, however, that the Society would be entitled to deduct from the annuities the proper income tax thereon under sect. 102 of the [1]Income Tax Act, 1842. On appeal, this decision was affirmed, and it was held that the deduction claimed was prohibited by Schedule D., r. 4, of the [1]Income Tax Act, 1842, and [2]sect. 102 of the same Act, but for which prohibition the deduction might have been made. The Court of Appeal also held that the case was governed by the rule of construction laid down in [3]*Alexandria Water Co.* v. *Musgrave.* But on appeal to the House of Lords, it was held that the Society ought not to be assessed upon the amount paid by it for the annuities, that the deduction prohibited by rule 4 of Schedule D. was a deduction on account of an annuity or annual payment made out of profits and gains, and that gross receipts were not to be treated as profits without regard to the payments to which, in consideration of those receipts, the Society had bound themselves. The rule was primarily designed to meet such a case as that in which a trader had contracted to make an annual payment out of his profits, as, for example, when he had agreed to make such a payment to a

[1] 5 & 6 Vict. c. 35. As to Schedule D. r. 4, see *ante*, p. 127.
[2] See *post*, pp. 157, 158, 249—251.
[3] See *ante*, p. 135.

former partner, or to a person who had agreed Chap. II.
to make a loan on the terms of receiving such
payment. The language of the 4th rule, when
read in connection with sect. [1]102 of the [2]Income
Tax Act, 1842, showed that the rule only related
to annuities payable out of profits and gains
"brought into charge" by virtue of the Act,
and the conclusion was not invalidated by the
fact that in the Act—for instance, in the 3rd
rule of schedule D.—the words "profits and
gains" were not always used in their proper or
ordinary sense. The decision in [3]*Alexandria
Water Co.* v. *Musgrave* was right upon the facts
of that case, the claim there being a claim to
deduct the company's debts for borrowed capital, and to diminish the amount of the profits
of the trading, but it did not govern [4]the present case. Sect. 102 of the [5]Income Tax Act,
1842, and sect. 40 of the [6]Income Tax Act,
1853, had no bearing upon the question. *Gresham Life Assurance Society* v. *Styles*, (in Queen's
Bench Division) 24 Q. B. D. 500; 38 W. R.
480; 62 L. T. 464; (in Court of Appeal) 25

[1] See *post*, pp. 157, 158, 249—251.
[2] 5 & 6 Vict. c. 35.
[3] *Ante*, p. 135.
[4] The case arose before the passing of the Customs and
Inland Revenue Act, 1888 (51 Vict. c. 8). See *post*, p. 250,
as to sect. 24 of this Act.
[5] 5 & 6 Vict. c. 35.
[6] 16 & 17 Vict. c. 34. See *post*, pp. 198, 199, as to sect. 40.

E.   H

Cases of
*Scottish
Union, &c.
Co.* v.
Smiles, and
*Northern
Assurance
Co.* v.
Russell.
1. Profits
of fire
insurance
and life
insurance
to be
reckoned
as one
undivided
income.

2. Interest
of invest-
ments from
which tax
has not
been de-
ducted at
the source
to be
reckoned
as profit.
3. Mode of
ascertain-
ing profits
of fire
insurance.

4. Mode of
ascertain-
ing profits

Q. B. D. 351; 38 W. R. 696; (in House of
Lords) 41 W. R. 270.

In the cases of the *Scottish Union and National
Insurance Co.* v. *Smiles,* and the *Northern Assurance Co.* v. *Russell* (26 Sco. L. R. 330), the following instructions were given by the Court:—

1. In assessing to the Income Tax the gains
of a Company carrying on the businesses both
of fire insurance and life insurance, the net profits and gains from the two branches of the
business must be massed together as one undivided income, assessable according to the rules
applicable to the first case under Schedule D.

2. The interest of investments which has not
suffered deduction of income tax at its source
must be taken into account in ascertaining the
assessable amount of profits and gains of the
Company.

3. Seeing that fire insurance policies are contracts for one year only, premiums received for
the year of assessment, or on an average of three
years, deducting losses by fire during the same
period and ordinary expenses, may be fairly
taken as profits and gains of the Company,
without taking into account, or making any
allowance for, the balance of annual risks unexpired at the end of the financial year of the
Company.

4. But this rule is not applicable to the ascer-
tainment of profits and gains upon "life" busi-

ness. Life policies are contracts of most variable Chap. II. endurance, and the premiums are in many cases of life not annual payments. The profits and gains insurance. can be ascertained only by actuarial calculation.

5. Where the gain is made by the Company 5. Profit on (within the year of assessment, or the three years an invest- prescribed by the Income Tax Act, Schedule D.) taxed. by realising an investment at a larger price than was paid for it, the difference is to be reckoned among the profits and gains of the Company.

Where a company, to extend its business, Case of opened a manufactory and fitted machinery, Westing- but subsequently closed it, removed a portion of Brake Co. the machinery, and re-opened the manufactory on a smaller scale, and thereby lost a portion of the original expenditure, it was held that this was a loss of capital, and that no deduction could be allowed in respect of such loss. *Smith* v. *Westinghouse Brake Co.* (unreported).

A company carrying on the business of iron- Case of founders claimed to deduct from the sum shown *Handyside.* in their own report as net profits a sum which they had written off under a provision in their articles of association to form a reserve fund for the purpose of "meeting contingencies, or of Reserve purchasing, improving, enlarging, rebuilding, contingen- restoring, reinstating, or maintaining the works, plant, and other premises, or property, of the company." The company had deducted a cer- tain sum for repairs, and the deduction had been

Chap. II.

allowed. It was held that they were not entitled to make the deduction claimed. [1]*Forder* v. *Handyside*, L. R., 1 Ex. D. 233; 35 L. T. 62; 24 W. R. 764.

Case of *Gillatt & Watts* v. *Colquhoun*.

Messrs. Gillatt & Watts paid a premium of 34,000*l.* for the lease of the house in which they carried on their business, and a rent of 250*l.* a year. The house was assessed to the income tax under Schedule A., at an annual value of 1,000*l.* Messrs. Gillatt & Watts contended that in making their returns for assessment under Schedule D. they were entitled to treat the 34,000*l.* paid in the first year as an actual expenditure in that year, so that, if they did not make any more than 34,000*l.*, they would have no income tax to pay at all, and that, the lease being for twenty-two years, they had a right to deduct in each year one twenty-second part of the 34,000*l.*, because the lease would diminish in value as every year was cut off from it. It was held that the principle contended for was

---

[1] The case of *Forder* v. *Handyside* was decided in the year 1876, before the passing of 41 & 42 Vict. c. 15, s. 12 (*ante*, pp. 60, 75), which permitted an allowance to be made in respect of depreciation of machinery. The case is referred to by A. L. Smith, J., in the course of his judgment in *Gillatt and Watts* v. *Colquhoun* (*infra*), as showing that the balance-sheet to be made out to show what profit a trader has made under Schedule D. is not to be worked out in the same way that the trader would make out his balance-sheet for his own information showing what profit or loss he has made.

wrong; that the right principle was, taking the premium into consideration, and the rent, to take what an actuary would put as the fair rent for the lease for the time over which the lease extended—that is, supposing no premium had been paid. It was found that the actual premium was not a fair premium, but one much too large, and, the case stated containing a finding that, the premises in question being assessed under Schedule A. at the sum of 1,000*l.*, that was, for the purposes of the case, to be taken as the "annual value" of the premises, the judges intimated that that should be taken as the fair rent the deduction of which should be allowed. [1] *Gillatt and Watts* v. *Colquhoun*, 33 W. R. 258.

[1] It may be gathered, from the observations of A. L. Smith, J., in delivering judgment in this case, that a freeholder carrying on his trade upon his own premises, would be entitled, in making his return of profits under Schedule D., to deduct a sum which would represent a fair rent for the premises. It will be remembered that special provision is made for the case of a person renting a dwelling-house of which part is used by him for the purpose of any trade or concern, enabling such person to make a deduction of so much, not exceeding two-thirds, of the rent paid by him as the Commissioners allow. (*Ante*, pp. 127, 130.) This provision seems intended to meet the case where the trader lives upon premises which he has hired, and carries on his trade there also, so that the premises are part dwelling-house, and part place of business. But where the owner of premises uses them solely for the purposes of the trade or concern which he carries on there, it would seem that he is entitled to deduct a fair rent.

Nothing is to be deducted which is not strictly part of the costs and expenses incurred in production. Therefore, although a brewer is entitled to deduct the annual cost of the buildings in which the beer is manufactured, the cost of the raw material used in the manufacture of beer, and the wages of the persons employed in the manufacture, and, it may be, under some circumstances, the cost of conveying the beer to the consumer, he is not entitled to deduct anything on account of premiums paid by him for leases of public-houses which he lets to tenants, whom he places under covenants to buy beer of him, any more than, if he chose to give dinners to publicans, and they said in return "We will buy a quantity of beer from you," he would be entitled to deduct the cost of the dinners; or than he would be entitled to deduct [1]the costs of

[1] As to the question whether the cost of advertisements may be deducted, the following observations were made by Grove, J., by way of illustration, in the course of his judgment in *Gillatt and Watts* v. *Colquhoun* (*ubi sup.*): "I may mention advertisements as one class of outlay, and in one case that was mentioned it was said to be a matter which ought to be deducted. No doubt it would be a most difficult question to settle, because it may differ in different trades. Some trades possibly may be founded very much upon advertisements; and there may be a trade of advertising which is founded upon the value of such advertisements. It is a question of degree, and I do not at present go the length of saying that in no case can advertisements ever be deducted."

advertisements by which he increased the sale Chap. II.
of his beer. *Watney* v. *Musgrave*, L. R., 5 Ex. D.
241; 49 L. J., Ex. 493; 42 L. T. 690; 28
W. R. 491.

The decision in the above-mentioned case of Case of
Watney v. *Musgrave* was held to be one affecting Brewery
investment of capital, and therefore to be con- Neale.
fined to the case itself, and inapplicable as a
guide in a case where a firm of brewers carried
on, in connection with their brewery business,
a business of banking and money lending, confined to the customers of the firm, and ancillary
to their business as brewers. The capital used
by the firm in the banking and money lending
business was held to be used only in the sense
that all money which is laid out by persons who
are traders is used; it was not invested in the
ordinary sense of the word. If the firm had
carried on two businesses, they would have been
entitled under [1] sect. 101 of 5 & 6 Vict. c. 35 to
set off a loss sustained in one business against a
profit made in the other, but as they carried on
not two businesses but one business, they were
entitled to write off, by way of deduction from
their taxable profits, such losses as they had sustained in the debts of the branch of the brewing
business relating to loans and advances. *Reid's
Brewery Co.* v. *Neale*, [1891] 2 Q. B. 1; 39

---

[1] See *ante*, pp. 129, 130.

W. R. 459; 60 L. J., Q. B. 340; 60 L. T. 294.

Case of
Russell v.
*Aberdeen
Town and
County
Bank.*

The Aberdeen Town and County Bank owned a building in which its business was carried on, and in which there was also accommodation provided for managers and agents of the Bank, who occupied portions of the building as their residences. The question raised was whether the Bank was entitled to deduct from its profits, before returning them for assessment under Schedule D., the whole value of their Bank premises, where such premises were in part occupied for residence by officers of the Bank. The Court of Exchequer (Scotland) decided that the Bank were entitled to make the deduction, and on appeal to the House of Lords the judgment was upheld. Lord Herschell said it was not disputed that the [1] annual value of premises exclusively used for business purposes is properly to be deducted in arriving at the balance of profits and gains. Probably this deduction was allowed because it was an essential element to be taken into account in ascertaining the amount of the balance of profits. For, if not, it could only be included by a

---

[1] It is believed that no difficulty will be made in allowing a deduction on account of annual value (which would be taxed under Schedule A.) of business premises owned by the person carrying on the business, whether such premises consist of land or buildings, although there may be, perhaps, some difficulty in pointing out how the right to such deduction is conferred. See *ante*, p. 149, note [1].

very broad extension of the terms actually used, as being a disbursement or expense, which is money wholly and exclusively laid out or expended for the purpose of the trade. But it was admitted, and, he thought, it must have been admitted, that in one way or another the deduction would have to be made. If the annual value of the premises belonging to the Bank, used for the purposes of their business, had to be deducted, there was no reason why any deduction should be made from that amount on account of the fact that the manager of the Bank for purposes of the business, or as part of his emolument (it mattered not which), occupied a portion of the Bank premises. And it made no difference whether the Bank manager would, or would not, be liable to income tax in respect of the value of his residence as part of the emoluments of his employment. *Russell* v. *Aberdeen and County Bank*, 13 App. Cas. 418.

Where a company borrowed money to be Case of *Arizona* employed in its business, and covenanted to pay Copper Co. v. *Smiles.* annual interest thereon, and to repay the capital with an additional bonus of 10 per cent., it was held that the bonus paid could not be claimed as a deduction. *Arizona Copper Co.* v. *Smiles*, 29 Sco. L. R. 134.

Second Source.—The second source from which the annual profits or gains chargeable under Schedule D.

H 5

Chap. II. arise [1] is " professions, employments, or vocations, not
contained in any other schedule ; " and " employ-
ment " extends to every employment by retainer in
any character whatever, whether such retainer shall
be annual or for a longer or shorter period, " and all
profits and earnings of whatever value." [2] The duty
to be charged on annual profits or gains arising from
this source is, like that on the annual profits or gains
arising from the first source, to be computed exclusively of the profits of lands, and [3] on an average of
profits of three years. [4] Friendly societies legally
established, and so conducting their business as not
to debar themselves from the benefit of the [5] exemption under Schedule C., are exempted from liability
to be charged under Schedule D., as under Schedule C.
In ascertaining the profits, [6] doubtful debts may be
estimated, as in the case of profits arising from the
first source.

Second Source—Deductions allowed.—[7] The deductions allowed in estimating the balance of profits and
gains upon which duty is charged under Schedule D.,

[1] 5 & 6 Vict. c. 35, s. 100, second case, and first rule of
second case.
[2] 5 & 6 Vict. c. 35, s. 100, second rule of rules applying to
first and second cases.
[3] 16 & 17 Vict. c. 34, s. 48.
[4] 16 & 17 Vict. c. 34, s. 49.
[5] See *ante*, p. 98.
[6] 16 & 17 Vict. c. 34, s. 50. See *ante*, p. 125.
[7] 5 & 6 Vict. c. 35, s. 100, rules applying to first and
second cases.

ånd which arise from the second source, are again, Chap. II.
except in the case of deduction on account of life insurance or deferred annuity, generally only negatively·
indicated by a reference to deductions *not* allowed,
which are the same, so far as the change of subject
will permit, as those allowed in the case of profits
arising from the first source; "profession, employment, or vocation," being substituted for "trade,
manufacture, adventure, or concern." [1] In addition,
however, to such deductions as are generally allowed,
there is one positively permitted in the case of a
clergyman, or minister, of any religious denomination, who is allowed to deduct from the profits, fees,
or emoluments of his profession, any expenses incurred by him wholly, exclusively, and necessarily,
in the performance of his duty or function as such

---

[1] 16 & 17 Vict. c. 34, s. 52. The words "profits, fees,
and emoluments of his profession," would seem to confine
the operation of this provision to cases in which the clergyman, or minister, is chargeable under Schedule D. But inasmuch as the section commences with the words "In assessing
the duty chargeable *under any schedule of this Act* upon any
clergyman, or minister," we must assume, unless the words
italicised have no meaning, that the deduction would be
allowed in cases where the clergyman, or minister, is chargeable under Schedules A., B., C., or E., provided only that he
enjoys that in respect of which he is charged as professional
emolument. A voluntary contribution made by a clergyman
towards the stipend of an assistant, is not an allowable deduction under this section, which applies to expenses incurred
by the clergyman in the personal performance of the duties
of his office. *Lothian* v. *Macrae*, 22 Sco. L. R. 219.

Chap. II. clergyman or minister. [1] A deduction is also allowed in respect of the rent of a dwelling-house, part of which is occupied for the purposes of a profession, the profits of which are chargeable under Schedule D.

Third Source.—[2] The third source can only be circuitously described. It is a source from which arise "profits of an uncertain annual value not charged in Schedule A." From the provisions which follow we may gather that the kind of profits intended are profits on securities bearing interest payable out of the public revenue (except [3] securities charged under Schedule C.), discounts, and interest of money not annual interest, and the profits arising from such trades as those of dealers in cattle and sellers of milk, who are concerned in an indirect way with land, but whose profits cannot be accurately estimated by the rent they pay for land in their occupation. The duty is charged upon the full amount of the profits or gains within the preceding year, ending on the day of the year immediately preceding the year of assessment, on which the accounts of the business (if profits of a business are in question) have been usually made up, or on the 5th day of April preceding the year of assessment. Land occupied by a dealer in cattle, or cupied by a dealer in a dealer in, or seller of, milk, where the land occupied

---

[1] See *ante*, pp. 127, 130.
[2] 5 & 6 Vict. c. 35, s. 100, third case. See *post*, pp. 222, 223.
[3] As to these securities, see *ante*, pp. 97, 98.

has been estimated or charged on the rent or annual
value, but is not sufficient for the keep and sustenance
of the cattle brought on the land, so that the rent or
annual value of the land cannot afford a just estimate
of the profits of such dealer, a return of such profits
is required, and such further sum must be charged
thereon as, together with the charge in respect of the
occupation of the land, makes up the full sum where-
with such trader ought to be charged. The same
deduction on account of life insurance, or purchase
of deferred annuity, is allowed as [1] in the case of
profits and gains arising from the first source. [2] All
annuities, yearly interest of money, or other annual
payments charged on any property of the person

---

[1] See *ante*, pp. 128, 129.

[2] 5 & 6 Vict. c. 35, s. 102. The practical effect of this
provision is, however, confined to cases in which the annual
payment is, by reason of the same being charged on property
in any of her Majesty's dominions abroad, or on any foreign
property, or foreign security, or otherwise, received without
any deduction of duty being made by the person liable to
make such payment (see *post*, pp. 197—201), or where any
such payment is made from profits or gains not charged by
the Income Tax Acts, or where any interest of money is not
reserved, or charged, or payable, for the period of one year.
In the case of the *Gresham Life Assurance Society* v. *Styles*
(see *ante*, p. 143) it was held by the Queen's Bench Division,
and by the Court of Appeal, that this section authorized a
society which sold annuities to deduct income tax from the
annuities paid. But the House of Lords decided that the
section had no such application. Such deduction may, however, now be made under sect. 24 of the "Customs and
Inland Revenue Act, 1888" (51 Vict. c. 8). See p. 250.

Chap. II. paying the same, or payable by virtue of any contract, are also charged with duty under the provisions applicable to the third case of Schedule D.

Case of *Strong.* Gift of money raised by voluntary subscription.　　　A gift of money raised by voluntary subscription and made annually to a minister of religion by his congregation is assessable—the annual gift being either "gain" under Schedule D., or "emolument" [1] under Schedule E. *In re George Walter Strong*, 15 Sco. L. R. 704. But a sum paid to a clergyman by way of allowance by a charitable society, not renewable save at the discretion of the society, and paid to the clergyman, not in respect of his services, but as being poor and deserving, is not assessable. *Turner* v. *Cuxson*, 22 Q. B. D. 151; 37 W. R. 254; 58 L. J., Q. B. 131; 60 L. T. 335; *ante*, p. 123.

Fourth Source.—[2] The fourth source is securities in what are called in the [3] Income Tax Act, 1842, "the British Plantations in America," or in any other of her Majesty's dominions out of Great Britain, and foreign securities, from which interest arises, except [4] such annuities, dividends, and shares as are charged under Schedule C. [5] It includes dividends, and shares of annuities, payable out of the revenue of any foreign state, and interest, dividends, or other annual

---

[1] As to Schedule E., see *post*, p. 166.

[2] 5 & 6 Vict. c. 35, s. 100, fourth case.

[3] 5 & 6 Vict. c. 35.

[4] As to these annuities, &c., see *ante*, pp. 97—101.

[5] 5 & 6 Vict. c. 80, s. 2, and 16 & 17 Vict. c. 34, s. 10.

payments, payable out of, or in respect of, the stocks,
funds, or shares of any foreign, or [1]colonial, company, society, adventure, or concern, or in respect of
any securities given by, or on account of, any such
company, &c., and [2] all annuities, pensions, or other
annual sums, payable out of the funds of any institution in India, which have been intrusted to any person, corporation, company, or society in the United
Kingdom, for payment to any person, corporation,
company, or society, in the United Kingdom. The
same deduction on account of life insurance, or
purchase of deferred annuity, is allowed as [3] in
the case of profits and gains arising from the first
source.

A company formed for the purpose of borrow-   *Case of Scottish*
ing money in this country and investing it   *Mortgage*
abroad at higher rates of interest, were charged   *Co. of New Mexico* v.
upon interest of money lent by them on the   *McKelvie.*
security of property in the United States of
America, a deduction being made of the expenses of management in America (which could
not have been received in this country as part of
the income derived from foreign securities, and
was, therefore, rightly deducted), and expenses

---

[1] 24 & 25 Vict. c. 91, s. 36 (the phrase "person entrusted
with payment" in this section, has the same extent of meaning as in sect. 96 of 5 & 6 Vict. c. 35, as to which see *post*,
p. 219, note [3]); 48 & 49 Vict. c. 51, s. 26.

[2] 31 & 32 Vict. c. 28, s. 5.

[3] See *ante*, p. 128.

of management in this country (which, whether rightly deducted or not, was allowed as a deduction by the Inland Revenue). The interest received by the company's agents in America was periodically brought into account in the books of the company kept at the head office in Glasgow, but of the funds raised by the company in this country there was retained a sum equivalent to the interest or gain realized from the American securities after defraying the working expenses in America, and out of this sum was paid all the working expenses in Great Britain, the interest to debenture holders and depositors, and a dividend at the rate of 7 per cent. to the shareholders. The company contended that under these circumstances the interest or gain realized from the American securities was not brought into this country, and therefore not chargeable. But it was held that the sum retained out of the funds raised in this country (the above-mentioned deductions being made) had been, in the process of book-keeping, converted into income (for otherwise the payments made out of it, which were clearly payments to be made out of income, would have been illegal), and that the company had been rightly charged.

The Crown may charge under the case most to its advantage.

It was held that the company were rightly charged under the fourth case, and that though they might have been charged under the first case, where a charge might be made under either of two cases, the Crown was entitled to charge under that case which was most to its advantage. (*Scottish Mortgage Co. of New Mexico* v. *McKelvie*, 24 Sco. L. R. 87 ; and see *Smiles* v. *Northern Investment Co. of New Zealand*, 24 Sco. L. R. 530.)

The Australasian Mortgage and Agency Company carried on an extensive and miscellaneous business in connection with the Australian colonies. The company were first of all wool-brokers, and they acted as parties both to buy and to sell wool, and they advanced money on the security of the goods in which they dealt, and they received a commission for their agency. Their trade was partly the trade of a broker and partly the trade of a banker, although they did not call themselves bankers. The advances made by them were made on second mortgages over real property in the colonies, and on liens and charges upon stock, wool, and other produce, and on the security of shipments of wool and other produce, some of which might be in warehouse in Australia, some in course of transit to this country, and some in warehouse in London. The advances were in the nature of bankers' advances or loans, the amounts of which fluctuate from time to time according as produce is realized or other payments are made. The company had its registered office in Scotland. It was sought to charge the company

Case of Smiles v. Northern Investment Co. of New Zealand.
Case of Smiles v. Australasian Mortgage and Agency Co.

upon the profits of a part of their business as if those profits were interest arising from securities in the colonies, so far as those profits were received in this country, under the fourth case of Schedule D. But it was held that that part of the business of the company which it was sought so to charge was proper trading, and not an investment of money upon securities, and that the company were chargeable under the first, and not under the fourth case of Schedule D. The case was distinguishable from the cases of the *Scottish Mortgage Co.* v. *McKelvie*, and *Smiles* v. *Northern Investment Co.* (*ubi sup.*). (*Smiles* v. *Australasian Mortgage and Agency Co.*, 25 Sco. L. R. 645.)

Fifth Source.—[1] The fifth source is possessions in the "British Plantations in America," or in any other of her Majesty's dominions out of Great Britain, and foreign possessions. The duty is charged upon the actual annual sums received in Great Britain upon an average of three preceding years, allowing such deductions only [2] as in the case of profits arising from the first source.

Sixth Source.—[3] The sixth source is such as produces annual profits or gains not falling under any

---

[1] 5 & 6 Vict. c. 35, s. 100, fifth case. As to the meaning of "possessions," see the case of *Colquhoun* v. *Brooks, ante,* pp. 117, 118.

[2] See *ante*, pp. 125 *et seq.*

[3] 5 & 6 Vict. c. 35, s. 100, sixth case.

of the preceding cases, and not charged by virtue of any other schedule. The duty is charged on the amount of the value of the profits and gains received annually, or according to an average of such period, greater or less than one year, as the case may require, and as shall be allowed by the Commissioners. The same deduction on account of life insurance, and purchase of deferred annuity, is allowed as [1] in the case of profits and gains arising from the first source.

Exemption from Duty and Abatement under Schedule D.—[2]Friendly societies legally established, and not assuring to any individual any sum which would Friendly societies. debar such society from the benefit of the exemption granted to friendly societies by 5 & 6 Vict. c. 35, in respect of their stocks, &c., chargeable under Schedule C., are exempted from the duty chargeable under Schedule D. [3]Trade unions duly registered under Trade the [4]Trade Union Acts, 1871 and 1876, and the rules unions. of which limit the amount assured to any member, or person nominated by or claiming under him, to a total sum not exceeding 200*l.*, and the amount of any annuity granted to any member or person nominated by him to a yearly sum not exceeding 30*l.*, are

[1] See *ante*, pp. 128, 129.
[2] 16 & 17 Vict. c. 34, s. 49. As to the exemption under Schedule C, see *ante*, p. 98.
[3] Trade Union (Provident Funds) Act, 1893 (56 Vict. c. 2, s. 1.
[4] 34 & 35 Vict. c. 31; 39 & 40 Vict. c. 22.

Chap. II.

exempt from income tax chargeable under Schedule D., in respect of the interest and dividends of the trade union applicable and applied solely for the purpose of [1]provident benefits. [2]A person whose income is less than 150*l.* a year is exempted from payment of income tax; and a person whose income, though exceeding 150*l.* a year, is less than 400*l.* a year, is entitled to an abatement in respect of 120*l.* of his income. The mode in which such exemption and abatement respectively may be claimed and allowed will be described [3]later on. [4]Abatements may be claimed on account of diminution of profits and gains within the year current at the time of making the assessment, which reduces the profits and gains for that year below the sum at which they were computed, and also in case the person charged ceases to carry on trade, or dies, before the end of such year. [5]And when a person sustains a loss in any trade, manufacture, adventure, or concern, or profession, employment, or vocation, carried on by him either solely or in partnership, he may obtain an adjustment of his liability by reference to the loss and to the aggregate amount of his income for the

Person whose annual income is less than 150l., or than 400l.

Person sustaining a loss in trade, &c.

---

[1] As to what are "provident benefits," see *ante,* p. 86.

[2] 39 & 40 Vict. c. 16, s. 8.

[3] See *post,* pp. 265—271, 294.

[4] 5 & 6 Vict. c. 35, ss. 133, 134. As to the mode in which such abatements are claimed and made, see *post,* pp. 303—306.

[5] 53 & 54 Vict. c. 8, s. 23. As to the mode in which the relief is claimed and made, and the time within which the claim must be made, see *post,* pp. 305, 306.

year, estimated according to the several rules and
directions of the Income Tax Acts. But if he
avails himself of this relief, he will not be entitled
to claim, or be allowed a deduction on the assessment
for a subsequent year by reference to the amount of
the loss in respect of which he has obtained relief.

In the case of *Tennant* v. *Smith* ([1892] A. C.
150; 61 L. J., P. C. 11; 66 L. T. 327) it was
held that an agent for a bank, who was bound,
as part of his duty, to occupy the bank house as
custodian of the whole premises belonging to the
bank, and also for the transaction of any special
bank business after bank hours; who was not
entitled to sub-let the bank house, or to use it
for other than bank business; and who, in the
event of his ceasing to hold his office, was under
obligation to quit the premises forthwith; claiming abatement on the ground that his total
income from all sources was less than 400*l.*,
cannot be compelled to bring into account the
yearly value of his privilege of free residence in
the bank premises.

Doubtful Debts may be valued.—[1] In ascertaining
the profits of any person chargeable under Schedule
D., the value of all doubtful debts due or owing to
the person who is to be charged may be estimated,
and in the case of the bankruptcy, or insolvency, of
the debtor, the amount of the dividend which may

[1] 16 & 17 Vict. c. 34, s. 50.

Chap. II. reasonably be expected to be received on any debt due from him is to be deemed the value thereof.

SECTION V.—SCHEDULE E.

Public Offices, &c.—Under Schedule E. the duty is charged [1] "for, and in respect of, every public office or employment of profit, and upon every annuity, pension, or stipend, payable by her Majesty, or out of the public revenue of the United Kingdom, except [2] annuities charged to the duties under Schedule C.," for every [3] twenty shillings of the annual amount thereof. [4] The following is an enumeration of the "public offices and employments of profit," upon which the duty is charged for all "salaries, fees, wages, perquisites, or profits," accruing therefrom, under Schedule E., viz. :—

Offices :—
1. Of Parliament.

1. Parliament. Any office belonging to either House of Parliament.

2. Of Courts of justice.

2. Courts of justice. Any office belonging to any Court of justice.

3. Of civil service.

3. Civil service, &c. Any public office held under the civil government of her Majesty, or in any county palatine, or the Duchy of Cornwall.

[1] 16 & 17 Vict. c. 34, s. 2.

[2] As to these annuities, see *ante*, pp. 97 *et seq.*

[3] Fractional parts of 20*s.* are charged with duty by the Act 16 & 17 Vict. c. 34, s. 3; but no duty is charged of a lower denomination than 1*d.*

[4] 5 & 6 Vict. c. 35, s. 146, r. 3.

4. Army, navy, &c. The office of any commis- Chap. II.
sioned officer in the army or navy, or in the militia 4. Of army,
or volunteers. navy, &c.

5. Ecclesiastical. Any office held under any 5. Ecclesiastical.
ecclesiastical body.

6. Public corporations, &c. [1] Any office held under 6. Of public
any public corporation, or under any company or corporations,
society. companies
or socie-
7. Public institutions. Any office under any public ties.
institution, or in any public foundation. 7. Of public
institutions.
8. County, municipal, &c. Any office in any
county, city, town, or place. 8. County, municipal, &c.

9. General. Every other public office or employ- 9. Gene-
ment of profit of a public nature. rally.

The profits [2] may be estimated either on the profits
of the preceding year, or on the fair average of one
year of the amount of the profits in the three years
preceding, such years in each case ending on the
5th day of April in each year, or on the other day
of each year on which the accounts of such profits
have been usually made up. And in estimating
the profits the following deductions may be made,
viz. :—

1. [3] The amount of duties, or other sums, payable First de-
or chargeable on the same, by any Act of Parliament, Duties, duction:

[1] Including offices, and employments of profit held in, or
under, any railway company. See 23 & 24 Vict. c. 14, s. 6.
[2] 5 & 6 Vict. c. 35, s. 146, fourth rule.
[3] 5 & 6 Vict. c. 35, s. 146, first rule.

Chap. II.
&c. payable by Act of Parliament.

where such duties, &c., have been actually paid by the person charged.

Second deduction: Official deductions.

2. [1]All official deductions and payments made upon the receipt of the salaries, fees, wages, perquisites, and profits.

Third deduction: Expenses of travelling and keeping a horse.

3. [2]The expenses of travelling in performance of the duties of the office or employment, necessarily incurred, or of keeping a horse necessary for the fulfilment of such duties, actually defrayed out of the emoluments of the office or employment, and money otherwise necessarily and actually expended in the performance of such duties.

Case of Bowers v. Harding.

An assessment was made upon George Harding under Schedule E. in respect of his office of national schoolmaster, and [3]of the office of national schoolmistress held by his wife, for which they received a joint salary of 150*l.* a year, and also of Harding's office of choirmaster, for which he received 10*l.* a year. He claimed a deduction of 30*l.* a year, in respect of expenses incurred by him in keeping a servant, in order

---

[1] 5 & 6 Vict. c. 35, s. 146, ninth rule.

[2] 16 & 17 Vict. c. 34, s. 51. The directors of a company who travel from their residences to the place of meeting of the company cannot, under this section, deduct their travelling expenses from the remuneration allowed them as such directors. *Revel* v. *Directors of Elworthy Brothers & Co., Limited* (not reported).

[3] By sect. 45 of 5 & 6 Vict. c. 35, the profits of a married woman, living with her husband, are to be deemed the profits of the husband. See *post*, p. 180.

that his wife might be able to perform her Chap. II.
duties as schoolmistress, which, in addition to
the deduction of 120*l.* a year, the statutory
abatement on all incomes less than 400*l.*,
and 12*l.* allowed for annual life insurance premium, would have entitled him to total exemption, as reducing his income from all sources
below 150*l.* a year. It was held that the deduction for expenses of keeping a servant could not
be allowed. *Bowers* v. *Harding*, [1891] 1 Q. B.
560; 39 W. R. 558; 60 L. J., Q. B. 474; 64
L. T. 201.

4. A deduction on account of life insurance and Fourth deduction:
purchase of deferred annuity, similar to [1]that For life
insurance.
allowed in case of profits, &c., chargeable under
Schedule D.

Mr. Glasson was principal bursar of St. John Case of
Langston
Baptist College, Oxford, and in that capacity v. *Glasson.*
received a stipend of 450*l.* a year. He was one
of several officers who received such stipends as
the president and fellows of the college at their
general meeting considered to be proper. He
was not one of the body who constituted the
college. The following are instructions given
by the Board of Inland Revenue to the officers
of Inland Revenue. "The members of a capi-
tular or collegiate body are not liable to direct

---

[1] See *ante*, p. 128.

assessment in respect of sums which they are, as members of the corporate body, legally entitled to receive out of the taxed income of the corporation. Salaries paid out of such income to persons who are not members are, however, chargeable by direct assessment, unless they are a charge by statute or otherwise on the revenue of the corporation." The question was, to which of the two categories the bursar belonged. If he was a member of the collegiate body, and was merely taking his 'share of the collegiate property, he would not be taxed, for then there would be no office, no salary, but he really would be receiving that which fell to his lot as one of that college body. But if he received a salary paid out of the college income, that salary was liable to be assessed and charged. It was held that the bursar fell under the latter of the two categories, and that he was chargeable with income tax in respect of his stipend. *Langston* v. *Glasson*, [1891] 1 Q. B. 567; 39 W. R. 476; 60 L. J., Q. B. 356; 65 L. T. 159.

Exemption when Income is under 150*l.*; *and Abatement when Income is under* 400*l.*—[1]A person whose income is less than 150*l.* a year is exempt from payment of income tax; and [1]a person whose income,

---

[1] 39 & 40 Vict. c. 16, s. 8.

though exceeding 150*l.*, is less than 400*l.* a year, is entitled to an abatement in respect of 120*l.* of his income. The mode in which the exemption and abatement respectively are claimed and allowed will be described [1]later on.

---

[1] *Post*, p. 309.

CHAPTER III.

ASSESSMENT AND COLLECTION.

WE have now to explain the modes in which the duties of income tax are assessed, and collected. The modes of assessment, and collection, differ according to the kind of property, or character of profits, to be charged. The simplest way to deal with the subject will be to take each schedule in turn, and describe with reference to the property, or profits, comprised in each the mode of assessment, and collection, prescribed.

SECTION I.—SCHEDULE A.

SUB-SECTION I.—ASSESSMENT.

Who are Commissioners for assessing Duty under Schedule A.—[1]The General Commissioners act in all matters relating to the duties in Schedule A., except [2]such] allowances in respect thereof as are made by the Special Commissioners, and except [3]assessments in respect of the annual value of, or profits or gains arising from, railways, [4]which are made by the Special Commissioners.

---

[1] 5 & 6 Vict. c. 35, s. 22.

[2] 5 & 6 Vict. c. 35, s. 22. As to allowances made by the Special Commissioners, see *post*, Chap. IV.

[3] 23 & 24 Vict. c. 14, s. 5.

[4] See *post*, p. 212.

Place of Charge.—[1] All properties chargeable to the Chap. III.
duties under Schedule A. are charged in the parish
or place where the same are situate, except in the
following cases :—

1. Canals, &c. The profits arising from canals, First case
inland navigations, streams of water, drains or levels, ception :
railways, and roads or ways of a public nature, and &c., rail-
belonging to, or vested in, any company of pro- roads, &c.
prietors or trustees, corporate or not corporate, may
be stated in one account, and charged in the city,
town, or place at, or nearest to, the place at which the
general accounts of such concern have been usually
made up.

2. Manors and royalties. The profits arising from Second
any manor or royalty which extends into different exception :
parishes may be assessed in one account in the parish and royal-
where the Court for such manor or royalty has been ties.
usually held. And the profits arising from all fines
received by the same person may be assessed in one
account where the person to be charged resides.

3. Lands occupied by the same person. All lands Third
occupied by the same person are to be brought into exception :
every account required to be delivered by such per- different
son, although situated in different parishes ; but the occupied
duties to be charged thereon are charged in each same
parish, in proportion to the value of the property person.
situate therein. But land situate in the same district
of Commissioners, although in different parishes, may

---

[1] 5 & 6 Vict. c. 35, s. 60, No. 4, rr. 1, 2.

Chap. III. be charged in either parish at the discretion of the
Commissioners, if they are satisfied that the proportion in each parish, either in respect of the quantity,
rent, or value of the lands, cannot be ascertained.   If
the lands extend into different districts of Commissioners, they are to be assessed in the district in which
the occupier resides.

Mode of proceeding to obtain Return.—[1]The Assessor
for each parish, being appointed as we have [2]before
explained, causes notices to be affixed on the door of
the church, or chapel, of the parish, and in other
specified situations, requiring [3]all persons who are
bound to make any list, declaration, or statement, to
make out and deliver the same to the Assessor, or to
the General Commissioners, or their Clerk, at a place
to be specified in the notice, within a time which must
not be more than twenty-one days.   The notices must
remain up for ten days before the day appointed for
the delivery of the list, &c. ; and every person who
defaces a notice renders himself liable to a penalty
not exceeding 20*l.*   Further, although the general
notice we have mentioned is to be deemed sufficient
notice to all persons resident within the place for
which the Assessor acts, [4]he must also give a similar

---

[1] 5 & 6 Vict. c. 35, s. 47.

[2] *Ante*, pp. 25 *et seq.*

[3] As to the persons bound to make out lists, &c., see *post*,
pp. 175—178.

[4] 5 & 6 Vict. c. 35, s. 48.

notice to every person chargeable in respect of any Chap. III.
property situate, or profits arising, within the limits
of such place. This additional notice may be served
by leaving it at the residence of the person to be
charged, or on the premises upon which the assessment is made; or, if given by a Surveyor, as may be
the case when Assessors are not appointed, or [1] when
the Assessor has neglected to give the notice to any
person to whom it ought to be given, or when any
person comes to reside in any parish, or place, after
the expiration of the notices given by the Assessor,
[2] may be sent by registered post.

Persons required to make out Lists, &c.—The persons who are required to make out lists, declarations,
and statements, and who are, therefore, affected by
the above-mentioned notices, are the following:—

1. Persons chargeable. [3] Every person chargeable 1. Persons charge-
with duty must, when required to do so, prepare a able with duty must
statement in writing containing (a) the [4] annual make out statement.
value of all lands and tenements in his occupation,
and (b) the amount of the profits or gains made by
him, and chargeable, from whatever source they arise.

2. Persons acting for others. [5] Every person who 2. Persons acting for others
receives money, or value, or profits, or gains, belong-

---

[1] 5 & 6 Vict. c. 35, s. 57.
[2] 43 & 44 Vict. c. 19, s. 16.
[3] 5 & 6 Vict. c. 35, s. 52.
[4] As to the meaning of "annual value" under Schedule A.,
see *ante*, pp. 48 *et seq.*
[5] 5 & 6 Vict. c. 35, s. 51.

ing to any other person, for which such other person is chargeable, or would be chargeable if resident in Great Britain, must prepare a statement in writing of such money, value, profits, or gains, and of the name and place of abode of every person to whom the same belongs, and whether such person is of full age, or a married woman living with her husband, or a married woman for whose payment of the duty the husband is not accountable, or resident in Great Britain, or an infant, idiot, lunatic, or insane person. If any other person is joined with the person delivering this statement in receiving such money, value, profits, or gains, *his* name and address must also be stated.

[1]If the person to whom the money, &c., belongs is an idiot or lunatic, or resident out of Great Britain, and so cannot be personally charged, the person making the statement must add a declaration that the amount of the profits, &c., has been estimated on all the sources mentioned in the schedules describing the same, as if he himself were to be charged in respect of property of his own.

3. Officers of companies. [2]The Chamberlain, or other officer acting as treasurer, auditor, or receiver, for the time being, of any corporation, fraternity, fellowship, company, or society, must prepare a statement in writing of the profits and gains of such corporation, &c.; and [3]must also do all such acts as

1 5 & 6 Vict. c. 35, s. 53.
2 5 & 6 Vict. c. 35, s. 54.
3 42 & 43 Vict. c. 21, s. 18.

are required to be done for assessing the officers and Chap. III.
persons in the employment of the corporation, &c.
The estimate of profits, &c., must be made on the
amount of the annual profits and gains before any
dividend is paid; but salaries, wages, or profits of any
officer of such corporation, &c., otherwise chargeable,
are not to be included in the statement.

4. Persons having lodgers, employés, &c. [1] Every 4. Persons having lodgers, employés, &c. must make out lists of names.
person, on being required to do so, must prepare a
list in writing of the names of lodgers or inmates
resident in his dwelling-house, and of other persons
chiefly employed in his service, whether resident in
his dwelling-house or not, and of any lodger or
inmate who has any ordinary place of residence elsewhere at which he is entitled, and desires, to be
assessed.

[2] The lists, &c., must be made out in the prescribed
form, and signed by the person making them, and
delivered to the Assessor of the parish, or place, in
which such person resides. In the case of statements
made by trustees, or agents, of persons incapacitated,
or abroad, the statements may be signed by all the
trustees, or agents, if more than one, or by one on
behalf of himself and his colleagues; and when the
statement is made by the person chargeable, or, as
before mentioned, by the agent of a person incapacitated, or resident out of Great Britain, or by the

[1] 5 & 6 Vict. c. 35, s. 50.
[2] 5 & 6 Vict. c. 35, ss. 50, 51, 52, 53, 54, 190, Sched. G.

I 5

Chap. III. officer of a corporation, &c., it must contain a declaration that the amount of profits which it shows has been estimated on all the sources contained in the schedules describing the same. [1] The penalty for neglecting to deliver lists, &c. is, if proceeded for by information before the Commissioners, a sum not exceeding 20l. and treble duty, the increased duty to be added to the assessment; if proceeded for in a court of law, 50l. But if any person who is required to deliver a list, &c., on behalf of another, delivers an imperfect list, &c., and declares that he is at the time unable to deliver a more perfect list, &c., giving reasons for such inability, and the Commissioners are satisfied with the reason given, further time may be granted for the delivery of a list, &c., as perfect as the nature of the case admits of. [2] And no person required to deliver a list of persons in his service or employ is liable to a penalty for omitting the name, or residence, of any such person not resident in his dwelling-house, if it appears that such person is exempt from payment of duty. [3] And a person who has not received a particular notice from the Assessor, [4] as before mentioned, is not liable to any penalty for having neglected to make a statement of income, if it appears to the Commissioners on inquiry that he is entitled to be exempt from payment of all duty.

[1] 5 & 6 Vict. c. 35, s. 55.
[2] 5 & 6 Vict. c. 35, s. 50.
[3] 5 & 6 Vict. c. 35, s. 56.
[4] *Ante*, pp. 174, 175.

Persons chargeable.—All persons who are in pos- session for their own benefit of profits arising from property, professions, trades, and offices, are "persons chargeable" with duty in respect thereof.

Persons chargeable in respect of Profits not their own. Persons charge-
—Besides those who are in receipt for their own able in
benefit of profits arising from property, professions, profits not
trades, and offices, and who are chargeable with duty their own;
in respect thereof, certain other persons are chargeable in respect of profits not their own, but which
they receive for others. Thus [1]the parent, guardian, parents, trustees,
or tutor of any infant or person under twenty-one guardians, tutors,
years of age, and the trustee, guardian, tutor, cura- curators,
tor, or committee of any infant, married woman, com- mittees;
lunatic, idiot, or insane person, having the management of the property of such infant, &c., whether such
infant, &c., is resident in Great Britain or not; and
[2]the executors or administrators of any person dying; executors and admi-
and [3]the factor, agent, or receiver, having receipt of nistrators;

[1] 5 & 6 Vict. c. 35, ss. 41, 108, 173; 43 & 44 Vict. c. 19, s. 92.
[2] 5 & 6 Vict. c. 35, s. 173; 43 & 44 Vict. c. 19, s. 92.
[3] The person not resident in Great Britain is, strictly speaking, to be charged, but *in the name of* his trustee, guardian, tutor, curator, committee, factor, agent, or receiver. (Sect. 41.) This, however, practically amounts to the trustee, &c. being chargeable, and he is responsible for doing all acts requisite for assessment. But see sect. 108. In *Tischler* v. *Apthorpe* (33 W R. 548; 52 L. T. 814, *ante*, p. 106), Mathew, J., referring to sect. 41 of 5 & 6 Vict. c. 35, said, "When one looks at the section, and then at sect. 44" (see below), "it is clear that sect. 41 is intended to aid the Commissioners in

Chap. III. any profits belonging to any person resident out of

factors, agents and receivers; Great Britain; [1] the receiver appointed by the Chancery Division of the High Court of Justice, or any

receivers appointed by the Chancery Division of the High Court of Justice; other Court in Great Britain having the direction and control of any property chargeable; [2] the husband of any married woman living with her husband (in

husbands of married women; respect of profits of the wife); [3] the wife of any man,

wives living separate from their husbands; living separate from her husband, whether he shall be only temporarily absent or otherwise (in respect of any allowance or remittance received from her husband, or from property of his out of Great Britain); are all chargeable in respect of the profits received by them in the characters aforesaid. So

bodies politic, &c., companies, &c.; [4] all bodies politic, corporate, or collegiate, companies, fraternities, fellowships, or societies of persons, corporate or not corporate, are chargeable, and the

recovering the tax, and not to alter the incidence of taxation in any way, for, under sect. 44, the agent who was charged under sect. 41 is entitled to recover from his principal, who is the person really liable, any payment he may have made. If the principal can be got at, there is no need to have recourse to sect. 41. But where the case contemplated by sect. 41 arises, of one resident abroad who cannot be reached by the Commissioners, then the Commissioners can come down upon the agent." This was adopted by Lord Esher, M. R., in *Werle & Co.* v. *Colquhoun,* 20 Q. B. D. 753; 36 W. R. 613; 57 L. J., Q. B. 323; 58 L. T. 756 (*ante,* p. 109).

[1] 5 & 6 Vict. c. 35, s. 43.

[2] 5 & 6 Vict. c. 35, s. 45.

[3] 5 & 6 Vict. c. 35, s. 45. Married women acting as sole traders, or having separate property, are chargeable as if unmarried.

[4] 5 & 6 Vict. c. 35, s. 40.

officer acting as treasurer, auditor, or receiver, for Chap. III.
the time being, is to do all acts requisite for assessment. [1] But parents, trustees, agents, factors, trustees,
&c. may
receivers, guardians, tutors, curators, or committees, retain
moneys
executors, or administrators, so charged may retain for payment of
from moneys coming to their hands when acting duties;
in such capacities enough to pay the duties charged,
and every such officer of a company, &c. is indem- officers of
companies
nified against the company, &c. for all payments indemni-
fied in
made by him in discharge of such chargeableness paying
duties;
as aforesaid. [2] A trustee who has authorized the trustees in
receipt of the profits arising from the trust property certain
cases only
by the person entitled thereto, or his agent (provided bound to
return
they have been actually so received), need, however, names of
cestuis que
do no more than return a statement of the name and trust;
residence of such person, and the case is the same
with any agent, or receiver, of any person of full and
agents,
age resident in Great Britain, not being a married &c. of
names of
woman, lunatic, idiot, or insane person, unless indeed persons
for whom
the testimony of the trustee, agent, or receiver, is they act.
required by the Commissioners, [3] for then such testimony must be given.

Occupiers chargeable for Owners of Land.—[4] The
occupier, that is, the person having the use, of any

[1] 5 & 6 Vict. c. 35, ss. 44, 73; 43 & 44 Vict. c. 19, s. 92.
[2] 5 & 6 Vict. c. 35, s. 42.
[3] 5 & 6 Vict. c. 35, s. 125.
[4] 5 & 6 Vict. c. 35, s. 63, No. 9, rr. 1, 2, 3. The occupier
may deduct the duties paid by him from his rent. See *post*,
pp. 197, 198.

Chap. III. lands or tenements for the time being, is chargeable with the duties under Schedule A., although he is not the owner of the lands and tenements, and although [1] he has not occupied them for the whole period for which the duty is levied. There are, however, the following exceptions to this rule, the reasons for which will be easily understood :—

First exception : Dwelling-house under the value of 10*l.* a year, and

1. Dwelling-house under the value of 10*l.* a year, or let for a period less than one year. [2] The owner, and not the occupier, is chargeable in the case of any dwelling-house in the occupation of a tenant, which, with the buildings or offices belonging thereto and the land occupied therewith, is under the value of

land or tenement let for a

10*l.* a year, and also in the case of any land or tenement let to any tenant for a less period than

---

[1] Every tenant on quitting the occupation is liable for any arrears at the time of so quitting, and for a proportionate part of the accruing duty up to the time of quitting. The amount for which the tenant quitting is so liable must be settled and levied by the Commissioners, and repaid to the occupier by whom the same has been paid. The executors, or administrators, of any tenant who dies before payment of any such assessment, is liable in like manner as the testator or intestate would have been if living. Every tenant quitting before the time of making the assessment, is liable for such portion of the year as has elapsed at the time of his so quitting, and the amount for which he is so liable must be adjusted, and settled, by the Commissioners; 5 & 6 Vict. c. 35, s. 63, No. 9, r. 3. These provisions can only have effect where the occupier cannot deduct the duty he has paid from the rent. See the last note.

[2] 5 & 6 Vict. c. 35, s. 60, No. 4, r. 3.

one year. But in default of payment by the owner the duty may be recovered from the occupier.

2. House occupied by foreign minister. [1] The owner, or person immediately entitled to the rent, and not the occupier, is chargeable in the case of any house or tenement occupied by any accredited minister from any foreign prince or state.

3. House let in apartments. [2] The landlord of any house or building let in different apartments or tenements, and occupied by two or more persons severally, is chargeable in respect of such house, &c. But in default of payment by him, the duty may be levied on the occupier or occupiers respectively. And [3] where any house is divided into distinct properties, and occupied by distinct owners, or their respective tenants, the duties are charged upon the respective occupiers.

Landowner chargeable for Owner of Rent-charge in lieu of Tithe.—[4] By an exception introduced in the case of the owner of a rent-charge confirmed under the [5] Act passed for the commutation of tithes, the owner of the land out of which the rent-charge issues pays the duty in respect of the land without any deduction on account of such rent-charge, though [6] on paying the rent-charge he will, of course, deduct the duty thereon.

Marginal notes:
Chap. III.
less period than one year.
Second exception : House occupied by foreign minister.
Third exception : House let in apartments.

[1] 5 & 6 Vict. c. 35, s. 60, No. 4, r. 7.
[2] 16 & 17 Vict. c. 34, s. 36.
[3] 5 & 6 Vict. c. 35, s. 60, No. 4, r. 13.
[4] 5 & 6 Vict. c. 35, s. 60, No. 2, r. 3.
[5] 6 & 7 Will. 4, c. 71.
[6] 5 & 6 Vict. c. 35, s. 60, No. 4, r. 10. See *post*, p. 200.

Chap. III. [1]But ([2]except in the Metropolis), on a due return of
any such rent-charge being made by the owner thereof
in order to an assessment upon him, the Commissioners acting in the matter may, if they think fit,
charge and assess the owner of the rent-charge in
respect thereof, allowing a deduction for the amount
of the parochial rates charged upon, or in respect of,
such rent-charge during the preceding year, and, in
case the assessment is made upon the owner of the
rent-charge, the amount of the rent-charge is allowed
as a deduction in the assessment of the land upon
which the same is charged.

Case of
Stevens v.
Bishop.

The owner of a tithe commutation rent-charge
assessed under section 32 of the Act of 1853,
may deduct the expenses of collection, where the
amount could not be realised without such
expenditure in collection.   Sect. 5 of the Act of
1853 makes the earlier statute of 1842 applicable to the income tax under the later Act.
The method of assessment under that Act is
contained in Schedule A.   Rule 1 of that
Schedule is the rule applicable.   Matters incapable of actual occupation may very well be within
that rule, but at any rate the words used in that
rule must be made to apply, inasmuch as sect.
5 of the Act of 1853 makes them applicable, for
the case cannot be brought under rule 2.   The

---

[1] 16 & 17 Vict. c. 34, s. 32.
[2] 32 & 33 Vict. c. 67, s. 77. As to the meaning of "Metropolis," see *ante*, p. 29, note [3].

value of the tithe rent-charge is, therefore, the **Chap. III.** amount at which it would let at a rack rent. This clearly could not exceed the gross amount of the tithe rent-charge less the reasonable remuneration for its collection, not the cost of a merely optional collection, but the expenditure without which the amount could not be realised. *Stevens* v. *Bishop*, 20 Q. B. D. 442; 36 W. R. 421; 57 L. J., Q. B. 283; 58 L. T. 669.

Other Persons chargeable.—[1]Subjects of the Queen whose ordinary residences are in Great Britain, but who have gone abroad for the purpose only of occasional residence, remain chargeable as if they had continued to reside in Great Britain. Persons temporarily in Great Britain become chargeable after residence, at one time, or at several times, for a period amounting to six months in any one year.

Proceedings after Notices given.—The notices having been given, [2]the Assessor appears before the Commissioners at the time appointed, and verifies upon oath the fixing of the general notices, and the delivery of the particular notices; and, if it appears that notices have not been served upon any persons, the Surveyor may cause notices to be served on them, as he may also cause notices to be served upon persons coming to reside in the parish after the Assessor's report.

[1] 5 & 6 Vict. c. 35, s. 39.
[2] 5 & 6 Vict. c. 35, ss. 57, 58.

Assessment—Period for which made.—[1] Every assessment is made for the year commencing on the 6th day of April in any year, and ending on the 5th day of April following; each of such days being reckoned inclusively.

Assessment in Case of Return made by Party chargeable.—[2] In the meantime, however, the Assessor proceeds to make his assessment, observing therein, in the case of each kind of property, the rules applicable thereto, which we have before explained; and using the returns made by the party chargeable. If he finds a difficulty in so doing, he applies for instruction, and assistance, to the Commissioners, or to the Surveyor. If he is not satisfied with the return made by the person to be charged, or if no return has been made, and if the annual value cannot otherwise be ascertained, he proceeds to estimate to the best of his judgment the annual value of the property of which no account, or no sufficient account, has been delivered, and to assess the same [3] except in the Metropolis; [4] taking as his guide the last assessment of the property for the purpose of the poor-rate in all cases in which the poor-rate has been made throughout by a pound-rate on the annual value as it would be estimated accord-

---

[1] 43 & 44 Vict. c. 19, s. 48.
[2] 5 & 6 Vict. c. 35, ss. 64, 74.
[3] See below.
[4] 5 & 6 Vict. c. 35, s. 64, No. 11, r. 1.

ing to Schedule A.; and in other cases, whenever Chap. III. possible, taking the assessment for the purpose of the poor-rate as his guide according to certain prescribed rules. In the Metropolis, as that word is defined by In the Metropolis the the [1] Valuation (Metropolis) Act, 1869—that is, valuation list is conthe unions, and parishes not in union, which were clusive either wholly or for the greater part in value, evidence of "gross" situate within the jurisdiction of the Metropolitan able" Board of Works appointed under the [2] Metropolis value. Management Act, 1855—[3] the valuation list made in pursuance of the [4] Valuation (Metropolis) Act, 1869, and for the time being in force, is conclusive evidence of the gross value, and rateable value, of the several hereditaments included therein, and of the fact that all hereditaments required to be inserted therein have been inserted therein, for the purpose of the [5] Income Tax Acts, in all cases where the tax is charged upon the gross value and not on profits. [6] "Gross value," as used in the Act we have just been quoting, is defined to mean "the annual rent which a tenant might reasonably be

[1] 32 & 33 Vict. c. 67. See *ante*, p. 29, note [3].

[2] 18 & 19 Vict. c. 120. The Metropolitan Board of Works no longer exists, having been abolished by the "Local Government Act, 1888" (51 & 52 Vict. c. 44).

[3] 32 & 33 Vict. c. 67, s. 45.

[4] 32 & 33 Vict. c. 67. The provisions of this Act relating to the making of valuation lists, and to appeals, contained in sects. 6—42, should be referred to.

[5] 5 & 6 Vict. c. 35, and any Acts continuing or amending the same. See 32 & 33 Vict. c. 67, s. 45 (2) (b).

[6] 32 & 33 Vict. c. 67, s. 4.

Chap. III. expected, taking one year with another, to pay for
a hereditament, if the tenant undertook to pay all
usual tenant's rates and taxes, and tithe commutation
rent-charge, if any, and if the landlord undertook
to bear the cost of the repairs, and insurance, and the
other expenses, if any, necessary to maintain the
hereditament in a state to command that rent;"
while the term "rateable value," as used in the same
Act, is defined to mean [1]"the gross value after deducting therefrom the probable annual cost of the
repairs, insurance, and other expenses as aforesaid."
The Assessor [2] may, however, estimate the value of
any dwelling-house which, with any ground occupied
therewith, is of less annual value than 10l., and
the value of which he is able to estimate, either
according to the prescribed rules, or of his own
knowledge, without requiring a return of the annual
value, unless the Surveyor objects to his so doing;
and this extends to land separately occupied. [3] He
is authorized to require any tenant to produce to him
the lease, or agreement, under which the tenant
holds; and, if the lease, or agreement, was made
within the period of seven years, and the rent
reserved expresses the full consideration, either in
money or in value, for the lease, the Assessor may
take such rent as the annual value of the property;
but always having regard to any increase of the

---

[1] 32 & 33 Vict. c. 67, s. 4.
[2] 5 & 6 Vict. c. 35, s. 65.
[3] 5 & 6 Vict. c. 35, s. 66.

amount of the reserved rent, by reason of any agree- Chap. III.
ment by the landlord to pay tenant's rates and
taxes, or to any decrease of the amount of the same
rent, by reason of any agreement by the tenant to
pay landlord's rates and taxes. [1] Express provision is made for cases in which the tenant has
undertaken to make certain improvements in the
property let, and the rent has been fixed with
reference to the estimated result of such improvements, but at a sum higher than the present annual
value of the property. [2] If the tenant holds under
a parol agreement made within the same period of
seven years, or for any reason has not the custody
of the lease under which he holds, it will be enough
if, instead of producing a lease or agreement, he
gives to the Assessor an account in writing, signed
by himself, of the actual amount of the annual rent
reserved; and the Assessor may make the assessment
according to such rent. [3] The penalty for delivering
a false account, or omitting to produce any lease or
agreement, with intent to conceal the annual value
of the property comprised therein, is 20*l.* and treble
duty.

Where there is an existing lease, made within Case of
the last seven years, by which the property which *Campbell*
is the subject of the assessment is let at rack- *Revenue.*
rent, the rent named is to be taken as the annual

---

[1] 5 & 6 Vict. c. 35, s. 66.
[2] 5 & 6 Vict. c. 35, s. 67.
[3] 5 & 6 Vict. c. 35, s. 68.

value. But if upon the face of the lease it clearly appears that what is called rent is payable, in part at least, for something which is not the subject of assessment, the clause does not apply. *Campbell* v. *Inland Revenue*, 17 Sco. L. R. 23. In this case a part of what appeared to be rent was in fact an annual instalment of a sum agreed to be paid for purchase of the goodwill of a business, and for stock in trade, the remainder only being rent properly so called.

Delivery of Certificates of Assessment.—The Assessor, having made his assessments, introduces the same into a certificate, the form of which is prescribed by the [1] Taxes Management Act, 1880, and delivers the certificate to the General Commissioners, with all returns made to him; and [2] the General Commissioners forthwith deliver the certificate to the Surveyor for examination. [3] The Surveyor has a right to examine every return, and every first assessment of the duties made for any parish, for any year; and every person who has any such return in his custody must deliver the same to the Surveyor, if he requests him to do so, taking the Surveyor's receipt for the same; and the Surveyor may take charge of any assessment so delivered to him, until he has taken such copies of, or extracts from, the same as may be necessary for his

---

[1] 43 & 44 Vict. c. 19.
[2] 43 & 44 Vict. c. 19, s. 50.
[3] 43 & 44 Vict. c. 19, s. 51; 5 & 6 Vict. c. 35, s. 161.

better information. [1]Any person who wilfully obstructs the Surveyor in the performance of his duty
in this respect is liable to a penalty of 50*l.* [2]The
Surveyor may also require the Assessor to give notice
to the overseers of the parish to deliver the rate books
of the parish, and a true copy of the last rate made,
to the Surveyor for his use, or to produce them to the
General Commissioners; and [3]he may at all times inspect, and take copies of, or extracts from, any book
kept by any parish officer, or other person, concerning
the poor-rates, or any other public taxes or rates;
and [4]if the occupier, or other person chargeable, has,
after due notice given, omitted to make the required
return, or has made a return with which the General
Commissioners are dissatisfied, the Surveyor may,
after having first obtained an order from the General
Commissioners, and after two days' notice to the
occupier, accompanied by such skilled persons as are
named in the order, view and examine any property
chargeable, in order to ascertain its annual value. A
similar power is given to Assessors.

Amendment of Assessment.—[5]If the Surveyor, upon
examination, discovers that any properties, or profits,
chargeable to the duties have been omitted, or that
any person chargeable has not made a full and proper

[1] 5 & 6 Vict. c. 35, s. 161.
[2] 5 & 6 Vict. c. 35, s. 75.
[3] 5 & 6 Vict. c. 35, s. 76.
[4] 5 & 6 Vict. c. 35, s. 78.
[5] 43 & 44 Vict. c. 19, s. 52.

Chap. III. return, or has made no return at all, or has not been charged, or has been undercharged, or has obtained any allowance, deduction, abatement, or exemption, not authorized, he corrects and amends the assessment. If the discovery should be made after the assessment has been signed and allowed in the manner [1]presently described, but within four months of the expiration of the year to which the assessment Surveyor's relates, the Surveyor certifies this error to the General certificate. Commissioners, who then sign and allow an addiAdditional tional first assessment, made in accordance with the first assessment. particulars certified by the Surveyor.

Allowance of Assessments.—[2]After the Surveyor has examined the assessments made, the General Commissioners take them into consideration; and, if the Surveyor has made no objections, and they are satisfied, they sign and allow the assessments. If the Surveyor makes an objection to any assessment, the Rectifica- Commissioners [3]rectify the same according to the best tion of assessments. of their judgment. The General Commissioners [4]have the same right as the Surveyor to require the overseers of any parish to produce the rate books,

[1] See below.
[2] 43 & 44 Vict. c. 19, s. 56.
[3] Except where they are specially authorized to do so, no assessment delivered to the General Commissioners is to be altered by them, except in case of, and upon, appeal. 43 & 44 Vict. c. 19, s. 57. See *post*, pp. 274—277.
[4] 5 & 6 Vict. c. 35, s. 75.

and [1]to inspect the rate books, and take copies of, or extracts from, them ; and, if the Surveyor alleges that the assessments have not been properly made, [2]they may summon Assessors and overseers before them, and examine them on their oaths.

Omissions from First, or Additional First, Assessments, how dealt with.—[3]An omission discovered by the Surveyor within the year following the year for which the person liable ought to have been charged, may be rectified by the Surveyor charging such person, Surcharge by Surand giving notice to him of the charge and the parveyor. ticulars thereof, and certifying to the General Commissioners the particulars of the omission and charge. The Commissioners, upon oath being made by the Surveyor, or other credible witness, of the service of the notice, sign and allow the certificate. The certificate must, however, be delivered to the General Commissioners, or to their Clerk, within the year following the year of assessment. [4]The person charged may, however, within ten days after receiving the notice, make an amended return, or give notice in writing to the Surveyor that he abides by the former return (if any) made by him, accompanying the same with a declaration, signed and attested, containing

[1] 5 & 6 Vict. c. 35, s. 76.
[2] 5 & 6 Vict. c. 35, s. 75.
[3] 43 & 44 Vict. c. 19, s. 63.
[4] 43 & 44 Vict. c. 19, s. 64.

E.   K

Chap. III.
Surveyor's
certificate
of objec-
tion to
supple-
mentary
return.
the particulars prescribed by the [1] Taxes Management Act, 1880. The Surveyor may object to the
return, or amended return; or may certify his satisfaction to the General Commissioners. In the former
case the Surveyor must give notice of his objection to
the person charged, and certify the return, or the
amended return, and the cause of his objection, to
the General Commissioners, who must thereupon
cause the assessment to be made upon the Surveyor's
certificate of objection, and allow no abatement,
except on the [2] appeal of the person charged. [3] To
make a false declaration in this respect is a misde-
meanour, and the penalty imprisonment for a period
not exceeding six months, and a fine not exceeding
treble the amount of duty charged.

*Apportionment of Assessment by General Commis-
sioners in Case of Divided Occupation.*—[4] If after the
assessment the land, &c., which is the subject of it
comes to be divided into two or more distinct occupations, the General Commissioners have power to
apportion the duty among the occupiers upon the
appeal of the parties interested.

Assessment of Railways by the Special Commissioner.
—[5] The annual value of, or profits or gains arising

---

[1] 43 & 44 Vict. c. 19.
[2] As to the mode of appealing, see *post*, pp. 274—278.
[3] 43 & 44 Vict. c. 19, s. 66.
[4] 23 & 24 Vict. c. 14, s. 4.
[5] 23 & 24 Vict. c. 14, s. 5.

from, any railway are, [1] as we have said, assessed by **Chap. III.** the Special Commissioners. The mode of assessment by the Special Commissioners [2] will be described when we treat of duties payable under Schedule D. The Special Commissioners, upon making an assessment upon any railway company, notify the amount of the assessment to the secretary or other officer of the company upon whom the assessment is made.

Time when Duties become payable.—Duties of income tax, except such as are payable by way of deduction, or are assessable in respect of [3] railways, [4] generally become payable on the 1st of January in the year for which the duties are charged; but duties of income tax included in any assessment signed and allowed on or after any such 1st of January become payable on the day after that on which the assessment is signed and allowed. Duties payable by way of deduction [5] must be deducted out of the sums in respect of which they are charged at the times when such sums become payable.

[1] See *ante*, p. 172.
[2] See *post*, pp. 245, 246.
[3] As to when duties assessed on railways become payable, see *post*, pp. 212, 213.
[4] 43 & 44 Vict. c. 19, s. 82.
[5] 5 & 6 Vict. c. 35, s. 158.

SUB-SECTION II.—COLLECTION.[1]

Proceedings after Assessment in order to the Collection of the Duties.—As soon as any assessments of income tax are signed and allowed by the General Commissioners, and [2] the time for hearing appeals has expired, the Clerk to the General Commissioners pre-

Duplicates of assessment.

pares [3] two duplicates of every assessment, in the prescribed form, which are then signed and sealed by the General Commissioners. One of the duplicates is handed by the Commissioners to the Collector of the parish for which the assessment is made, with a warrant for collecting the duty. The other duplicate is delivered to the Surveyor of the district. [4] Assessments not made, or against which any appeal is depending, when the first assessments are signed and allowed, when made, or determined, are included in a separate form of assessment and duplicate, and then collected in the same manner as the duties charged by the first assessments. When the duties become payable, [5] the Collector demands the sums

[1] Sect. 9 of the Taxes Management Act, 1880 (43 & 44 Vict. c. 19), contains a general saving of all powers for recovery of income tax contained in the Acts relating to income tax then in force, in cases not provided for by that Act, and so far as the same are not inconsistent with the express provisions of that Act.

[2] As to the time for hearing appeals, see *post*, p. 275.

[3] 43 & 44 Vict. c. 19, s. 83.

[4] 43 & 44 Vict. c. 19, s. 84.

[5] 43 & 44 Vict. c. 19, s. 85.

from the persons charged with the same, and upon Chap. III.
payment he gives a receipt in [1]the prescribed form. .

*Cases in which Persons chargeable may deduct Sums
paid by them for Duty from Payments made by them.—*
It will be convenient to mention here the cases in
which persons charged with duty under Schedule A.
are authorized to deduct the whole, or part, of what
is paid by them for duty from payments which they
make to others, and so become in some sense collectors of the duty from the persons ultimately liable
thereto. The cases referred to are the following :—

1. [2] Where the occupier, not being the owner, of First case:
any lands, tenements, or hereditaments, pays the Occupier
of lands,
duties assessed upon such lands, &c., he may deduct &c. deducts out
out of the next rent payable to the landlord so much of rent
payable to
of what he has paid for duty as a rate upon the rent landlord
amount of
payable equivalent to the rate of duty charged would duty
thereon.
amount to. But the whole sum to be deducted from
the rent must not exceed the sum actually paid for
duty by the occupier. [3] If the rate of income tax
has varied during the period for which the rent is
paid, so that the amount to be deducted cannot be
calculated, except by taking a proportionate amount

[1] That is, the form prescribed by the Board. 43 & 44 Vict.
c. 19, ss. 5, 15 (3). The receipt is not liable to stamp duty,
ante, pp. 41, 42.

[2] 5 & 6 Vict. c. 35, s. 60, No. 4, r. 9; 16 & 17 Vict. c. 34,
s. 40. As to the cases in which occupiers are chargeable for
owners, see *ante,* pp. 181—183.

[3] 27 & 28 Vict. c. 18, s. 15.

Chap. III. of several rates of income tax, such proportionate amount may be deducted from the rent by the occupier. [1]A mortgagee in possession, not in actual occupation of the land, &c. mortgaged, is liable to the same deduction as any other landlord would be.

Second case : Mortgagee in possession and in actual occupation of lands, &c. mortgaged must allow duty on interest in accounts between himself and mortgagor.

2. [2]A mortgagee in possession, and in actual occupation of the lands, &c. mortgaged, in the settlement of accounts between himself and the mortgagor, must allow the duty payable in respect of the amount of interest due upon such mortgage, as so much interest received by him on account of such interest. [3]The provision we have just quoted for the case of a variation in the rate of income tax applies here, so that if the income tax has varied during the period through which the interest has accrued a proportionate amount of the several rates of income tax chargeable must be allowed.

Third case : Persons

3. [4]Every person liable to the payment of any rent, or any [5]yearly interest of money, or any an-

---

[1] 5 & 6 Vict. c. 35, s. 60, No. 4, r. 11.

[2] 5 & 6 Vict. c. 36, s. 60, No. 4, r. 11.

[3] 27 & 28 Vict. c. 18, s. 15.

[4] 16 & 17 Vict. c. 34, s. 40.

[5] The words "or other annual payment" shows that the payments before referred to are annual payments. Rent means annual rent, and yearly interest cannot mean interest for less than a year. The interest upon short loans, not intended to be continued, and not continued, beyond a year, is not "yearly interest" within the meaning of the section. But a common mortgage, although expressed to be for six

nuity or other annual payment, as a charge on any property, whether the same is payable half-yearly, or at any shorter or more distant periods, is authorized, on making such payment, to deduct thereout the amount of the rate of duty payable at the time when such payment becomes due; and the person to whom such payment is to be made must allow such deduction upon penalty of a forfeiture of 50l. for refusing to do so. But the sum deducted must not be greater than the amount of the duty actually paid. [1]The provision above mentioned for the case of a variation in the rate of income tax applies to the cases we are now considering.

4. [2]Any person paying any rent-charge under the [3]"Drainage Advances Acts" may from time to time deduct thereout, in respect of the duty chargeable, one-third part of the sum which the rate of such duty, computed on such rent-charge, amounts to; and the deduction must be allowed by the receiver

months, is not, as a matter of business or in fact, a short loan. *Goslings and Sharpe* v. *Blake*, 23 Q. B. D. 324; 37 W. R. 774.

[1] 27 & 28 Vict. c. 18, s. 15.

[2] 16 & 17 Vict. c. 34, s. 42. Although sect. 15 of 27 & 28 Vict. c. 18, in terms applies only to cases within the 40th section of 16 & 17 Vict. c. 34, reason would seem to prescribe the application of the provision made by the first-named section to this case of a rent-charge under the Drainage Advances Acts.

[3] 9 & 10 Vict. c. 101; 10 & 11 Vict. c. 11; 11 & 12 Vict. c. 119; 13 & 14 Vict. c. 31; 19 & 20 Vict. c. 9.

Chap. III. and collector of the rent-charge upon receipt of the residue of the rent-charge then due.-

Fifth case: Owner of lands subject to rent-charge in lieu of tithes, &c. may deduct duty thereon.
5. [1]When any lands, &c. are subject to the payment of any rent-charge under the [2]Act passed for the Commutation of Tithes, or otherwise, or any annuity, fee farm rent, rent service, quit rent, stipend to any licensed curate, or other rent or annual payment charged thereon, the owner, not being the occupier, if he has allowed to the occupier any deduction from his rent in respect of duty paid by him under Schedule A., and the owner being also the occupier, may deduct out of every such rent-charge, &c., a proportionate part of the duty; and such deduction must be allowed by the person receiving, or entitled to, the rent-charge, &c.

Penalties for refusing to allow deduction.
[3] If any person refuses to allow any deduction authorized to be made out of any payment of annual interest of money lent, or other debt bearing annual interest, secured by mortgage or otherwise, he forfeits for every such offence treble the value of the

---

[1] 5 & 6 Vict. c. 35, s. 60, No. 4, r. 10. We may repeat here, *mutatis mutandis*, the observation made on the preceding page, note [2].

[2] 6 & 7 Will. IV. c. 71.

[3] 5 & 6 Vict. c. 35, s. 103. If a tenant does not deduct the property tax paid by him from the next rent, he cannot afterwards recover it as money paid; but if the tenant abstains from deducting the tax upon the promise of the landlord to repay the amount of the tax, there is a good consideration for the promise, and the tenant may sue upon it. *Lamb* v. *Brewster*, L. R. 4 Q. B. D. 220; 48 L. J., Q. B. 421; 40 L. T. 537; 27 W. R. 478.

principal money or debt; and if any person refuses **Chap. III.**
to allow any deduction authorized to be made out of
any rent or other annual payment before mentioned,
he forfeits the sum of 50*l*. All contracts, covenants,
and agreements made for payment of any interest,
rent, or other annual payment aforesaid, without
allowing such deduction, are void.

A tenant who had been assessed, and had Case of *Swatman*
paid income tax under Schedule A. in respect v. *Ambler.*
of land occupied by him, claimed to make the
deduction from his next payment of rent. The
landlord was not in fact liable to be assessed.
He had, before the payment of the tax by the
tenant, claimed exemption, and the exemption
was, but subsequently to the payment, allowed.
It was held that the tenant had nevertheless
a right to make the deduction from his rent.
Swatman v. *Ambler*, 24 L. J., Ex. 185.

A lessee of land for a term of years had Case of *Edmonds*
power to dig brick earth and make and sell v. *East-*
bricks. He paid (1) for surface rent 17*l*. 10*s*. *wood.*
a year; (2) for royalty, or brick rent, 100*l*. a
year; (3) for every 1,000 bricks above the first
million made in any year 2*s*. It was held that
the lessee was assessable under Schedule A. in
respect of all three kinds of rent, and might
make the deduction from his rent. *Edmonds* v.
Eastwood, 27 L. J., Ex. 209.

A coal-mine was sold upon terms that the Cases of *Taylor* v.
purchaser should pay the purchase-money by *Evans,* and

K 5

half-yearly instalments, which varied according to the amount of coal gotten, the minimum instalment being 150*l.* a year. It was held that the purchaser was not entitled to make the deduction from the instalments payable by him. *Taylor* v. *Evans*, 25 L. J., Ex. 269. A somewhat similar case was *Foley* v. *Fletcher*, 28 L. J., Ex. 100.

S. enjoyed an annuity charged upon real property, which was to be paid " free and clear of all taxes and assessments." He refused to allow the owner of the property to make any deduction from the annuity. S. was held liable to the penalty imposed by the Income Tax Acts for refusing to allow the deduction of income tax authorized by those Acts from " rents or annual payments." *Attorney-General* v. *Shield*, 28 L. J., Ex. 49.

Section 103 of 5 & 6 Vict. c. 35 does not apply to rent-charges granted by will; so that, if a testator by his will grants a rent-charge to be paid free of income tax, the annuitant is entitled to have the full amount paid to him, without the tax being deducted. *Festing* v. *Taylor*, 32 L. J., Q. B. 41.

If Payment of Duty is refused—Remedy by Distress.—If any person charged refuses to pay the duty on demand made, the Collector [1] must distrain

---

[1] 43 & 44 Vict. c. 19, s. 86. The Crown's right of distress is universal (per James, L. J., *In re W. J. Henley & Co.*, 26

upon the premises charged with the duty, or must distrain the person charged by his goods and chattels; for which he requires no other authority than [1] the warrant delivered to him upon his appointment. [2] For the purpose of levying a distress in such a case, the Collector may, if necessary, obtain a warrant from the General Commissioners, authorizing him to break open, in the daytime, any house or premises, calling to his assistance any constable, or other peace officer, for the parish; but such last-mentioned warrant must be executed by, and in the presence of, the Collector. [2] Every distress levied by a Collector must be kept by him for five days, at the cost of the person refusing to pay; and, if the duty is not paid within the five days, the distress must be appraised, that is, a value must be set upon it, by two inhabitants of the parish, or other sufficient persons, and then sold by public auction by the Collector or his deputy. If anything remains of the proceeds of sale, after deducting the duty, and the cost of taking, keeping, and selling the distress, it

W. R. 885), and therefore the statute provides that the distress may be either upon the premises charged, *or* upon the goods and chattels of the person charged, which may be elsewhere than upon the premises. The section above referred to adds, " and upon all such other goods and chattels as the Collector is hereby authorized to distrain," words which may have an application in cases of goods taken in execution, or seized by virtue of any process or assignment; see below.

[1] See *ante*, p. 33.
[2] 43 & 44 Vict. c. 19, s. 86.

Chap. III. is restored to the owner. [1]If, at the time any duty

Goods taken in execution, &c., income tax being in arrear. of income tax becomes in arrear, any goods or chattels belonging to the person charged are taken in execution, or are seized by virtue of any other process, except at the suit of a landlord for rent, or by virtue of any assignment, the person by whom the goods, &c., are so taken or seized must pay to the Collector all arrears of duty due at the time of execution, or seizure, or payable for the year in which the same is levied or made, not exceeding one year's duty; and if payment is not made by him the Collector must distrain, and sell, the goods, &c., as if no such execution, or seizure, had been levied, or made.

If Payment of Duty is refused—Remedy by Committal of Defaulter.—[2]If any duty of income tax is not paid within ten days after demand, and no sufficient distress is to be found, the General Commissioners may, by warrant under their hands and seals, commit the person refusing to pay to prison, there to be kept without bail until payment is made, or security given for payment, of the duty, and of the cost of apprehending and conveying the defaulter to prison. [3]Any person so imprisoned may be liberated upon the warrant of the General Commissioners, issued to the keeper of the prison, by the direction of the Treasury, or the Board.

[1] 43 & 44 Vict. c. 19, s. 88.
[2] 43 & 44 Vict. c. 19, s. 89.
[3] 43 & 44 Vict. c. 19, s. 91.

If Payment of Duty is refused—Remedy by Suit in
the High Court.—[1] The duties when assessed may be
recovered, with full costs of suit and all charges
attending the same, from the person charged therewith, by suit in the High Court, as a debt due to
the Crown; or by any other means by which any
debt of record, or otherwise due to the Crown may
at any time be sued, or prosecuted, for, or recovered;
as well as by the summary means before described.
A [2] schedule of arrears certified to the High Court as
[3] prescribed, and a [4] schedule of defaulters purporting
to be made in pursuance of the [5] Taxes Management Act, 1880, and certified to the High Court
under the hands of the Board, is sufficient evidence
of a debt due to the Crown, and sufficient authority
to a judge of the High Court to cause process to be
issued against any defaulter named in any such
schedule, to levy the sum in arrear and unpaid by
the defaulter, and the production of a schedule of
arrears or of defaulters purporting to be made in
pursuance of the [5] Taxes Management Act, 1880,
and purporting to contain the name of a defaulter,
is sufficient evidence of the sum mentioned in such
schedule having been duly charged and assessed upon

---

[1] 43 & 44 Vict. c. 19, s. 111.
[2] As to schedules of arrears, see *post*, p. 208.
[3] That is, in the form prescribed by the Board. 43 & 44
Vict. c. 19, s. 15 (2).
[4] As to the schedules of defaulters, see *post*, pp. 210, 211.
[5] 43 & 44 Vict. c. 19.

Chap. III. such defaulter, and of the same being due and owing, and in arrear, to the Crown.

Proceeding in case the Person charged removes from Place of Assessment.—[1] In case a person charged to any duty of income tax removes from the parish, &c. in which the assessment was made without paying the duty charged upon him, the General Commissioners for such parish, &c. sign, and transmit by the intervention of the Board, a certificate of the facts to the General Commissioners for the parish, &c. to which the defaulter has removed, and the last-mentioned Commissioners raise and levy the duty, and cause it to be paid to the Collector of Inland Revenue. If the removal is only from one parish, &c. within the jurisdiction of one set of Commissioners to another parish within the same jurisdiction, the Commissioners authorize the Collector for such last-mentioned parish, &c., by certificate, to raise and levy the duty.

Account by Collectors.—[2] The Board may appoint in each year days of receipt for each county, [3] division,

---

[1] 43 & 44 Vict. c. 19, s. 90.

[2] 43 & 44 Vict. c. 19, s. 100.

[3] "Division" means and includes any hundred, rape, lathe, stewartry, or district, or any place of separate jurisdiction under the Land Tax Acts. 43 & 44 Vict. c. 19, s. 5.

parish, or [1] group. [2] On the appointed day, which- Chap. III. will be some day after the 1st of January in every year, every Collector must account for the full amount of the duties given him in charge to collect; but, if required by the Board to do so, he must remit weekly or oftener to the Exchequer, in anticipation of the receipt, the amount of his collection, in the manner prescribed by the Board. He must [3] on the appointed day of receipt (1) produce to the Collector of Inland Revenue, or to the Surveyor, whenever he is required by either of them to do so, his duplicate of assessment, showing the sums collected by him duly written off; (2) pay over to the Collector of Inland Revenue, or otherwise, as, and if so, required to do by the Board, all moneys received by him and then in his hands and unaccounted for; for which he is entitled to receive receipts or discharges; (3) deliver then, or within three days afterwards, to the General Commissioners [4] schedules of arrears in the [5] prescribed form, with affidavits subscribed, to be made on his oath, or affirmation, and signed by him, setting forth the christian and surname of each defaulter in his parish, or group, from whom he has demanded, but

Collector on appointed day must, 1. Produce his duplicate of assessment; 2. Pay over moneys received, if required; 3. Deliver schedules of arrears.

[1] "Group" means any parishes united or grouped for the purposes of collection of the duties of income tax. 43 & 44 Vict. c. 19, s. 5.

[2] 43 & 44 Vict. c. 19, ss. 100, 101.

[3] 43 & 44 Vict. c. 19, s. 103.

[4] As to the schedules of arrears, see *post*, p. 208.

[5] That is, in the form prescribed by the Board. 43 & 44 Vict. c. 19, s. 15 (2).

Chap. III. has not then received, payment of the duties given
him in charge to collect, and the respective sums
then in arrear from each such defaulter. The
Collector must also answer any lawful question
demanded of him by the Collector of Inland
Revenue, or Surveyor, touching the duties given him
in charge to collect; and [1] may be put upon his oath,
or made to affirm if he is a person allowed by law to
substitute an affirmation for an oath, by the Collector
of Inland Revenue, who is authorized to administer
an oath or affirmation for the purpose. The substance
of the answers given by the Collector to the questions put to him must be reduced into writing in his
presence, and he must then sign them.

The Schedules of Arrears.—[2] The schedule of arrears,
being made, and delivered to the General Commissioners, [3] as we have described, remains with them
for forty days, and during that period the Collector
gives notice to the defaulters named in it, who are
at liberty within the same period to pay their arrears
with costs, and have the arrears discharged from the
schedule. If they continue in default, the Commissioners may use any lawful means, within the same
period of forty days, for the recovery of the arrears;
[4] but at the expiration of that period the schedule of

[1] 43 & 44 Vict. c. 19, s. 104.
[2] 43 & 44 Vict. c. 19, s. 105.
[3] *Ante*, p. 207.
[4] 43 & 44 Vict. c. 19, s. 111.

arrears may be certified to the High Court by either the Collector of Inland Revenue, or the General Commissioners ; [1] the schedule itself, when so certified, being transmitted to the Board. The Board, again, on receiving the schedule of arrears, may direct the Collector to use any method allowed by law for the recovery of any arrears therein included ; but otherwise they forward the schedule to the High Court, certifying it under their hands ; [2] and the schedule so certified to the High Court by the General Commissioners and by the Board is sufficient evidence of a debt due to the Crown, and sufficient authority to a judge of the High Court to cause process to be issued against any defaulter named in the schedule to levy the sum in arrear, and unpaid by him.

Schedules of Deficiencies.—Besides the schedule of arrears, which he is bound to return, [3] every Collector must also make out a schedule of deficiencies, which is to contain the names, surnames, and places of abode of all persons within his district of collection from whom he has not been able to collect the duties for any of the following causes, viz. :—

1. That the defaulter became bankrupt before the First day on which the duties became payable, and had not goods and chattels sufficient whereon to levy such duties within the district of collection, at any time since the duties became payable.

First cause: Bankruptcy of defaulter.

---

[1] 43 & 44 Vict. c. 19, s. 106.
[2] 43 & 44 Vict. c. 19, s. 111.
[3] 43 & 44 Vict. c. 19, ss. 108, 109.

Chap. III.

Second cause: Removal of defaulter.

2. That the defaulter removed from the district of collection before the day on which the duties became payable, without leaving therein goods and chattels sufficient as aforesaid.

Third cause: That defaulter has no goods and chattels.

3. That there were not, nor are, any goods and chattels of the defaulter whereon the duties, or any part thereof, might, or may, be levied.

An oath or affirmation is indorsed, and certified, on the schedule, that the sum for which the defaulter is returned in default is due, and wholly unpaid, either to the Collector, or to any other person for the Collector, to the best of the knowledge and belief of the Collector; and that the return is made for one or other of the causes above mentioned; and the schedule must contain, besides the particulars aforesaid, the particular reason for returning the defaulter, and the particulars of the sum or sums charged upon him. The oath, or affirmation, indorsed upon the schedule is made, or subscribed, by the Collector.

Schedules of Discharge and Default.—[1]The General Commissioners, after examining the Collector upon oath, or affirmation, (1) ascertain the sums which, according to the [2]Income Tax Acts, or the [3]Taxes

[1] 43 & 44 Vict. c. 19, ss. 108, 109.

[2] "Any Act, or part of any Act, relating to the assessment of any person, land, tenement, heritage, property, or profits whatsoever, to the income tax." 43 & 44 Vict. c. 19, s. 5. The phrase used in the place under reference is "the Tax Acts," the definition of which includes the definition above given of "Income Tax Acts."

[3] 43 & 44 Vict. c. 19.

Management Act, 1880, have been, or may be, dis- charged for a cause specially allowed by such Acts, and make out their schedules of discharge containing such sums; (2) make out their schedules of defaulters containing (a) the sums with which each defaulter ought to be charged, and the particulars thereof; and (b) the sums which have not been collected by reason of the Collector's neglect, and [1]for which he shall be held liable, and [2]which ought to be re-assessed on the parish. The schedules so made out by the General Commissioners are transmitted to the Board, and deposited at their head office.

Insupers.—[3]In case there is a failure on the part of the persons responsible for doing any of the following acts, viz.:—

1. Assessing the duties in any parish[4]—

2. Returning the duplicates of the assessments [5]of the duties made for any parish—

3. Raising or paying the several sums charged upon any person for the duties in any parish[6]—to do any of them, the Board may at any time after such failure, set *insuper* (as it is called) all sums appearing in arrear, and make a return by certificate thereof to

---

[1] See 43 & 44 Vict. c. 19, s. 112 (3).

[2] See 43 & 44 Vict. c. 19, s. 112 (4), and *post*, p. 212.

[3] 43 & 44 Vict. c. 19, s. 112.

[4] As to assessment, see Chap. III., sub-sect. 1.

[5] See *ante*, p. 196.

[6] This default would be on the part either of Collectors or persons charged with duty.

Chap. III. be delivered to the [1]Queen's Remembrancer. The
return must specify [2]certain particulars; and any
persons charged with the duties who ¯may be in
default are liable to process; and, in the case of a
When parish set *insuper* for a sum not accounted for to the
parish
liable to Collector of Inland Revenue, and contained in the
reassess-
ment. duplicate of assessment delivered to him, the parish
is liable to be re-assessed, except when by special
enactment relieved from liability to re-assessment.[3]

*Collection of Duties of Income Tax assessed upon
Railways.*—[4]The duties assessed upon railway companies in England are paid by four quarterly payments, namely, the first quarterly payment on or
before the 20th day of June; and the second, third,

---

[1] The "Queen's Remembrancer" is an officer of the Supreme
Court for revenue purposes.

[2] See 43 & 44 Vict. c. 19, s. 112. The particulars to be
specified are—(1) the parish, division, and county where the
failure has happened; (2) the cause of such failure; (3) the
names of any two or more of the General Commissioners
for the division in which the failure has happened; (4) the
names of the Assessors, and Collectors, and the several persons belonging to such parish charged with the duties, who
have failed to pay them.

[3] No parish is answerable for the acts, neglects, or defaults of a Collector appointed by the Board, or who gives
security to the Crown. 43 & 44 Vict. c. 19, s. 79 (1), *ante*,
p. 37.

[4] 43 & 44 Vict. c. 19, s. 95. We have, for convenience
sake, mentioned the assessment of railway companies in
England at this place; but it appears from the enactment just
quoted that such assessment is now made under Schedule D.

and fourth quarterly payments, on or before the **Chap. III.**
20th days of September, December, and March,
respectively, in each year. The duties upon railway
companies are assessed by the Special Commissioners,
who, when authorized to make, sign, or allow, any
assessment, have all the powers and authorities in
relation to assessment, appeal, collection of duty,
which the General Commissioners have.

SECTION II.—SCHEDULE B.

ASSESSMENT AND COLLECTION.[1]

What we have said of the assessment and collection
of duties charged under Schedule A. is equally
applicable, *mutatis mutandis*, to duties charged under
Schedule B.

SECTION III.—SCHEDULE C.

This schedule, it must be remembered, comprises
interest, annuities, and dividends, payable out of
public revenue. The annuities, &c., are paid through
certain persons, or corporations, entrusted with the
duty of paying the same, who are directed to deduct
the tax from the annuity, &c., before paying it to the
person entitled. Those mentioned in the [2]Income
Tax Act, 1842, and in the second section of the Act
5 & 6 Vict. c. 80 (and the list is no doubt an exhaustive

---

[1] See note [1], p. 196, *ante.*
[2] 5 & 6 Vict. c. 35.

Chap. III. one) are [1]The Bank of England, [2]The Commissioners for Reduction of the National Debt, [3]The Bank of Ireland, [4]persons entrusted with the payment of annuities, &c., payable out of the revenue of any colony or settlement, [5]persons entrusted with the payment of annuities, &c., payable out of the revenue of any foreign state, or acting therein as agents, or in any other character, and [6]the Exchequer or other public office. The methods of assessing, and collecting, the duties under Schedule C. may conveniently be described together. They differ, as will be seen, very materially from the methods employed to assess, and collect, the duties under Schedules A. and B.

ASSESSMENT AND COLLECTION.[7]

Who are Commissioners for Assessing the Duties under Schedule C.—[8]The Special Commissioners whom we now proceed to mention, are, with reference to the duties placed under their jurisdiction, respectively, the Commissioners appointed to act in all matters

---

[1] 5 & 6 Vict. c. 35, s. 89.

[2] *Ibid.*

[3] 5 & 6 Vict. c. 35, s. 90. This section was repealed by the Statute Law Revision Act, 1874, No. 2, (37 & 38 Vict. c. 96), but see 16 & 17 Vict. c. 34, s. 11.

[4] 5 & 6 Vict. c. 35, s. 96.

[5] 5 & 6 Vict. c. 80, s. 2.

[6] 5 & 6 Vict. c. 35, s. 97.

[7] See note [1], p. 196, *ante.*

[8] 5 & 6 Vict. c. 35, s. 23.

relating thereto, [1] but they have no power to summon **Chap. III.** any person to be examined before them. All enquiries by, or before, such Special Commissioners are answered by affidavit, taken before one of the General Commissioners in his district.

Annuities, &c. payable by the Bank of England.—The Governor and Directors of the Company of the Bank of England [2] are, as [3] we have said, Commissioners for the purpose of assessing and charging the duties payable under the [4] Income Tax Acts in respect of all annuities payable to the company at the receipt of the Exchequer, and the profits attached to the same and divided amongst the several proprietors, and in respect of all annuities, dividends, and shares of annuities, payable out of the revenue of the United Kingdom, and entrusted to the said Governor and Company for payment, [5] including dividends paid upon coupons attached to stock certificates issued under the [6] National Debt Act, 1870. [7] As often

[1] The Special Commissioners have this power when acting as General Commissioners (see *ante*, p. 18), or on appeal, as in certain cases arising under Schedule D. (see *post*, pp. 302, 303). 5 & 6 Vict. c. 35, s. 23.

[2] 5 & 6 Vict. c. 35, s. 24.

[3] See *ante*, pp. 6, 7.

[4] "Any Act, or part of any Act, relating to the assessment of any person, land, tenement, heritage, property, or profits whatever, to the income tax." See *ante*, p. 210, note [2].

[5] 33 & 34 Vict. c. 71, s. 36.

[6] 33 & 34 Vict. c. 71.

[7] 5 & 6 Vict. c. 35, s. 89.

Chap. III. as payments become due upon the said annuities, &c., true accounts are made out in writing at the Bank, in books provided for the purpose, of the annuities (with the profits attached to the same) which are paid to the said company in respect of its corporate stock, and of the annuities, &c., entrusted to the company for payment, and of the amount of duty chargeable thereon. In these books the separate account of each person entitled to any share of the said annuities, &c., is distinguished, so that each such share may be distinctly assessed; and the Governor and Directors of the Company of the Bank of England, acting in their capacity as such Commissioners as aforesaid, make an assessment of the duty which appears to be payable on such accounts to the best of their judgment, and then deliver the books of assessment, signed by them, to the [1] Commissioners for Special Purposes. [2] The last-named Commissioners cause two certificates on parchment to be made out under their hands and seals, containing the total amounts of duty, and of the annuities, &c. upon which the duty is charged, contained in each assessment, and transmit one of such certificates to the Governor and Directors of the Company, as Commissioners for making the assessment, and the other certificate to the [3] Head Officer of Inland Revenue.

---

[1] That is, the Board, and such persons as the Treasury appoint. *Ante*, pp. 5, 6.

[2] 5 & 6 Vict. c. 35, s. 89.

[3] The Receiver-General of Inland Revenue.

[1]The Governor and Directors of the Bank of England, Chap. III. on receiving notice from the Special Commissioners by certificate of the amount of each assessment, set apart and retain the amount of duty so assessed from each annuity, &c., before paying the same to the person entitled, who [2]is bound to allow what is so set apart and retained under penalty of a forfeiture of fifty pounds; and [3]all moneys so set apart and retained are paid into an account kept at the Bank of England with the Receiver-General of Inland Revenue.

Annuities, &c. payable by the Bank of Ireland.—The Governor and Directors of the Company of the Bank of Ireland [4]are Commissioners for assessing and charging the duties payable under the [5]Income Tax Acts, in respect of all annuities, dividends, and shares of annuities, payable by them out of the revenue of the United Kingdom. [6]The duties chargeable upon such annuities, &c., are assessed and charged by the

---

[1] 5 & 6 Vict. c. 35, s. 93.
[2] 5 & 6 Vict. c. 35, s. 103.
[3] 5 & 6 Vict. c. 35, s. 94; 12 & 13 Vict. c. 1, s. 17.
[4] 16 & 17 Vict. c. 34, s. 11.
[5] " Any Act, or part of any Act, relating to the assessment of any person, land, tenement, heritage, property, or profits whatever, to the income tax." See *ante*, p. 210, note [2].
[6] 5 & 6 Vict. c. 35, ss. 91, 93, 94. Sect. 91 is repealed by the Statute Law Revision Act, 1874, No. 2 (37 & 38 Vict. c. 96), but the exemption of persons resident in Ireland from liability to the duties under this schedule is abrogated by 16 & 17 Vict. c. 34, s. 11.

E.   L

Chap. III. Governor and Directors of the Company of the Bank of Ireland, communicated to the [1]Special Commissioners certified by them, and afterwards set apart and retained, and paid into the account kept at the Bank of England with the Receiver-General of Inland Revenue, in a manner precisely similar to [2]that in which the duties chargeable upon annuities, &c. entrusted for payment to the Bank of England are dealt with.

Annuities payable by the Commissioners for the Reduction of the National Debt.—The Commissioners for the Reduction of the National Debt [3]are, as [4]we have said, Commissioners for assessing and charging the duties payable under the [5]Income Tax Acts in respect of all annuities payable by them out of the revenue of the United Kingdom. The duties chargeable upon such annuities [6]are assessed and charged by the Commissioners for the Reduction of the National Debt, communicated to the Special Commissioners, certified by them, and afterwards set apart and retained, and paid into the account kept at

---

[1] The Board, and such persons as the Treasury appoint. *Ante*, pp. 5, 6.

[2] See *ante*, pp. 215—217.

[3] 5 & 6 Vict. c. 35, s. 28.

[4] *Ante*, p. 7.

[5] "Any Act, or part of any Act, relating to the assessment of any person, land, tenement, heritage, property, or profits whatever, to the income tax." See *ante*, p. 210, note [2].

[6] 5 & 6 Vict. c. 35, ss. 89, 94; 12 & 13 Vict. c. 1, s. 17.

the Bank of England with the Receiver-General of Chap. III.
Inland Revenue in a manner precisely similar to
[1]that in which the duties charged upon annuities, &c.
entrusted for payment to the Bank of England are
dealt with by them.

*Annuities payable out of the Public Revenue of any
Colony, &c.*—[2]The Special Commissioners are Commissioners for assessing the duties in respect of
annuities, dividends, and shares of annuities, payable [3]out of the Revenue of any foreign state, or

[1] See *ante*, pp. 215—217.

[2] The Board, and such persons as the Treasury appoint.
Ante, pp. 5, 6.

[3] 5 & 6 Vict. c. 35, ss. 29, 96; 5 & 6 Vict. c. 80, s. 2.
See *ante*, p. 97. A somewhat extended application is given
to these sections by 29 & 30 Vict. c. 36, s. 9. The following
are to be deemed persons entrusted with the payment of such
dividends—(1) The agent or other person having the ordinary
custody of the book or list in which the name of the person
entitled to the dividend, &c. is entered or registered (where
such is the case) (29 & 30 Vict. c. 36, s. 9); (2) any banker,
or person acting as a banker, who sells or otherwise realizes,
coupons or warrants for, or bills of exchange purported to be
drawn or made in payment of, any dividends (save such as
are payable in the United Kingdom only), and pays over the
proceeds to any person, or carries the same to his account;
(3) any person who, by means of coupons received from any
other person, or otherwise on his behalf, obtains payment of
any dividends elsewhere than in the United Kingdom; (4)
any dealer in coupons who purchases coupons for any
dividends (save such as are payable in the United Kingdom
only) otherwise than from a banker or person acting as a
banker, or another dealer in coupons (48 & 49 Vict. c. 35,
s. 26). The term "coupons" includes warrants for, or bills

L 2

Chap. III. [1]out of the public revenue of any colony, or settlement, belonging to the Crown of the United Kingdom, [2]or out of the stocks, funds, or shares, of any foreign or [3]colonial company, which are entrusted for payment to any person other than the Governor and Company of the Bank of England and the Commissioners for the Reduction of the National Debt; and every such person entrusted with the payment of any such annuities, &c., must deliver into the Head Office of Inland Revenue in England an account in writing, containing the names and residences of the persons to whom such annuities are payable, and a description of such annuities, &c , within one month after the accounts have been required by public notice in the London Gazette; and must also, on demand by the inspector appointed for that purpose by the Board, deliver to him for the use of the Special Commissioners true accounts of the

of exchange purporting to be drawn or made in payment of any dividends. Customs and Inland Revenue Act, 1888 (51 Vict. c. 8), s. 24. A person entrusted with the payment of dividends, who performs all necessary acts, so that the income tax thereon may be assessed and paid, is entitled to receive as remuneration an allowance of so much (not being less than threepence) in the pound of the amount paid as may from time to time be fixed by the Treasury. But no banker is to be obliged to disclose any particulars relating to the affairs of any person on whose behalf he may be acting. *Id.* s. 25.

[1] 5 & 6 Vict. c. 35, s. 96.
[2] 16 & 17 Vict. c. 34, s. 10.
[3] 24 & 25 Vict. c. 36, s. 9.

amounts of the annuities, &c., payable by him. The Chap. III. Special Commissioners assess the duties upon such annuities, &c., and give notice of the assessment to the persons entrusted with payment of the annuities, &c., who must pay the duties thereon on behalf of the persons entitled thereto, out of the moneys in their hands, into the account kept at the Bank of England with the Receiver-General of Inland Revenue, under a penalty of 100*l.* over and above the duties charged, for payment of which they are also personally answerable, and are acquitted of the duties paid by them [1] as in the case of annuities paid by the Bank of England.

Interest payable out of the Public Revenue on Securities issued at the Exchequer or other Public Office.— [2] The Commissioners for assessing the profits of offices in the Exchequer, or other public office, [3] are Commissioners also for assessing the duties upon any interest payable out of the public revenue on securities issued at the Exchequer, or other public office. They act in that capacity in the same manner as [4] the Commissioners who assess the profits arising from annuities payable out of the public revenue in other cases. The Commissioners authorized to act in relation to such securities as aforesaid appoint Assessors, and Collectors, of the duties arising from such securities from amongst

[1] *Ante*, pp. 210—217.
[2] *Ante*, pp. 6, 7.
[3] 5 & 6 Vict. c. 35, s. 97.
[4] *Ante*, pp. 215—217.

Chap. III. the officers entrusted with the payment or discharge
of such securities; and the Assessors, and Collectors, so
appointed compute the duties upon the securities at
the time the same are paid or discharged; and after
computation of the duties enter the same in a certificate
of assessment, and certify the same to the proper
officer appointed for the payment or discharge of such
securities.   Such last-mentioned officer is empowered
to stop and detain the duty, and to pay the same into
the Bank of England, to the credit of the Receiver-
General of Inland Revenue, in discharge of the
assessment.   Every person receiving, or purchasing,
any such security in circulation, with current interest
thereon, is entitled to deduct from such interest the
proportion of duty which will become chargeable
thereon, as if the interest were then due, and charged
with the said duty.   [1] The penalty for not allowing
any such deduction is the same as in other cases of
payment of interest.

Small Annuities, &c.—The following general provision with regard to annuities, dividends, or shares
of annuities, the half-yearly payment on which does
not amount to 50s., must be noticed, viz. :—[2] that the
respective Commissioners for assessing annuities, &c.
chargeable under Schedule C. are not required to
make any assessments upon such small annuities as
above mentioned, but they must be accounted for,

---

[1] *Ante*, p. 199.
[2] 5 & 6 Vict. c. 35, s. 95.

and charged, under the [1] third case of Schedule D., **Chap. III.** by which profits of an uncertain value are directed to be charged, [2] except in the case of dividends payable upon coupons annexed to stock certificates issued under the [3] National Debt Act, 1870, from which income tax is to be deducted, although the dividend represented by the coupon does not amount to 50s.

Time for Payment.—The duties under Schedule C. being payable by way of deduction, [4] are not governed by the general rule, under which duties payable otherwise than by deduction become payable on the 1st of January in every year, but [5] must be deducted out of the moneys in respect of which they are charged at the times when such moneys become payable.

SECTION IV.—SCHEDULE D.

This schedule, it will be remembered, is to a large extent, although not exclusively, supplementary to the other schedules; and comprises (1) undertakings in connection with lands, &c., not mentioned in Schedule A.; (2) profits of professions not contained in any other schedule; (3) profits of an uncertain annual value not charged in Schedule A.; (4) income

[1] *Ante*, p. 156.
[2] 33 & 34 Vict. c. 71, s. 36.
[3] 33 & 34 Vict. c. 71.
[4] 43 & 44 Vict. c. 19, s. 82.
[5] 5 & 6 Vict. c. 35, s. 158.

Chap. III. arising from colonial and foreign securities; (5) income arising from colonial and foreign possessions; (6) profits not falling under any of the preceding heads. The provisions, therefore, for the assessment and collection of the duties under this schedule are many and various. We will deal with the provisions for assessment, and the provisions for collection, separately.

SUB-SECTION 1.—ASSESSMENT.

Period for which Assessment made.—[1] Every assessment is made for the year commencing on the 6th day of April in any year, and ending on the 5th day of April following, each of such days being reckoned inclusively.

Place of Charge.—[2]The place in which the duty is to be charged depends to some extent upon the character of the person charged, thus:—

1. Householder *not* engaged in trade, &c.

1. Every householder *not* a person engaged in any trade, manufacture, adventure, concern, profession, employment, or vocation, is charged in the parish or place in which his dwelling-house is situated—

2. Person engaged in trade, &c.

2. Every person engaged in any trade, &c., is charged in the parish or place in which such trade, &c., is carried on or exercised—

3. Person not a house-

3. Every person not a householder, and not engaged in any trade, &c., who has any place of

---

[1] 43 & 44 Vict. c. 19, s. 48.
[2] 5 & 6 Vict. c. 35, s. 106.

ordinary residence, is charged in the parish, or place, Chap. III.
in which he ordinarily resides—

4. Every person not before described is charged in
the parish, or place, in which he resides at the time the
general notices (described *ante*, p. 174) are given—
and, in order to ascertain the place of charge, everyone who delivers a list or statement, as described *ante*,
pp. 175, 178, is required to deliver at the same time
a declaration in writing, signed by him, declaring in
what place he is chargeable ; and if he is engaged in
any trade, &c., and, if so, where it is carried on.
But we must supplement what we have said about
the place of charge by noticing the following provisions, viz. :—

1. [1]That where any trade is carried on in Great
Britain by the manufacture of goods, wares, or merchandise, the assessment must be at the place of
manufacture, though the sale of such goods, &c., is
elsewhere.

2. [1]That every person not engaged in any trade,
&c., who has two or more houses, or places, at which
he is ordinarily resident, must be charged in the
parish, or place, in which he is ordinarily resident at
the beginning of each year, as the year is computed
for the purposes of the Income Tax Acts, or in which
he comes ordinarily to reside after such general
notices as aforesaid are given.

*holder,
and not
engaged in
trade, but
having an
ordinary
residence.*

*4. Persons
not before
described.*

*1. When
trade
carried on
in Great
Britain.*

*2. Persons
not en-
gaged in
trade
having
two or
more re-
sidences.*

----

[1] 5 & 6 Vict. c. 35, s. 106. As to the computation of the
year, see *ante*, p. 1.

L 5

Chap. III.   **3.** [1]That the duty to be assessed in respect of the

3. Profits arising from foreign or colonial possessions, &c.
profits or gains arising from foreign possessions, or foreign securities, or in "the British plantations in America," or in any other of her Majesty's dominions, may be assessed in that one of the following places— London, Bristol, Liverpool, and Glasgow—at, or nearest to, which such property shall have been first imported into Great Britain, or at, or nearest to, which the person who has received remittances, money, or value from thence, and arising from property not imported as aforesaid, resides, as if such duty had been assessed upon the profits or gains arising from trade or manufacture carried on in such one of the said places : Provided that

(a) Profits, &c. arising from foreign, or colonial, possessions, imported partly into port of London, partly into outports of Bristol, Liverpool, or Glasgow.
(a) Whenever the produce, or the profits or gains, arising from such possessions, or securities, shall have been imported partly into the port of London, and partly into the outports of Bristol, Liverpool, or Glasgow, or shall have been received by any person partly in the City of London, and partly in any of the said outports, within the period of making up the account on which the duty is chargeable, the whole of the duty must be assessed and charged by the Commissioners acting for the City of London.

(b) Profits, &c. of foreign, or colonial, possessions, imported
(b) Whenever such produce, &c., shall have been within such period wholly imported into, or received at, the said outports of Bristol, Liverpool, and Glasgow, and different parts thereof, shall have been

[1] 5 & 6 Vict. c. 35, s. 108.

imported into, or received at, two or more of such outports, the duty chargeable thereon must be assessed and charged in one account at such one of the said places at which the major part in value of such produce, &c., has been so imported or received.

4. [1] That the profits arising from the London Docks, the East and West India Docks, and the Saint Katharine's Dock must be assessed by the Commissioners acting for the City of London.

Who are Commissioners for assessing Duty under Schedule D.—Subject to the right which, as [2] we shall presently explain, the person to be charged has of choosing the kind of Commissioners by whom he shall be assessed, and as a general rule, [3] the General Commissioners act in all matters relating to the duties in Schedule D.; [4] except in the case of railways, the annual value of, or profits and gains arising from, which, are assessed by the Special Commissioners; and except as follows :—

1. [5] The Governor and Directors of the Company of the Bank of England are Commissioners for assessing and charging the duties in respect of all profits of

Margin notes: Chap. III. wholly into out-ports of Bristol, Liverpool, and Glasgow, and partly in one and partly another, or others of such outports. Profits arising from London Docks, &c.

1. Duties upon profits, &c. of Bank of England

[1] 5 & 6 Vict. c. 35, s. 109.
[2] *Post*, p. 244.
[3] 5 & 6 Vict. c. 35, s. 22. In certain particulars relating to the assessment of the duties under Schedule D., the Additional Commissioners, or the General Commissioners acting as Additional Commissioners, act. See *post*, pp. 234 *et seq.*
[4] 29 & 30 Vict. c. 36, s. 8.
[5] 5 & 6 Vict. c. 35, s. 24.

Chap. III. assessed by its governor and directors. the company chargeable under Schedule D., and of all pensions and salaries payable by the company, and of all profits chargeable with duty and arising within any office or department under the management and control of the said Governor and Company.

2. Duties upon salaries, &c. payable by Commissioners for Reduction of National Debt assessed by them. 2. [1]The Commissioners for the Reduction of the National Debt are in like manner Commissioners for assessing and charging the duties in respect of all salaries and pensions payable in any office or department under their management or control.

3. Duties upon dividends, &c. payable out of or in respect of stock, &c. of any foreign company, &c. assessed by the Special Commissioners. 3. [2]The Special Commissioners [3]are Commissioners for assessing and charging the duties upon all interest, dividends, or other annual payments, payable out of, or in respect of, the stocks, funds, or shares of any foreign company, society, adventure, or concern, or in respect of any security of any such company, &c., and entrusted for payment to any person, corporation, &c., in this country.

4. Certain duties assessed by 4. [4]Subject to a certain power of control in the Treasury (who may determine that in any particular department, not being one of her Majesty's Courts

---

[1] 5 & 6 Vict. c. 35, s. 28.

[2] That is, the Board, and such persons as are appointed by the Treasury. *Ante*, pp. 5, 6.

[3] 16 & 17 Vict. c. 34, s. 10. "Person entrusted with payment" in this section has the enlarged meaning given to the same phrase in sect. 96 of 5 & 6 Vict. c. 35, and sect. 2 of 5 & 6 Vict. c. 80. See *ante*, p. 219, note [3]. 48 & 49 Vict. c. 51, s. 26.

[4] 5 & 6 Vict. c. 35, s. 30.

civil, judicial, or criminal, or an ecclesiastical, or Chap. 111.
commissary, Court, Commissioners shall not be ap- the Lord
pointed; and how the officers of such department cellor, &c.
shall be assessed), the Lord Chancellor, the judges,
and the principal officer, or officers, of each Court, or
public department of office under her Majesty,
whether civil, judicial, or criminal, ecclesiastical or
commissary, military or naval, respectively, have
authority to appoint Commissioners in relation to the
offices in each Court, or department, respectively from
amongst the officers of each Court, or department of
office, respectively. The persons so appointed, or any
three or more of them, not in any case exceeding seven,
are Commissioners in relation to the offices in each
such Court, or department of office, respectively.
Where the Commissioners of one department act
in relation to any other department, the Assessors,
and Collectors, for such other department are appointed from the officers of such last-mentioned
department. Notice of the appointment of Commissioners must be given to the Treasury within a
certain time; and if no appointment of Commissioners
is made within the time limited, of which failure to
notify the appointment in due time is conclusive
proof, the Commissioners acting in their several
districts in relation to the duties upon lands and
tenements, on notice of the default being given to
them, act also in relation to the duties on offices, and
employments of profit exercised within the same
districts respectively.

Chap. III.

5. Certain duties assessed by the Speaker and principal clerks of the Houses of Parliament, &c.

5. [1] The Speaker, and the principal clerk, of either House of Parliament, the principal, or other, officers in the several counties palatine, and the Duchy of Cornwall, or in any ecclesiastical Court, or in any inferior Court of Justice, whether of law, or equity, or criminal, or justiciary, or under any ecclesiastical body or corporation, whether aggregate or sole, appoint Commissioners from amongst the persons executing offices in either House of Parliament, or in their respective departments of office, and the persons so appointed, or any three of them, not in any case exceeding seven, are Commissioners in respect of the places, offices, and employments of profit, in each House of Parliament, and in each such department, respectively. The names of the persons so appointed Commissioners must be transmitted to the Treasury within a certain time, and in default the Treasury appoint Commissioners; or, if the Treasury make no appointment, the Commissioners acting in relation to the duties on lands and tenements in their several districts, on notice of the default being given to them, act in relation to the duties on such offices, or employments of profit, exercised within the same districts respectively. [2] If in any Court, or department of office, there are not a sufficient number of officers proper to be appointed Commissioners, the Treasury may direct that the

---

[1] 5 & 6 Vict. c. 35, s. 31.
[2] 16 & 17 Vict. c. 34, s. 26.

Commissioners for any other department may act; Chap. III. and in default of both appointment and direction the General Commissioners in their respective districts act.

Where the Assessment is made by the General Commissioners or by the Special Commissioners at the Request of the Person chargeable.

Notices, Lists, and Statements, &c.—What we have said of [1] the period for which the assessment is made, of [2] the mode of proceeding to obtain a return, of [3] the persons who are required to make out lists, &c., and of [4] the proceedings taken by the Assessor after notices given, in treating of the assessment of the duties under Schedule A., is applicable in the case of the duties in Schedule D. The only qualification that we have to introduce is, [5] that where the General Commissioners acting for any parish, or place, have had inserted in the notice that an office is opened for the receipt of statements of profits chargeable under Schedule D., and a proper person appointed to receive the same, and the time and place of attendance, in that case the statements are to be delivered at, and to, the appointed office, and person; [6] and that the statement may be delivered sealed up, if superscribed with

[1] *Ante*, p. 186.
[2] *Ante*, pp. 174, 175.
[3] *Ante*, pp. 175—177.
[4] *Ante*, pp. 185 *et seq.*
[5] 5 & 6 Vict. c. 35, s. 49.
[6] 5 & 6 Vict. c. 35, s. 110.

Chap. III. the name, and place of abode, of, or place of exercising the profession, or carrying on the trade, by, the person by whom the same is made.

Trade or profession carried on jointly or in partnership.

Where Trade, &c., is carried on by two or more Persons, jointly.—[1]Where a trade or profession is carried on by two or more persons jointly, the return must be made and stated jointly, and the duty is computed in one sum, and separately from any other duty chargeable on the same persons, or either, or any of them. The partner who is first named in the deed, or other instrument, of partnership, or, if there is no such deed or instrument, the partner who is named singly, or with precedence to the other partner or partners, in the usual style of the partnership, or if such precedent partner is not an acting partner, the preceding acting partner, if resident in Great Britain, must make the return on behalf of himself and of the other partner, or partners. If no such partner is resident in Great Britain the return must be made by the agent, manager, or factor, resident in Great Britain, for the partners. No separate return may be made in the case of a partnership by any partner, except for the purpose of claiming exemption,

Change in partnership.

or of accounting for a separate concern. [2]If amongst any persons engaged in any trade or profession in partnership any change takes place in the partnership by

---

[1] 5 & 6 Vict. c. 35, s. 100, third rule applying to first and second cases.

[2] *Ibid.*, fourth rule applying to first and second cases.

death, or dissolution of partnership, as to all or any Chap. III.
of the partners, or by admitting any other partner
into the partnership, before the time of making the
assessment, or within the period for which the assessment is made, or if any person has succeeded to any
trade, or profession, within the respective periods
aforesaid, the duty is charged according to the profits
and gains of the business derived during the period of
assessment notwithstanding such change, or succession, unless the partners, or the person succeeding to
the business, can prove to the satisfaction of the Commissioners that the profits and gains of the business
have fallen short, or will fall short, from some specific
cause, since the change, or succession, took place, or by
reason thereof. [1]Every statement of profits charge- Statement
of profits
able under Schedule D. must include every source must include every
chargeable thereunder on the person delivering the source.
statement on his own account, or on account of any
other person. But in cases where the same person is
engaged in separate partnerships, or in different
trades, &c., in more places than one, a separate assessment is made in respect of each trade, &c., at the place
where such trade, &c., if singly carried on, ought to be
charged. Every statement made on behalf of any
other person for which such person is chargeable, or
on behalf of any corporation, fellowship, fraternity,
company, or society, must include every source of

---

[1] 5 & 6 Vict. c. 35, s. 100, fifth rule applying to first and
second cases.

Chap. III. profit chargeable under Schedule D., and must be
delivered in the division in which such person, corporation, &c., would be chargeable if acting on his,
or their, own behalf.

Case of
The
Rhyope
Coal Co.

The Rhyope Coal Company was an ordinary
partnership for the purpose of working certain
mines in the county of Durham until the 21st
December, 1875, when the assets of the company
were sold to the Rhyope Coal Company, Limited.
The shareholders in the new company were the
partners in the old; the only change effected
being that the old partners were incorporated as
a limited company, in which they held the same
interests as in the old company, but divided into
partially paid up shares. The working of the
mines never ceased. It was held that the case
was within the fourth rule above stated. It was
also held that an extraordinary depression in
trade may be a "specific cause" within the
meaning of the same rule. *Rhyope Coal Company* v. *Foyer*, L. R., 7 Q. B. D. 485.

*Assessment in Case of Return made by Person
chargeable.*—If required by the person chargeable,
the assessment may be made by the [1] Special Commissioners, as we shall presently explain; but otherwise
[2] the statement is laid before the Additional Commis-

[1] That is, the Board, and such persons as the Treasury
appoints. *Ante*, pp. 5, 6.
[2] 5 & 6 Vict. c. 35, s. 111.

sioners, or the [1] General Commissioners acting as Chap. III. Additional Commissioners in their respective districts, who appoint meetings for taking all statements delivered to them into consideration. The Surveyor has power to examine such statements, and the meetings of the Commissioners are appointed within a reasonable time after the examination has been made by the Surveyor. If the Additional Commissioners are satisfied that the statements are *bonâ fide*, and properly made, and if no objection to them is made by the Surveyor, they direct an assessment to be made of the duties chargeable on such statement. The Additional Commissioners [2] then cause certificates of the assessments made by them to be made out, and entered in books provided for the purpose, and sign the assessments, which are then delivered under cover and sealed up, together with the statements made by the persons assessed, to the General Commissioners; and after the expiration of fourteen days from the delivery of the certificates to the General Commissioners, and after notice of such delivery has been given to the Surveyor, the assessments are also delivered to the persons charged. [3] Any person charged, who feels himself aggrieved by an assessment made by the Additional Commissioners, may appeal to the General Commissioners,

---

[1] As to General Commissioners acting as Additional Commissioners, see *ante*, pp. 23, 24.

[2] 5 & 6 Vict. c. 35, s. 117.

[3] 5 & 6 Vict. c. 35, s. 118.

Chap. III. and of this right of appeal we shall treat [1] hereafter. If no appeal is made, and the General Commissioners approve the assessment, [2] they confirm the same. If, however, the Surveyor, upon examining the statement made by any person chargeable, objects to the same, and his objection is overruled by the Additional Commissioners, [3] he may require such Commissioners to state specially, and sign, the case upon which the question arises, together with their determination thereon; and the case, so stated and signed, is delivered to the Surveyor, to be transmitted by him to the General Commissioners for the district, who are bound to return the case so submitted to them, with their answer thereon, with all convenient speed; and the assessment is altered, or confirmed, in accordance with the opinion of the General Commissioners. [4] And after an assessment has been made by the Additional Commissioners, the Surveyor may at all reasonable times examine the same before it has been delivered to the General Commissioners; and, if he discovers any error therein, which in his judgment requires amendment, he may certify the same to the Additional Commissioners, who must, if sufficient cause is shown, amend the same, as in their judgment the case may require; [5] or, if they decline to amend the assessment, the

---

[1] See *post*, pp. 296 *et seq.*
[2] 5 & 6 Vict. c. 35, s. 122.
[3] 5 & 6 Vict. c. 35, s. 112.
[4] 5 & 6 Vict. c. 35, s. 115.
[5] 5 & 6 Vict. c. 35, s. 116.

Surveyor may state his objection in writing, and the Additional Commissioners must then certify the objection, and their reasons for making the assessment, and any information they have acquired bearing upon the assessment, to the General Commissioners; and the Surveyor must give notice to the person charged, in order that he may appear before the General Commissioners and support the assessment. The Additional Commissioners are not, however, bound in every case themselves to make an assessment; [1]for they may, if they think proper, deliver to the General Commissioners the case in writing relative to the statement of the person chargeable, as it appears to them; and the General Commissioners must then enquire into the merits of the statement, and the assessment is made in accordance with their determination.

Assessment in case no Return is made by the Person chargeable.—[2]Whenever any person, not otherwise charged to the duties, makes default in delivering a statement, or delivers a statement with which the Additional Commissioners are not satisfied, or to which the Surveyor has made an objection in writing, or whenever the Additional Commissioners have received any information of the insufficiency of a statement delivered, they must make an assessment upon such person in such sum as, according to the

---

[1] 5 & 6 Vict. c. 35, s. 114.
[2] 5 & 6 Vict. c. 35, s. 113.

Chap. III. best of their judgment, ought to be charged upon him. Such assessment is subject to appeal, as we shall [1] presently describe.

Amendment of Assessment.—[2] If the Surveyor discovers that any profits have been omitted from the first assessment, or that any person chargeable has not made a full and proper, or any, return, or has been undercharged in the first assessment, or has obtained any allowance, abatement, or exemption, not authorized, the Additional Commissioners must, at any time after the first assessment has been signed and allowed, but within four months after the expiration of the year to which the first assessment relates, make an assessment on any such person in an additional first assessment in such sum as, according to their judgment, ought to be charged on such person, subject to objection by the Surveyor, and [1] to appeal.

Enquiries by the General Commissioners.—[3] Whenever the General Commissioners are dissatisfied with any assessment returned to them by the Additional Commissioners, or require further information respecting the same, they may put any question in writing touching such assessment, or any sums which have been set against, or deducted from, the profits

---

[1] *Post*, pp. 296 *et seq.*
[2] 43 & 44 Vict. c. 19, s. 52.
[3] 5 & 6 Vict. c. 35, s. 123.

or gains to be estimated in such assessment; and Chap. III. may demand an answer in writing from, and signed by, the person to be charged; and may issue their precept requiring true and particular answers to be given to the questions put within seven days after service of the precept; and every such person must answer according to the precept within the time limited, in writing, or, within the same time, tender himself before the General Commissioners, to be examined by them *virâ voce;* but he is permitted to give his answers in writing or *virâ voce*, as the case may be, without having taken any oath; and may object to any question, and peremptorily refuse to answer any question. The substance of such answers as he may give *virâ voce* must be reduced into writing in his presence, and read to him; and he may alter any part thereof, and alter or amend any particular contained in his answers in writing, before being called upon to verify the same on oath, [1] which the General Commissioners may afterwards, if they think it necessary, require him to do. [2] The General Commissioners may also summon in like manner any person whom they may think able to give evidence respecting the assessment made upon any other person to appear before them to be examined; and may examine every such person so summoned on oath, except the clerk, agent, or servant of the person to be charged, or other person confidentially

---

[1] 5 & 6 Vict. c. 35, s. 124.
[2] 5 & 6 Vict. c. 35, s. 125.

'Chap. III. intrusted, or employed, in the affairs of the person to be charged, who can only be examined in the same manner, and subject to the same restrictions, as is, or are, provided for the *vivâ voce* examination of any person touching the assessment made on him. The penalty for refusing to appear when summoned, or to be sworn, or to answer any lawful question put, is a sum not exceeding twenty pounds, and treble duty.

Where Objection made by Surveyor, and allowed by General Commissioners, a Schedule required.— [1] Whenever the General Commissioners allow an objection to any assessment made by the Surveyor, they direct their precept [2] to the person charged, to return to them within the time limited in the precept a schedule containing such particulars as the Commissioners shall demand, for their information; and the schedule must be delivered complete to the satisfaction of the Commissioners. The precept is delivered to the person to whom it is directed, or left at his last or usual place of abode, or if he has removed from the jurisdiction of the Commissioners, or cannot be found, or if his place of abode is not known, the precept is fixed on or near to the door of the church or chapel of the place where the Commis-

---

[1] 5 & 6 Vict. c. 35, s. 120.

[2] The section mentions only " the person appealing." But the schedule is required, not only in the case of an appeal (as to which see *post*, pp. 298 *et seq.*), but also in the case mentioned in the text.

sioners meet in execution of their office; and the precept is then binding upon the person to whom it is directed, and he must make the required return within the time limited, under [1]a penalty of a sum not exceeding twenty pounds and treble duty. [2]The Surveyor has free access at all reasonable times to the return, and may take copies, or extracts, of or from the same as he thinks necessary; and [3]he may, within a reasonable time to be allowed by the General Commissioners, after he has had examination of the schedule, object to the same or any part thereof in writing. If the Surveyor objects, he must deliver a notice in writing of the objection to the person to be charged, or leave the same at the last, or usual, place of abode of such person, under cover, sealed up, and directed to him, in order that he may, if he thinks fit, appeal against the objection to the General Commissioners. [4]If, upon receiving the objection of the Surveyor to any schedule, the General Commissioners disallow the objection, they may confirm, or alter, the assessment according to the schedule, as the case may require. [5]If the person charged appeals, the assessment cannot be confirmed, or altered, until the appeal is heard. [6]If, upon hearing the appeal, the General

[1] 5 & 6 Vict. c. 35, s. 128.
[2] 5 & 6 Vict. c. 35, s. 120.
[3] 5 & 6 Vict. c. 35, s. 121.
[4] 5 & 6 Vict. c. 35, s. 122.
[5] 5 & 6 Vict. c. 35, s. 121.
[6] 5 & 6 Vict. c. 35, s. 122.

Chap. III. Commissioners are satisfied with the schedule, and have received no information of its insufficiency, they may also confirm, or alter, the assessment according to the schedule, as the case may require. But, if the General Commissioners think that the schedule should be verified, they direct the Assessor to give notice to the person charged to appear before them; and he must appear accordingly and verify the contents of his schedule upon oath, and sign the same; and after such verification the General Commissioners make a final assessment. [1]The General Commissioners have the same powers of putting questions in writing, and calling upon the person questioned to verify his answers upon oath, with reference to any schedule, as we have [2]before described them to have with reference to an assessment. [3]In any case in which any person required to return a schedule neglects to do so, and in any case in which a schedule has been objected to by the Surveyor, and the objection has not been appealed against in proper time, and in any case in which a person called upon to verify his schedule or his answers, or examination in writing, neglects to do so, as well as in any case in which the General Commissioners agree to allow the objections made by any Surveyor, the General Commissioners, according to the best of their judgment, settle and

---

[1] 5 & 6 Vict. c. 35, ss. 123, 124.
[2] *Ante*, pp. 238—240.
[3] 5 & 6 Vict. c. 35, s. 126.

ascertain in what sums such person ought to be
charged, and make a final assessment. [1]Any person,
however, who has delivered a schedule, may, if he
discovers any omission or wrong statement therein,
deliver an additional schedule rectifying such omission or wrong statement; and upon doing so is
exempt from liability to any proceeding for such
omission or wrong statement; and, if he has neglected
to deliver a schedule within the time limited, he
may deliver a schedule at any time before any proceeding has been taken to recover the penalty;
and upon doing so is not liable to any proceeding for
recovering the penalty. Even after proceedings have
been commenced for recovering the penalty, the
General Commissioners may, upon proof that no-
fraud or evasion was intended, stay the proceedings.
upon such terms as they think fit; or, if any proceeding has been commenced in any Court, the Judge-
of the Court may, upon a certificate from the General.
Commissioners that in their judgment no fraud or
evasion was intended, stay the proceedings on such
terms as he may think fit. And if an imperfect
schedule has been delivered, if the person delivering
the same gives a sufficient reason why a perfect
schedule cannot be delivered, the Commissioners
may give further time for delivery of the schedule.
These provisions apply equally to statements as
to schedules, and to the Commissioners to whom

[1] 5 & 6 Vict. c. 35, s. 129.

M 2

Chap. III. statements are to be delivered, as to the General Commissioners.

Assessment by Special Commissioners on Request of Person chargeable.—[1] Any person chargeable, who does not claim the exemption granted to persons whose annual incomes are less than 150*l.*, may require that all proceedings in order to an assessment upon him be taken before the [2] Special Commissioners instead of the Additional Commissioners or General Commissioners. He must deliver a notice of his request, with the list, declaration, and statement of his profits and gains, to the Assessor of the parish, to be by him transmitted to the Surveyor of the district in which he is chargeable. The Surveyor thereupon examines the list and statement, and assesses the duty according to his judgment, and delivers a certificate of the assessment, with the list, declaration, and assessment, to the Special Commissioners, who examine the same, and make, or sign and allow, such an assessment as appears to them just and proper. The person charged, and also the Surveyor, [3] has a right of appeal against the assessment so made. [4] The

---

[1] 5 & 6 Vict. c. 35, s. 131. As to the exemption, see *ante*, p. 164.

[2] That is, the Board, and such persons as the Treasury appoints. *Ante*, pp. 5, 6.

[3] As to the appeal, see *post*, pp. 302, 303.

[4] 5 & 6 Vict. c. 35, s. 132.

Special Commissioners, when authorized to make, sign, or allow, any assessment, have all the powers which may be exercised by the General Commissioners, or by the Additional Commissioners in relation thereto.

Chap. III.

Special Commissioners, when authorized to make assessment, have all the powers of General Commissioners.

Where the Assessment is made by the Special Commissioners.

Procedure—Powers of Special Commissioners, &c.—
[1]In every case in which an assessment is made by the Special Commissioners, they notify the amount of the assessment to the person charged. In the case of interest, dividends, or other annual payments, payable by [2]foreign or colonial companies, and of [3]all dividends, interest, and other annual payments, where the right or title of the person to whom the same is payable is shown by the registration or entry of the name of such person in any book or list ordinarily kept in the United Kingdom, which, [4]as we have said, are assessed by the Special Commissioners, [5]all persons entrusted with the payment of such annuities, &c., or acting therein as agents, or in any other character, or having the custody of such book, or making such list, must without further

---

[1] 5 & 6 Vict. c. 35, s. 131.
[2] 16 & 17 Vict. c. 34, s. 10; 24 & 25 Vict. c. 91, s. 36.
[3] 29 & 30 Vict. c. 36, s. 9.
[4] *Ante,* p. 228.
[5] 5 & 6 Vict. c. 80, s. 2. As to the extent of the phrase "person entrusted with payment," see *ante,* p. 219, note [3].

Chap. III. notice deliver to the Board an account in writing containing a description of the annuities, &c., intrusted to them for payment, and other prescribed particulars, within one month after the same has been required by public notice in the "London Gazette;" and must also, on demand by the inspector authorized for that purpose by the Board, deliver to him for the use of the Special Commissioners true accounts of the annuities, &c. payable by them. The Special Commissioners make the assessment on such annuities, &c., and give notice of the amounts of the assessments made by them to the respective persons intrusted with the payment of the annuities, &c. The penalty which any person intrusted with the payment of the annuities, &c., who neglects, or refuses, to deliver an account as aforesaid, incurs, is 100*l.* over and above the duty. As [1] we have said, the Special Commissioners have, in all cases in which they are authorized to act, the same powers as the Additional or the General Commissioners.

Assessments entered in Books, &c.—[2] The General Commissioners, and the Special Commissioners when authorized to act, enter the several amounts of the sums assessed by them in their Books of Assessment; and from time to time make out and transmit to the Board accounts of the amount of duty assessed by them containing prescribed particulars.

---

[1] *Ante*, p. 245.
[2] 5 & 6 Vict. c. 35, s. 136; 12 & 13 Vict. c. 1, s. 17.

SUB-SECTION 2.—COLLECTION.[1]

When Assessment made by General Commissioners.—
[2] All assessments made by the General Commissioners
are entered in books with the names, and descriptions, and places of abode, of the persons, corporations, or societies, charged thereunder ; and the
entries are either numbered progressively or distinguished by letters as the Commissioners think proper.
If any person charged by any such assessment
declares his intention of paying the duty to the
proper officer for receipt within the time limited for
payment, and the Commissioners are satisfied with
such declaration, they deliver to such person, or to
anyone attending on his behalf, a certificate under
the hands of two of the Commissioners, specifying
the amount of the sums to be paid within one year
upon such assessment. The certificate is numbered
or lettered with the same number or letter as the
entry in the book of the Commissioners to which
such certificate relates, without naming, or otherwise
describing, the person charged ; and the certificate is
a sufficient authority to the receiving officer to receive
from time to time from any person producing the
certificate the amount of the sums contained therein ;
and on payment of the sums contained in any such
certificate the receiving officer gives a certificate for

[1] See note, p. 196, *ante.*
[2] 5 & 6 Vict. c. 35, s. 137.

Chap. III. the same, acknowledging the payment. [1]If no declaration is made by the person charged, or if the Commissioners are not satisfied with the declaration, they
deliver a duplicate of the assessment made upon
such person to the Collector, with their warrant for
collecting the same. If after a declaration as aforesaid is delivered, the duty is not paid in accordance
therewith, the name of the defaulter, and the amount
of the duty assessed upon him, is inserted in the
duplicate of the Collector, and the warrant for collecting the same is then of like force as if the name
and sum had been inserted therein at the time of
issuing the warrant. [2]The General Commissioners
are empowered to deliver to the receiving officers
duplicates of the assessments made by them, containing the sums assessed upon every person to
whom a certificate has been delivered by letter or
number, without naming such persons, with their
warrants for receiving the duties when the same
become payable. [3]The duty payable on every such
assessment must be paid by the person charged to
the receiving officer before the day appointed for
payment; and the certificate required to be given
on payment must be delivered to the General
Commissioners, or to one or more of them, or to
their clerk at his office, before the time when the
duty is payable, and their, or his, receipt taken for

[1] 5 & 6 Vict. c. 35, s. 138.
[2] 5 & 6 Vict. c. 35, s. 139.
[3] 5 & 6 Vict. c. 35, s. 140.

the same. If the duty is not paid, or the certifi- cate delivered as aforesaid, the General Commissioners deliver a duplicate of all sums assessed on the defaulter, together with their warrant, to such Collector as they may appoint to levy the sum in arrear and unpaid. The duties mentioned in the warrants delivered to the receiving officers are collected and levied as the duties under any other of the schedules are collected and levied. [1] The duty may, if the person chargeable so pleases, be paid in advance, and in that case an allowance by way of discount of 2*l.* 10*s.* per cent. per annum will be made.

Deduction of Duty from Interest, &c.—[2] Every person liable to the payment of any yearly interest of money, or any annuity, or annual payment, as a personal debt, or obligation by virtue of any contract, may, on making such payment, deduct the amount of the rate of duty, which at the time when such payment becomes due is payable. [3] If the rate of income tax has varied during the period through which such payment has accrued, a proportionate amount of the several rates of income tax chargeable may be deducted. [4] A refusal to allow any

[1] 5 & 6 Vict. c. 35, s. 141 ; 52 & 53 Vict. c. 42, s. 10.
[2] 5 & 6 Vict. c. 35, s. 102 ; 16 & 17 Vict. c. 34, s. 40. As to the meaning of " yearly interest," see *ante*, p. 198, note [5].
[3] 27 & 28 Vict. c. 18, s. 15.
[4] 5 & 6 Vict. c. 35, s. 103 ; 16 & 17 Vict. c. 34, s. 40. Where interest, &c. has been paid out of profits chargeable under Schedule D. without deduction, the Commissioners

M 5

Chap. III. such deduction renders the person refusing liable in some cases to forfeit treble the value of the debt, and in others to a penalty of fifty pounds.

[1] And upon payment of any interest of money, or annuities, charged with income tax under Schedule D., and not payable, or not wholly payable, out of profits and gains brought into charge to such tax, the person by or through whom such interest, or annuities, shall be paid is to deduct thereout the rate of income tax in force at the time of such payment, and is forthwith to render an account to the Commissioners of Inland Revenue of the amount so deducted, or of the amount deducted out of so much of the interest, or annuities, as is not paid out of profits or gains brought into charge, as the case may be; and such amount is to be a debt from such person to Her Majesty, and recoverable as such accordingly, and [2] the provision in sect. 8 of 13 & 14 Vict. c. 97

may grant a certificate which will entitle the person charged to make the deduction. See *post*, p. 292.

[1] Customs and Inland Revenue Act, 1888 (51 Vict. c. 8), s. 24 (3). This enactment was suggested by the case of *Gresham Life Assurance Society* v. *Styles* (*ante*, pp. 143—145), and " for the first time made it compulsory upon the persons liable in payment to retain income tax, upon their making payment out of the capital which they employ in trade, of any interest of money or annuities charged with the tax under Schedule D., and not payable or wholly payable out of profits brought into charge to such tax." Lord Halsbury, L. C., in that case.

[2] This section makes money received for duty a debt to the Crown from the person receiving it, and provides for its recovery.

in relation to money in the hands of any person for Chap. III.
legacy duty applies to money deducted by any person
in respect of income tax.

Under the above enactment a Railway Company which has made no profits during the
period its works were under construction, but
has during that period paid interest upon its
share and debenture capital out of a fund provided for the purpose, is bound to deduct income
tax from the payments of interest so made, and
the income tax so deducted becomes a debt to
the Crown. *Lord Advocate* v. *Forth Bridge Railway Co.*, 28 Sco. L. R. 576.

A debtor assigned to trustees a fund in Court, Case of
upon trust to pay a fixed sum yearly to his cre- *Crane* v.
ditors in payment of their debts *pro ratâ* with *Kilpin.*
interest until payment. It was held that the
trustees were entitled to deduct income tax on
the payments made by them in respect of interest.
Crane v. *Kilpin*, L. R., 6 Eq. 334.

*Where the Assessment is made by the Special Com-
missioners.*—[1] All persons entrusted with payment
of annuities, dividends, or shares of annuities, or
interest, payable out of the revenues of any foreign
state, or by foreign or colonial companies, and on all

[1] 5 & 6 Vict. c. 35, ss. 29, 96; 16 & 17 Vict. c. 34, s. 10;
24 & 25 Vict. c. 91, s. 36; 29 & 30 Vict. c. 36, s. 9. The
phrase "person entrusted with payment," has the same extent of meaning in the first three sections quoted, as to which
see *ante*, p. 219, note [3].

Chap. III. dividends, &c., the right to which of the person to whom the same may be payable is shown by the registration or entry of the name of such person in any book or list ordinarily kept in the United Kingdom, and on all annuities, pensions, or other annual sums payable out of the funds of any institution in India, entrusted to any person in the United Kingdom for payment to any persons resident in the United Kingdom, on receiving the [1] notice of the amount of the assessments thereon given by the Special Commissioners, must pay the duty on such annuities, &c., on behalf of the persons, corporations, and companies, entitled to the same out of the moneys in their hands. The persons entrusted with payment of the annuities, &c., must from time to time pay the duties assessed thereon into the Bank of England to the account kept there with the Receiver-General of Inland Revenue. [2] The Special Commissioners, when authorized to act in relation to the assessment, have all the powers of the General, or Additional, Commissioners in relation to the collection of the duties.

Section V.

Schedule E.—Assessment and Collection.[3]

Who are Commissioners for assessing the Duties under Schedule E.—[4]The Commissioners authorized to

---

[1] See *ante*, p. 221.
[2] 5 & 6 Vict. c. 35, s. 132.
[3] See note [1], p. 196, *ante*.
[4] 5 & 6 Vict. c. 35, ss. 30, 31, 34.

assess the duties chargeable under Schedule E. upon the salaries, &c., attached to the offices which [1] we have mentioned as included in this schedule, are the [2] respective Commissioners for all the offices in each department, and the assessment is made in the respective places in which such Commissioners respectively execute their offices. In all cases of duty chargeable under this schedule in which the Commissioners just referred to have no jurisdiction, [3] the assessment is made by the General Commissioners, [4] except in the case of offices, and employments of

[1] See *ante*, pp. 166, 167.

[2] For an enumeration of these Commissioners, see *ante*, pp. 7—10.

[3] 5 & 6 Vict. c. 35, s. 22. The General Commissioners are Commissioners for assessing the duty upon all offices, and employments of profit (not being public offices, or employments of profit, under her Majesty), in any county, riding, shire, city, liberty, town, or place, whether in the appointment of the lieutenant, custos rotulorum, justices or magistrates, commissioners for aids or taxes, or sheriff, of such county, &c., or of any trustees, or guardians of any trust, or fund, in such county, &c., and for all parochial offices in such county, &c. (except corporate offices in cities, corporate towns, boroughs, or places, or offices in cinque ports, in assessing the duties on which the mayor, aldermen, and common council, or the principal officers or members of the city, &c., or any three or more of them, not exceeding seven, act as Commissioners: *ante*, pp. 9, 10). 5 & 6 Vict. c. 35, s. 32. This section was repealed by sect. 9 of the Customs and Inland Revenue Act, 1876 (39 & 40 Vict. c. 16), but was revived, with respect to the duties chargeable under Schedule E., by sect. 7 of the Customs, Inland Revenue, and Savings Bank Act, 1877 (40 & 41 Vict. c. 13).

[4] 23 & 24 Vict. c. 14, s. 6. See *post*, pp. 259, 260.

Chap. III. profit held in or under any railway company, the assessment upon which is made by the Special Commissioners. [1]Every person to be assessed for his office, or employment, is deemed to have exercised the same at the head office of the department under which such office or employment is held; and every office is deemed to belong to, and to be assessed by, or under, the principal officers of that department by, or under, whom the appointment to such office is made; but when such appointment is made by any inferior officer, the office is assessed by the same Commissioners as assess such inferior officer. But when any such appointment is made under the Great, or Privy, Seal, or under the Royal Sign Manual, or under the hands or seals of the Treasury, and the office is not exercised in the department of the Treasury, the officer holding the same is assessed in the department in which he exercises his office. But this is without prejudice to the right of the Commissioners of the district to assess the profits of offices within their respective jurisdictions, although such offices are not held under their appointment. [2]In all cases in which any annuity, or pension, is payable out of any particular branch of the public revenue, and at the office of that branch of revenue, the Commissioners acting for that department have authority to assess and levy the duty upon same as a salary, or wages, payable thereout.

[1] 5 & 6 Vict. c. 35, s. 147.
[2] 5 & 6 Vict. c. 35, s. 146, r. 10.

Assessment—Period for which made.—[1]The assessment in respect of annuities, pensions, or stipends, mentioned in Schedule E. is in force for one whole year, unless the same ceases, or expires, within the year by lapse, death, or otherwise; from which period the assessment is discharged. [2]The assessments are in force for one year, commencing, and payable, at the like periods as the assessments in parishes are made payable.

Qualification of Commissioners for Duties on Offices, &c.—[3]No qualification is required of any of the officers or persons who are Commissioners for the duties on offices, or employments of profit, or on pensions, stipends, or annuities, chargeable under Schedule E., and who act as such Commissioners by virtue of their several offices, other than such offices respectively.

Proceedings in order to Assessment.—[4]The Commissioners meet as soon after their appointment as they conveniently can in some convenient place, and, after qualifying themselves by taking [5]the prescribed oaths, they may elect a Clerk, and Assessors: and, [6]in

[1] 5 & 6 Vict. c. 35, s. 146, r. 1.
[2] 5 & 6 Vict. c. 35, s. 154.
[3] 5 & 6 Vict. c. 35, s. 156.
[4] 5 & 6 Vict. c. 35, s. 150.
[5] *Ante*, p. 10.
[6] As to the cases in which the duties may be stopped or detained, see *post*, pp. 257, 258.

cases in which the duties cannot be stopped and detained at the departments of office of the Commissioners respectively, or for which they respectively act, they may also elect separate Assessors from the officers in their respective departments. Such Assessors, within a time fixed by the Commissioners, deliver to them their certificates of assessment in writing under their hands, and verified upon oath, of the full and just annual value of all offices, and employments of profit, chargeable with duty, and of all pensions, and stipends, and of the names and surnames of the several officers, and persons, entitled to pensions, or stipends, and of the duties they ought to pay. The Assessors [1] assess themselves as well as all other persons whom they ought to assess; and may have free access to all documents and papers whatever in their respective offices touching the salaries, &c. of any person chargeable belonging to their respective offices. They may also, whenever necessary, require returns from the persons chargeable, in order that they may make a true assessment; but, [2]unless such a return is required by the Assessors, no person chargeable is to be liable to a penalty for not returning a statement of the profits arising from his office, pension, or stipend, in pursuance of any general notice. [3]Lists or accounts of all salaries, fees, wages, perquisites, and profits, pensions, and stipends, must

---

[1] 5 & 6 Vict. c. 35, s. 150.
[2] 5 & 6 Vict. c. 35, s. 151.
[3] 5 & 6 Vict. c. 35, s. 154.

be delivered upon the request of the Assessors by the officers or their deputies, receivers, and paymasters, in every office for which Commissioners are appointed for raising the duties, to, or by, whom the same salaries are paid, or payable; as well as by any agent by whom the same are payable. The penalties for not delivering such lists or accounts upon request are the same as those exacted for not delivering the other returns required by the [1] Income Tax Act, 1842. The assessments made by the Assessors must be brought by them to the Commissioners appointed in regard of the same, who must sign the assessments.

Stoppage of Duties.—[2] In all cases in which any salaries, fees, or wages, or other perquisites, or profits, or any annuities, pensions, or stipends are payable at any public office, or by any officer of her Majesty's household, or by any of her Majesty's receivers, or paymasters, or by any agents employed in that behalf, the duties payable in respect thereof are detained and stopped thereout, if not otherwise paid; and, whenever such duties are assessed by the General Commissioners in their respective districts, they must transmit an account of the amount of the duty assessed to the office where the salaries, &c., are payable, in order that the duty assessed may be there stopped or detained. [3] In all cases in which the salaries, &c., of any officer chargeable do not arise out of any of

---

[1] 5 & 6 Vict. c. 35.
[2] 5 & 6 Vict. c. 35, s. 146, r. 5.
[3] 5 & 6 Vict. c. 35, s. 146, r. 6.

Chap. III. the offices mentioned, but out of some other office, or employment of profit, chargeable with duty, and the salaries, &c., are payable at such office by any officer thereof, or by any receiver, or by any agent, employed in that behalf, the duties chargeable on such salaries, &c., are also stopped or detained thereout, if not otherwise paid. [1]Such portion of the duties on offices, or employments of profit, or on annuities, pensions, or stipends, charged with any sum of money payable to any other person, is deducted out of the sum payable to such other person as a like rate on such sum would amount to; and all such persons, their agents, or receivers, must allow such deductions and payments upon receipt of the residues of such sums. [2]And such portions of the duties charged on any office, or employment of profit, executed by any deputy, or clerk, or other person employed under the principal in such office, and paid by such principal out of his salary, &c., is deducted out of the salary, &c., so payable as a like rate on such salary, &c., would amount to; and all such deputies, &c., must allow to their respective principals such deductions and payments on receipt of the residues of such salaries, &c. [3]Every person refusing to allow any deduction of duty authorized to be made incurs a penalty of fifty pounds. [4]In estimating the duty payable for any

---

[1] 5 & 6 Vict. c. 35, s. 146, r. 7.
[2] 5 & 6 Vict. c. 35, s. 146, r. 8.
[3] 5 & 6 Vict. c. 35, s. 103.
[4] 5 & 6 Vict. c. 35, s. 146, r. 9.

such office, or employment of profit, or any pension, annuity, or stipend, all official deductions and payments made upon receipt of the salaries, fees, wages, perquisites, and profits thereof, or in passing the accounts belonging to such office, or upon the receipt of such pension, annuity, or stipend, must be allowed, to be deducted, if a due account thereof is rendered to the Commissioners and proved to their satisfaction.

Additional Assessment.—[1]Where any person who holds, or exercises, any public office, or employment of profit, becomes entitled to any additional salary, fees, or emoluments, during any year of assessment beyond the amount for which any assessment was made upon him, or beyond the amount at which at the commencement of the year of assessment he was liable to be charged, an additional or supplemental assessment is from time to time, as often as the case requires, made upon such person for the additional salary, &c., so that he may be assessed and charged for the full amount of the whole of the salary, &c., which he receives, or becomes entitled to, during the year of assessment.

Duties in respect of Offices, &c., in or under any Railway Company.—[2]The Special Commissioners,

---

[1] 16 & 17 Vict. c. 34, s. 53.

[2] 23 & 24 Vict. c. 14, s. 6; 40 & 41 Vict. c. 13, s. 7. A railway company is not liable to be assessed in respect of wages paid by them to persons employed by them at weekly wages. It would seem that any such persons, if their in-

Chap. III. when they have assessed the duty payable in respect of any office, or employment of profit, in or under any railway company, notify the particulars thereof to the secretary, or other officer, of the company, and the assessment is then deemed to be an assessment upon the company, and is paid, collected, and levied accordingly. The company, or their secretary, or other officer, may deduct or retain out of the fees, emoluments, or salary of each person in their employment the duty charged in respect of his profits or gains.

When any Office, &c., is executed by Deputy.— [1]When any office, or employment of profit, chargeable with duty is executed by deputy, and the deputy is in receipt of the profits thereof, he is answerable for, and must pay the assessment charged thereon, and may deduct the same out of the profits of such office, or employment. And where the salaries, fees, wages, emoluments, or profits of any officer, or officers, in any such office are receivable by one or more of the said officers for the use of such officer, or officers, or as a fund to be divided amongst such officers in certain proportions, the officer, or officers, receiving such salaries is, or are, answerable for the duties charged thereon, and must pay the

---

comes amount to 150*l.* a year, are liable to be assessed under Schedule D. *Attorney-General* v. *The Lancashire and Yorkshire Railway Company*, 33 L. J., Ex. 163.

[1] 5 & 6 Vict. c. 35, s. 153.

same, and deduct them out of the funds provided for such respective offices, or employments, before any division or apportionment thereof. In case of refusal to pay, or non-payment, the deputy, or receiver, is liable to such distress, and to all such other remedies, and penalties, respectively, as is, or are, prescribed against any person having the office or employment.

Delivery of Duplicates of Assessments to Collectors.— [1] The respective Commissioners for duties upon offices, in all cases in which Collectors are authorized to be appointed, cause like duplicates of assessment to be made, and delivered to the Collectors, with like warrants to collect the duties, as [2] are given to Collectors for any parish or place; and the Collectors of the duties on offices have like authority to demand and levy the said duties as [2] is given to Collectors of any parish or place. [3] In all cases in which the duties on any salaries, fees, wages, perquisites or profits of any public office are detained and stopped out of the same salaries, &c., the respective Commissioners cause like duplicates to be delivered to the proper officers in the respective offices, who keep true accounts of all moneys stopped and detained, and are answerable for the same.

[1] 5 & 6 Vict. c. 35, s. 154.
[2] See *ante*, p. 196.
[3] 5 & 6 Vict. c. 35, s. 154.

CHAPTER IV.

ALLOWANCES, ABATEMENTS, RELIEFS, AND CORRECTION
OF ERRONEOUS ASSESSMENTS.

IN the preceding portion of this book we have dealt
with the authorities concerned in assessing, and collecting, the income tax, with the property, and profits,
upon which the tax is charged, and with the machinery by means of which the tax is assessed, and
collected. We have now to describe the methods by
which persons charged obtain the allowances and
abatements, which they are entitled to claim, and
secure the rectification of erroneous assessments made
upon them. In dealing with this subject we shall
adopt the plan we have previously employed, and
divide the present chapter into sections corresponding
with the five Schedules under which the duties of
income tax are charged.

SECTION I.—SCHEDULE A.

*Allowances to Ecclesiastical Persons in respect of
Tenths, &c.*—As [1]we have already seen, [2]allowances
are made for the amount of the tenths, and first

---

[1] *Ante*, pp. 72, 73.
[2] 5 & 6 Vict. c. 35, s. 60, No. 5, rr. 1, 2, 3.

fruits, duties and fees on presentations, paid by any ecclesiastical person within the year preceding that in which the assessment is made; for procurations, and synodals, paid by ecclesiastical persons, on an average of seven years preceding that in which the assessment is made; and for repairs of collegiate churches and chapels, and chancels of churches, or of any college or hall in any of the universities of Great Britain by any ecclesiastical or collegiate body, rector, vicar, or other person, bound to repair the same, on an average of twenty-one years preceding that in which the assessment is made. [1] The allow- ances in respect of the charges enumerated may be made to the ecclesiastical, or collegiate, body, rector, vicar, or other person, liable to such charges respec- tively in one sum, either by deducting the same from the assessment made upon him (with deductions so made we have not now to deal), or by certificate. [2] In case the allowance has not been made by way of deduction from the assessment, the person entitled thereto must claim the allowance at any time [3] within three years after the expiration of the year of assess- ment, before the General Commissioners for the district in which the property charged with the pay- ments in respect of which the allowance is made is situate. The General Commissioners, upon due proof before them that the claimant is entitled to the

Allow- ances may be made either by deduction from as- sessment,

or by certificate and order.

---

[1] 5 & 6 Vict. c. 35, s. 60, No. 5.
[2] 5 & 6 Vict. c. 35, s. 61.
[3] 23 & 24 Vict. c. 14, s. 10.

Chap. IV. allowance which he claims, certify the particulars
and amount of the allowance to the Special Commissioners at the [1]Chief Office of Inland Revenue in
England, and the Special Commissioners then grant
an order for the payment of such allowance, directed
either to the Receiver-General of Inland Revenue, or
to an officer for receipt, or collector, of the duties, or
to a distributor, or sub-distributor, of stamps, as may
be most convenient for the person entitled to the
allowance, and upon the delivery of the order to
the Receiver-General or other officer to whom the
same is directed, he pays the amount of the allowance to the person entitled thereto, taking a receipt
by indorsement upon the order.

*Allowance for Diminished Value of Machinery by
wear and tear.*—In the case of any [2]concern chargeable under Schedule A. by reference to the rules of
Schedule D., [3]when any machinery or plant is let for
the purposes of the concern, to the person, or company, by whom the concern is carried on, upon such
terms that the burden of maintaining and restoring
the machinery, or plant, falls upon the lessor, he is
entitled, on claim made to the General, or Special,

---

[1] 12 & 13 Vict. c. 1, s. 17.

[2] See *ante*, p. 54.

[3] 41 & 42 Vict. c. 15, s. 12. We are dealing now, it will
be observed, only with the claim to repayment made by the
lessor of machinery, &c. As to the deduction for diminished
value of machinery, &c., by wear and tear made upon assessment of any such concern as above mentioned, see *ante*, p. 60.

Commissioners in the [1]manner prescribed by sect. 61 of the [2]Income Tax Act, 1842, to have repaid to him such a portion of the sum which has been assessed and charged in respect of the machinery or plant, and deducted by the lessee on payment of the rent, as represents the income tax upon such an amount as the Commissioners think just and reasonable as representing the diminished value by reason of wear and tear of such machinery or plant during the year. But no such claim is allowed unless it is made within twelve calendar months after the expiration of the year of assessment.

Exemption of Persons whose Income is less than 150*l. a year from Duty, and Mode of claiming Exemption.*—[3]Any person chargeable to the duties either by way of assessment or deduction, is exempt if his annual income is less than 150*l.*; and, if he has paid, or been charged with, duty, he is entitled to be repaid the amount of all payments, and deductions, made by, or against, him on account of duty, except, of course, such sums paid, or charged, on account of duty as he is entitled to charge against any other person, or to deduct out of any payment to which he may be, or become, liable. The modes of proceeding to claim the exemption differ according as the

[1] See *ante*, p. 263.
[2] 5 & 6 Vict. c. 35.
[3] 5 & 6 Vict. c. 35, ss. 163, 164; and 39 & 40 Vict. c. 16, s. 8.

E.   N

Chap. IV. claim is made before assessment, or after the duty has been charged by way of deduction, and are as follows :—

1. Mode of proceeding in case claim is made before assessment.

1. [1] If the claim is made before assessment, the claimant within the time limited for delivering the lists, declarations, and statements, required from him, or within such further time as the Commissioners for special cause assigned allow, must deliver to the Assessor of the parish or place in which he resides, a notice of his claim to exemption, with a declaration and statement [2] in the prescribed form, signed by him, setting forth all the particular sources from which his income arises, and the amount of that part of his income which arises from each source specified, and every sum of annual interest, or other annual payment, reserved, or charged thereon, by which the income is diminished, and also every sum which the claimant has charged, or is entitled to charge, against any other person, for, or on account of, the duty, or which he is entitled to deduct or retain from or out of any payment to which he is, or may become, liable. [3] The claim must be made to the Commissioners of the district in which the claimant resides, whether he is personally

[1] 5 & 6 Vict. c. 35, s. 164.

[2] The Board have a general authority to prescribe, supply, and approve forms. 43 & 44 Vict. c. 19, s. 15.

[3] 5 & 6 Vict. c. 35, s. 169.

charged in such district or not. [1] The claim may be made by any guardian, trustee, attorney, agent, or factor, acting for the claimant, in any case in which satisfactory proof is afforded that the claimant is unable to attend in person, as well as in cases in which such guardian, &c., is authorized to act for another for the purpose of being assessed on his account in the first instance. [2] The Surveyor is at liberty to peruse and examine, and to take copies of, or extracts from, the declaration and statement delivered by the claimant, or on his behalf. The notice, declaration, and statement, when received by the Assessor, is transmitted by him to the Commissioners, and if the Surveyor does not object to the declaration within forty days, the Commissioners may allow the claim to exemption, and discharge the assessment upon the claimant, either in his own name, or in the name of his lessee or tenant. If it appears that any property, or profits, of the claimant is, or are, assessed, or liable to be assessed, in any other district, the Commissioners certify to the Board the allowance of the claim to exemption, and the Board direct the assessment made upon the property, or profits, of the claimant in such other district to be discharged, either in his own

[1] 5 & 6 Vict. c. 35, s. 170.
[2] 5 & 6 Vict. c. 35, s. 164.

N 2

name, or in the name of his lessee or tenant. If the Surveyor objects to the claim to exemption in writing, and suggests that he has reason to believe that the income of the claimant, or any other particulars required to be set forth in the declaration or statement, is, or are, not truly set forth in any specified particular, the merits of the claim to exemption are heard and determined on appeal before the General Commissioners, as other appeals are heard and determined before them; and if the claim is allowed on appeal, the General Commissioners issue all necessary certificates consequent thereon.

2. Mode of proceeding in case claim is made after the duty has been charged.

2. If the claim to exemption is made after the duty has been charged by assessment or by way of deduction, [1]then, if the claim has been allowed by the General Commissioners, and it is proved to their satisfaction that the claimant has been charged to, and has paid, any duty by way of deduction from any rent, annuity, interest, or other annual payment, to which he is entitled, and from which deduction is authorized, the General Commissioners certify to the Special Commissioners at the head office of Inland Revenue in England the amount, and the particulars, or nature, of the payment out of which, and the name, and place of abode, of the person by whom, such deduction has been made,

[1] 5 & 6 Vict. c. 35, s. 165; 12 & 13 Vict. c. 1, s. 17.

and other prescribed particulars ; and thereupon Chap. IV.
the Special Commissioners issue to the claimant
an order directed to the Receiver-General of
Inland Revenue, or to an officer for receipt, or
Collector, of the duties, or to a distributor, or
sub-distributor, of stamps, for repayment of the
duty certified to have been paid by him; and
such duty is accordingly repaid in the same
way as the allowances mentioned [1] before.
[2]But every claim for repayment of duty must
be made within three years after the end of the
year of assessment to which the claim relates.

[3]The annual value of lands, &c., belonging to, or How
occupied by, any person claiming exemption on the value of
ground of his yearly income being less than 150*l.* is estimated
estimated, for the purpose of ascertaining his title to for the
purpose of
such exemption, according to the [4]rules and direc- claiming
deduction
tions contained in the Schedules A. and B. respec- on account
of yearly
tively. The income arising from the occupation by income
being less
such claimant of lands, &c., is deemed, for the pur- than 150*l.*
pose aforesaid, to be equal in England to one-half of
the full annual value thereof, estimated according to
such rules and directions. Where the claimant is
proprietor as well as occupier, the amount deemed to
be the income arising from the occupation as aforesaid, is added to the full annual value of the lands, &c.,

[1] See *ante*, p. 264.
[2] 23 & 24 Vict. c. 14, s. 10.
[3] 5 & 6 Vict. c. 35, s. 167.
[4] See *ante*, pp. 48 *et seq.*

Chap. IV. and the aggregate amount is deemed, for the purpose aforesaid, to be the income of the claimant arising from the lands, &c., of which he is proprietor and occupier. The income arising from any lease of, or composition for, tithes is deemed, for the purpose aforesaid, to be equal to one-fourth of the full annual value of such tithes estimated as aforesaid.

Coparceners, joint tenants, and tenants in common and partners may claim severally. [1]Coparceners, joint tenants, or tenants in common, of the profits of any property, and joint tenants or tenants in partnership of lands or tenements, being in the actual and joint occupation thereof in partnership, and entitled to the profits thereof in shares, and personally labouring therein, or managing the same, may severally claim the exemption according to their respective shares and interests; and the claims, when duly proved to the satisfaction of the Commissioners to whom the same are made, may be proceeded upon as in the case of several interests. But the profits so arising are not in any case charged separately to the duty, in respect of the occupation of lands, where lands are let, or underlet, without relinquishment of the possession by the lessor, or where the lessee or tenant is not exclusively in the possession or occupation of the lands so let. [2]All claims for repayment of duty must be made within three years next after the end of the year of assessment to which the claim relates.

[1] 5 & 6 Vict. c. 35, s. 168.
[2] 23 & 24 Vict. c. 14, s. 10.

Abatement of Duty allowed to Persons whose Income
is under 400*l. a year.*—[1] Any person chargeable to the
duties, either by way of assessment or deduction, if
his annual income exceeds 150*l.* a year, but is less
than 400*l.* a year, is entitled, if he has paid, or been
charged with, duty, to be relieved from so much of
the duties assessed upon, or paid by, him as an assessment, or charge, of the said duties upon 120*l.* of his
income amounts to. The relief, if not given by
reduction or abatement of the assessment, upon the
person entitled to relief, is given by the repayment
to him of so much of the excess as he has paid, in
the same way as repayment is made to a person
entitled to exemption on account of his annual income
being less than 150*l.* a year.

*Abatement of Duty in respect of Premiums paid on
Life Assurances and Purchases of Deferred Annuities,
and Mode of claiming same.*—Any person who has
been assessed under Schedule A., and has paid the
duty assessed upon him, or has been charged with
it by way of deduction, may, if he has effected a life
assurance, or purchased a deferred annuity, as [2] before
explained, make a claim to the Commissioners for
Special Purposes for repayment of such a proportion
of the duty paid by him as the amount of the annual
premium paid by him bears to the whole amount of

---

[1] 39 & 40 Vict. c. 16, s. 8.
[2] *Ante*, pp. 87—89.

Chap. IV. his profits and gains on which he is chargeable under all, or any of, the schedules, and, on proof of the facts to the satisfaction of the Commissioners, is entitled to have such repayment made.

Allowances in respect of Payments out of Tithe Rent-Charge.—[1] As we have already explained, allowances are made for parochial rates, taxes, and assessments, charged upon, or in respect of, any rent-charge confirmed under the Act passed for the commutation of tithes, on the amount paid in the year in which the assessment is made. [2] These allowances are not made by way of deduction from the assessments, but by certificate in [3] the manner explained with reference to allowances for tenths, &c.

Allowances in respect of Land Tax, Drainage Charges, &c.—[1] As we have already explained, allowances are made for the amount of the land tax charged on lands, &c., under the 38 Geo. III. c. 5, where the land tax has not been redeemed, and for drainage, and other, charges. These allowances seem to be made by way of deduction from the assessment; so that with regard to them no further explanation is necessary.

Allowances for Colleges and Halls in Universities, Hospitals, &c.—[4] As we have already explained,

---

[1] *Ante*, p. 73.
[2] 5 & 6 Vict. c. 35, s. 60, No. 5, and s. 61.
[3] *Ante*, pp. 262—264.
[4] *Ante*, pp. 75, 76.

allowances are made for the duties charged on any Chap. IV. college or hall in any of the Universities of Great Britain in respect of public buildings and offices belonging to such college or hall in certain cases ; and on any hospital, public school, or almshouse, in respect of the public buildings, &c., belonging to such hospital, public school, or almshouse, in certain cases. [1] These allowances are directed to be made by the General Commissioners in their respective districts.

Allowances for Rents of Lands, &c., belonging to Hospitals, &c.—[2] As we have already explained, allowances are made for the duties charged on the rents and profits of lands, &c., belonging to any hospital, public school, or almshouse, or vested in trustees for charitable purposes. [3] These allowances are made by the Special Commissioners, on proof before them of the due application of such rents and profits to charitable purposes only, and in so far as the same are applied to charitable purposes only. The claim may be made, and proved, by any steward, agent, or factor, acting for such hospital, school, almshouse, or trust for charitable purposes, by affidavit taken before any Commissioner in the district in which the claimant resides. The affidavit must state the amount of the duties chargeable, and

[1] 5 & 6 Vict. c. 35, s. 61, No. 6.
[2] *Ante*, p. 82.
[3] 5 & 6 Vict. c. 35, s. 61, No. 6, and s. 62.

N 5

Chap. IV. the application of the rents and profits on which the duties are charged. The Special Commissioners give a certificate of the allowance, and an order for payment thereof in the manner [1]before explained. [2]The claim must be made within three years next after the end of the year of assessment to which the claim relates. [3]The claim to exemption of any trade union entitled thereto under the "Trade Union (Provident Funds) Act, 1893," must be claimed, and will be allowed, in the same manner.

Appeal against first Assessment—Notice of Day for. —As soon as the assessments for any parish or place have been allowed and signed by the General Commissioners in the manner we have [4]before described, [5]they cause notice that the assessments have been signed and allowed, and of the day for hearing appeals from the assessments, to be given, either by delivering to the Assessor of such parish, &c., a copy of the assessments, for the inspection of the persons charged thereby, and a public notice of the day of appeal to be affixed on, or near to, the church door, or on any other public place in the parish; or by delivering to each person charged the amount of his assessment with a note of the day of appeal. The notices must be given at least fourteen days before

[1] *Ante,* p. 264.
[2] 23 & 24 Vict. c. 14. s. 10.
[3] 56 Vict. c. 2, s. 2. See *ante,* p. 86.
[4] *Ante,* pp. 192, 193.
[5] 5 & 6 Vict. c. 35, s. 80; 43 & 44 Vict. c. 19, s. 57.

the day fixed for appealing. [1]The Clerk to the Com- Chap. IV.
missioners informs the Surveyor of the day fixed for .
appealing. Any person aggrieved by an assessment Time for appealing
upon him included in any first, or additional first, against first, or
assessment may give ten days' notice of objection in additional
writing to the Surveyor within the time limited for first, assessment.
hearing appeals, and, upon giving such notice, he
becomes entitled to appeal to the General Commissioners against the assessment within twenty-one
days after the day on which he received notice of the
assessment. The General Commissioners cause notice
of the day of appeal to be given to every appellant.
The Commissioners are bound to meet from time to
time, with or without adjournment, for the purpose
of hearing appeals, until all appeals have been determined. Except in cases in which they are [2]specially
authorized to rectify assessments otherwise, no assessment delivered to the General Commissioners may
be altered by them before the time for hearing and
determining appeals, and then only in cases of
charges appealed against, and upon hearing the
appeal on a day duly appointed. Any person altering any assessment wrongfully after it has been
allowed becomes liable to a penalty of 50*l.*

Proceedings on Appeal.—[3]The appellant must
appear before the General Commissioners on the day

[1] 43 & 44 Vict. c. 19, s. 57.
[2] *Ante*, pp. 191, 192.
[3] 43 & 44 Vict. c. 19, s. 57.

appointed, in person; no barrister, solicitor, or person practising the law, being allowed to plead for him. However, in cases in which persons are chargeable in respect of property or profits not their own, they may of course appeal, and appear upon the appeal, as if the assessment had been made in respect of property or profits to which they were beneficially entitled. [1]No abatement, or reduction, in the charge made upon any assessment, or surcharge, may be made by the General Commissioners, upon the hearing of any appeal, unless the appellant proves to them by evidence given by him upon oath, or affirmation, or by other lawful evidence produced by him, that he is overcharged in the assessment, or surcharge, against which he appeals. The Surveyor may attend the hearing of the appeal. He may be present during the whole time occupied by the Commissioners in hearing and in determining the appeal; and he may give his reasons in support of the assessment, or surcharge, appealed against, and produce any lawful evidence in support of such assessment, or surcharge.

Valuation in certain cases. [2]If upon the appeal any dispute arises about the annual value of any lands, &c., [3]situate elsewhere than in the Metropolis, and the General Commissioners

---

[1] 43 & 44 Vict. c. 19, s. 57.

[2] 5 & 6 Vict. c. 35, s. 81.

[3] 32 & 33 Vict. c. 67, s. 77. In the "Metropolis" the Valuation List is conclusive as to "annual value," *ante*, p. 187.

think it necessary, or [1]the appellant requires them, Chap. IV. to have a valuation of such lands, &c., made by a skilled person, they may direct the appellant to have a valuation made by any person they may name; and the costs of the valuation abide the final determination of the Commissioners, and are in their discretion. [2]The Commissioners have power to rectify the assessment appealed against, not only by reducing it in case the appellant proves that he has been overcharged, but also by increasing it in case it is proved that he has not been sufficiently charged. [3]When the General Commissioners have determined the appeal, their determination is final, unless a case for the opinion of the High Court has been required in the way we shall [4]presently describe; and is then capable of alteration only by order of the High Court; and [5]precludes the Surveyor from afterwards making a further charge for the same year on the person whose case is determined by the appeal, in respect of the property or profits included in the assessment appealed against and determined. The appeal is made, as we have said, to the General Commissioners of the district within which the assessment was made; but [6]if the person assessed has

[1] 16 & 17 Vict. c. 34, s. 47.
[2] 5 & 6 Vict. c. 35, ss. 81, 82; 43 & 44 Vict. c. 19, s. 57.
[3] 43 & 44 Vict. c. 19, s. 57.
[4] *Post*, pp. 280—282.
[5] 43 & 44 Vict. c. 19, s. 58.
[6] 16 & 17 Vict. c. 34, s. 55.

Chap. IV. moved out of such district without appealing, the Board may, if they think fit, upon his application, authorize the Commissioners of the district to which he has removed to hear and determine his appeal, as if it had been prosecuted before the General Commissioners for the district in which he was assessed.

Appeal for Apportionment in Case of Divided Occupation.—[1] If after assessment made, the land, &c., which is the subject of it has been divided into two or more distinct occupations, any of the occupiers may appeal to the General Commissioners for the district to settle and adjust what proportion of the duty charged shall be paid by each occupier. The General Commissioners thereupon make an apportionment of the duty, and the apportioned duty is collected and levied in like manner as the duty charged by an original assessment.

Relief to Owners who are also Occupiers for Purposes of Husbandry when Profits fall short of Assessment.— We have [2] already stated the relief afforded to owners who are also occupiers, and also to occupiers, of land for the purposes of husbandry only, in case of the profits and gains arising from the occupation of the lands during the year falling short of the sum on which the assessment was made. [3] The appeal is

---

[1] 23 & 24 Vict. c. 14, s. 4.
[2] *Ante*, pp. 87, 95.
[3] 14 & 15 Vict. c. 12, s. 3, which fixes the procedure. The

made to the Commissioners by whom the assessment was made within three calendar months after the expiration of the year of assessment. Notice in writing of the appeal must be given to the Surveyor of the district. If the abatement is allowed, and the whole sum assessed has been paid, the amount of the sum overpaid is certified and repaid, in the same way as an [1]overpayment of duty under Schedule D. is certified and repaid.

Relief for Losses caused by Flood or Tempest.— [2]Whenever loss is sustained by any flood or tempest on the growing crops, or on the stock, on lands let to a tenant at a reserved rent without fine, or lands so let are by flood, or tempest, rendered incapable of cultivation for any year, and the owner has in consideration of the loss agreed to make an abatement in the rent paid by the tenant for any year, the General Commissioners may, upon proof of the facts by oath, make an abatement in the assessment made in respect of the property in such lands for the same year for

abatement allowed was extended to all occupiers of land for the purposes of husbandry, not being also the owners thereof, and to all owners of land being also the occupiers thereof, and occupying the same for the purposes of husbandry, and obtaining their livelihood principally by husbandry, by 16 & 17 Vict. c. 34, s. 46; and to all owners of land occupying the same for the purposes of husbandry, by 43 & 44 Vict. c. 20, s. 52.

[1] *Post*, pp. 303 *et seq.*
[2] 5 & 6 Vict. c. 35, s. 83.

Chap. IV. which an abatement has been made in the rent; and may also make an abatement in the assessment made in respect of the occupations of the lands for the same year. [1]If, in such a case, the owner is an infant, idiot, lunatic, or under other disability, and incapable of consenting to any abatement in the rent, the abatement may nevertheless be made in the assessment made in respect of the occupation. [2]And if in such a case, the owner of the lands is also the occupier, the abatement may still be made in the several assessments in respect of the property in, and occupation of, the lands. [3]The penalty for making a false or fraudulent claim for abatement is the forfeiture of 100*l.*

Case for Opinion of the High Court.—[4]When the General Commissioners have determined any appeal, either the appellant or the Surveyor may, if he is dissatisfied with the decision as being [5]erroneous in point of law, declare his dissatisfaction to the Commissioners who heard the appeal, immediately after their decision is announced; and having done so may, within twenty-one days after the determination, address a notice in writing to the Clerk of the Commissioners

---

[1] 5 & 6 Vict. c. 35, s. 84.
[2] 5 & 6 Vict. c. 35, s. 85.
[3] 5 & 6 Vict. c. 35, s. 86.
[4] 43 & 44 Vict. c. 19, s. 59.
[5] There is no appeal on a question of fact from the decision of the Commissioners.

requiring the Commissioners to state and sign a case Chap. IV. for the [1]opinion of the High Court. He must, however, pay a fee of twenty shillings to the Clerk before he is entitled to have the case stated. The case sets forth the facts, and the determination of the Commissioners, and is delivered to the person requiring it, who must, within seven days after receiving the case, transmit it to the High Court of Justice, and previously, or at the same time, give notice in writing of the case having been stated on his application, and a copy of the case to the other party, Surveyor or appellant, as the case may be. The High Court hear and determine the question or questions of law arising on the case transmitted, and thereupon reverse, affirm, or amend, the determination of the Commissioners; or they may remit the matter to the Commissioners with their opinion thereon. They may make such order in relation to the matter, including an order as to costs, as they see fit; and the orders so made of the High Court are [2]final, and conclusive on all parties. But the High Court may, if they think fit, send the case back for amendment before delivering judgment.

[1] The Court will decline to express any opinion on points of law not raised before the Commissioners. *Bray* v. *Justices of Lancashire*, 22 Q. B. D. 484; 37 W. R. 392; 58 L. J., M. C. 54.

[2] Unless the orders are appealed. See below. The decision of the High Court upon a case stated is an "order," not a "judgment," and the appeal must be brought within twenty-one days. *Onslow* v. *Commissioners of Inland Revenue*, 25 Q. B. D. 465; 38 W. R. 728.

The jurisdiction of the High Court in this respect may be exercised by a Judge sitting in Chambers, and in vacation as well as in term time. An appeal lies from the decision of the High Court, or of any Judge, to the Court of Appeal, and thence to the House of Lords. But notwithstanding that a case so stated is pending before the High Court, the income tax must be paid according to the assessment of the Commissioners by whom the case was stated; and if the amount of the assessment is afterwards altered by the High Court, the difference, if too much duty has been paid, is repaid with such interest as the High Court may allow, and if too little duty has been paid, is deemed arrears, except that it involves no penalty, and is payable and recoverable as arrears.

Income tax must be paid notwithstanding pendency of case.

Appeal from Additional first Assessment.—[1]An additional first assessment allowed by the General Commissioners is subject to appeal in the same manner as a first assessment.

Appeal from Surveyor's Charges.—A certificate by the Surveyor of the particulars of any omission to assess any person liable to the duties, and of the charge which ought to be made upon such person, allowed by the General Commissioners, is [2]subject to appeal in the same manner as a first assessment, except that the person charged has [3]ten days after

[1] As to additional first assessments, see *ante*, p. 192.
[2] 43 & 44 Vict. c. 19, s. 63.
[3] 43 & 44 Vict. c. 19, s. 64.

service of the notice of charge in which to deliver an amended return, and [1] the delivery of such amended return, if objected to by the Surveyor, is a sufficient notice of appeal; or if the person charged makes no amended return within the ten days, he may, on the day appointed for hearing appeals, appear before the Commissioners, who must hear and determine the case, although no notice of appeal has been given. If the Commissioners have no meeting within the time limited for hearing appeals from the charges of the Surveyor, or if the Surveyor has not had notice of a meeting of the Commissioners, they must sign and allow the certificates at their first meeting held thereafter, and afterwards hear and determine all appeals.

Appeal against Surcharges.—[2] Appeals against surcharges are heard and determined in the same manner as appeals against first assessments. But if the person surcharged is prevented by absence, or sickness, or other sufficient cause, from appealing within twenty-one days after the date of the notice of charge, or from attending in person within such time, the Commissioners may postpone the hearing of the appeal for such time as they may think necessary. The "sufficient cause" above mentioned must be proved before the Commissioners on the oath or solemn affirmation

---

[1] 43 & 44 Vict. c. 19, s. 65.

[2] 43 & 44 Vict. c. 19, s. 67.

of the person appealing, or otherwise. [1] If the surcharge is allowed by the Commissioners, in whole or in part, the assessment on the amount of the surcharge allowed is made in treble the rate of duty; but the General Commissioners may remit, in whole or in part, the treble duty, and charge the single duty only, when they are of opinion :—

(a) That the original return would have enabled the Surveyor to amend the assessment;

(b) That there was no intention to defraud the revenue ;

(c) That the person charged was prevented from making an amended return by sickness, or other sufficient cause;

(d) That there was reasonable cause of doubt or controversy on the part of the appellant on the subject-matter of appeal.

Appeal in respect of Duties charged upon Mines of Coal, &c., Quarries, may be to the Special Commissioners. —[2] Any person assessed to the duty chargeable under Schedule A. in respect of any mine of coal, tin, lead, copper, mundic, iron, or any other mine, or any quarry of stone, or slate, may, if he thinks fit, appeal against such assessment to the Special Commissioners instead of to the General Commissioners, upon giving due notice of his intention to do so; and thereupon the

---

[1] 43 & 44 Vict. c. 19, s. 68.
[2] 23 & 24 Vict. c. 14, s. 7.

appeal is heard and determined by two or more of the Chap. IV.
Special Commissioners, in like manner as an [1]appeal
against an assessment of the duties under Schedule D.

Relief from Double Assessments.—[2]Whenever any
person has been assessed, either on his own account
or on behalf of another, and is by any error or mistake again assessed for the same cause, and on the
same account, and for the same year, he may apply
to the General Commissioners acting for the division
or place for which he has been assessed by error or
mistake, for the purpose of being relieved from such
double assessment; and the General Commissioners,
on due proof thereof to their satisfaction, must cause
the assessment, or such part thereof as is a double
charge, to be vacated. The proof may be made either
by a certificate of the assessment made upon the
applicant under the hands of the Commissioners by
whom he has been rightly assessed for the matter or
cause in question, certifying that such matter or cause
is included in an assessment made by them on the
applicant, on the same account and for the same year,
or by other lawful evidence given of those facts upon
the oath of any credible witness. [3]And whenever it
is proved to the satisfaction of the Board that a person has been assessed more than once to the duties
for the same cause, and for the same year, they must

---

[1] See *post*, pp. 301 *et seq.*
[2] 5 & 6 Vict. c. 35, s. 171.
[3] 43 & 44 Vict. c. 19, s. 60.

Chap. IV. direct the whole, or such part of such one or more of the assessments as appears to be an overcharge, to be vacated ; and thereupon the same is by such order vacated accordingly. [1] And whenever it is proved to the satisfaction of the Board that any such double assessment has been made, and has not been vacated, and that payment has been made of both assessments, they may order the Receiver-General of Inland Revenue, or any officer for receipt, to repay the sum so erroneously and doubly assessed and paid. [2] But the claim for repayment must be made within three years next after the end of the year of assessment to which the claim relates. Relief from a double assessment must be obtained in the manner indicated in the enactments above referred to, and cannot be obtained by means of a Petition of Right. *The Holborn Viaduct Land Co., Limited*, v. *The Queen*, (unreported).

SECTION II.—SCHEDULE B.

Mode of appealing against Assessment, and of claiming Exemptions, Allowances, and Abatements.—The mode of appealing against an assessment under Schedule B., and of claiming such of the exemptions, allowances, and abatements, mentioned under the head of Schedule A., as may be claimed upon any assessment under

---

[1] 5 & 6 Vict. c. 35, s. 171; 12 & 13 Vict. c. 1, s. 17.
[2] 5 & 6 Vict. c. 35, s. 171.

Schedule B., is similar to that adopted in the case of an appeal, or claim, having reference to an assessment under Schedule A. [1]The notices of first assessments given by the Assessors, and of the days fixed for appeals, include assessments under Schedule B., as well as assessments under Schedule A. [2]If an occupier of lands for purposes of husbandry only seeks an [3]adjustment of his liability with reference to the amount of a loss sustained and to the aggregate amount of his income for the year, he must give a notice in writing to the Surveyor for the district, within six months after the year of assessment, of intention to apply to the General Commissioners for such relief; and the Commissioners, on proof to their satisfaction of the amount of the loss, and of payment of income tax upon the aggregate amount of the appellant's income, will give a certificate authorizing repayment of so much of the sum paid for income tax as would represent the tax upon income equal to the amount of the loss. Such certificate may extend to give exemption or relief by way of abatement in accordance with the provisions of the Income Tax Acts. Upon receipt of the certificate, the Commissioners of Inland Revenue are to cause repayment to be made in conformity therewith. Any fraud or contrivance in making any such application is punish-

[1] 5 & 6 Vict. c. 35, s. 80; 43 & 44 Vict. c. 19, s. 57.
[2] 53 & 54 Vict. c. 8, s. 23.
[3] See *ante*, p. 95.

Chap. IV. able by a penalty of 50*l*., recoverable as a penalty imposed by virtue of the [1] Taxes Management Act, 1880.

SECTION III.—SCHEDULE C.

[2] *Claim of Exemption of Property of Friendly Society invested in Public Securities in Bank of England.*— [3] Any such exemption may be claimed and the right thereto proved by any trustee, or treasurer, of the society, or by any member of the society, before the Special Commissioners.

[4] *Claim of Exemption of Stock, &c., of Charitable Institutions—By whom made.*—[5] The application of the stock, &c., to charitable purposes may be proved before the Special Commissioners by any agent, or factor, on behalf of the institution, or by any of its members, or trustees. [6] The claim to exemption by any trade union entitled thereto under the "Trade Union (Provident Funds) Act, 1893," is to be claimed and allowed in the same manner as is prescribed by law in the case of income applicable and applied to charitable purposes.

[1] 43 & 44 Vict. c. 19.
[2] As to this claim, see *ante*, p. 98.
[3] 5 & 6 Vict. c. 35, s. 88, r. 1.
[4] As to this claim, see *ante*, p. 100.
[5] 5 & 6 Vict. c. 35, s. 88, r. 3.
[6] 56 Vict. c. 2, s. 2; see *ante*, p. 100.

[1] *Claim of Exemption of Stock, &c., belonging to her*
Majesty in the Books of the Bank of England, and to any accredited Minister of any Foreign State resident in Great Britain, if standing in the name of any Trustee— By whom made.—[2] The property in the stock, &c., may be proved before the Special Commissioners by the trustee in whose name it stands.

All Claims of Exemption under Rules in Schedule C.— To whom and where to be made.—[3] All claims of exemption under any of the rules contained in Schedule C. must be made to the Special Commissioners at the head office of Inland Revenue in England, according to the following rules:—

1. Every claim must be in writing, in [4] the pre- First rule: scribed form; and the Special Commissioners Form of must require the same to be verified on the affidavit of every such person, as they may think necessary. The Special Commissioners have authority to require from every person whom they may think proper to examine touching such claim, true answers upon oath to all such questions as they may think material.

2. Whenever the Special Commissioners allow Second any such exemption, they give an order for rule: Order for

[1] As to this claim, see *ante*, p. 101.
[2] 5 & 6 Vict. c. 35, s. 88, r. 5.
[3] 5 & 6 Vict. c. 35, s. 98.
[4] That is, in such form as the Board direct.

E.   O

Chap. IV.

payment
following
allowance
of ex-
emption
claimed.

payment of the sums retained for the duties on the annuities, dividends, and shares, in respect of which they have allowed such exemption, to the respective claimants, or to the attorneys, or agents, who have been authorized to receive the annuities, &c., on behalf of the claimants, and the payment is made in the same manner as [1]is provided with respect to allowances granted under No. 5 of Schedule A. [2]But the claim must be made within three years next after the end of the year of assessment to which the claim relates.

Claim of Exemption by a Person whose Yearly Income is less than 150l., and of Abatement by a Person whose Yearly Income is less than 400l.—[3]This exemption, and abatement, respectively, may be claimed by persons chargeable under Schedule C.; but, inasmuch as the claim is not made under the rules contained in that schedule, it would seem that it must be made in the manner described when [4]we were treating of similar claims made by persons chargeable under Schedule A. The same remark applies to the claim for abatement allowed on account of life assurance, and purchase of deferred annuities.

---

[1] See *ante*, p. 263.
[2] 23 & 24 Vict. c. 14, s. 10.
[3] 5 & 6 Vict. c. 35, ss. 163—170; 39 & 40 Vict. c. 16, s. 8.
[4] *Ante*, pp. 265—269, 271.

Relief against Double Assessment.—The duties under Schedule C. being levied by way of deduction from the annuities, &c., upon which they are charged, it is difficult to see how a case of double assessment can arise with reference to them; but if any such case does occur, [1]the enactments [2]we have quoted in dealing with cases of double assessment under Schedule A., which oblige the Board, upon proof of the double assessment being made, [3]within the time limited, to their satisfaction, to vacate the erroneous assessment, and to order the repayment of duty paid under it, will enable a person so charged by error under Schedule C. to obtain the relief to which he is entitled.

Case for Opinion of the High Court.—In case, too, of any appeal to the Special Commissioners, the appellant, if dissatisfied with their determination, as being erroneous in point of law, [4]may have a case submitted for the opinion of the High Court; the procedure being similar to that [5]we have described when dealing with cases for the opinion of the High Court having reference to the duties charged under Schedule A. [6]An appeal lies from the decision of

[1] 5 & 6 Vict. c. 35, s. 171; 43 & 44 Vict. c. 19, s. 60.
[2] *Ante*, pp. 285, 286.
[3] Three years. 23 & 24 Vict. c. 14, s. 10.
[4] 43 & 44 Vict. c. 19, s. 59. See *ante*, p. 280, note [5].
[5] *Ante*, pp. 280, 282.
[6] 41 & 42 Vict. c. 15, s. 15.

the High Court to Her Majesty's Court of Appeal; and from thence to the House of Lords.

Section IV.—Schedule D.

Deductions on Payment of Interest of Money, &c., from Profits charged under Schedule D.—[1] Whenever it is proved to the satisfaction of the Commissioners acting for the district in which the person making the application resides, that any interest of money, annuity, or other annual payment, is annually paid out of the profits and gains *bonâ fide* accounted for, and charged, under Schedule D., without any deduction on account thereof, such Commissioners may grant a certificate under the hands of any two of them, in the [2] prescribed form, and such certificate will entitle the person so assessed, upon payment of such interest, &c., to deduct so much as the duty upon such interest would amount to; and such deduction must be allowed by the person entitled to receive such interest, &c. But no such certificate is required when such payments are made out of the profits or gains arising from lands, tenements, or hereditaments, or of any office, or employment of profit, or out of any annuity, pension, or stipend, or any dividend or share in public annuities, in order to authorize the making of such deductions.

[1] 5 & 6 Vict. c. 35, s. 104.
[2] The Board have a general authority to prescribe, supply, and approve forms.   43 & 44 Vict. c. 19, s. 15.

Exemption in Case of Charitable Institutions from **Chap. IV.**
Duties on Interest chargeable under Schedule D.—
[1] Every corporation, fraternity, or. society of persons,
and trustee, for charitable purposes only, is entitled
to the same exemption in respect of any yearly
interest, or other annual payment, chargeable under
Schedule D., in so far as the same is applied to
charitable purposes only, as [2] is allowed to such corporation, &c., in respect of any stock, or dividends,
chargeable under Schedule C., and applied to like
purposes. The exemption is allowed by the Special
Commissioners, on due proof before them ; and the
amount of the duties paid by such corporation, &c.,
in respect of such interest or annual payment, either
by deduction or otherwise, is repaid under the order
of the Special Commissioners in the [3] same manner
as sums allowed by them in pursuance of any
exemption contained in Schedule C. are repaid.
[4] The claim to exemption by any trade union entitled thereto under the " Trade Union (Provident
Funds) Act, 1893," is to be claimed and allowed in
the same manner as is prescribed by law in the case
of income applicable and applied to charitable purposes.

If it was the intention of those who framed Case of
Trustees
the section above referred to, to effectuate an *of Psalms*
and Hymns
v. Whit-
[1] 5 & 6 Vict. c. 35, s. 105.   *well.*
[2] See *ante*, p. 100.
[3] See *ante*, p. 288.
[4] 56 Vict. c. 2, s. 2.

intention similar to that expressed in Schedule
C., with regard to stock of charitable institutions,
that intention has not been effectuated. Certain
trustees published a hymn book, and in accordance with the directions of the trust deed distributed the profits among widows and orphans
of Baptist ministers and missionaries. It was
held that such profits were ordinary trade profits,
not "yearly interest" or an "annual payment"
within the meaning of this section, and were,
therefore, not exempt from income tax. *The
Trustees of Psalms and Hymns* v. *Whitwell*, 7 T.
L. R. 164.

*Exemption in Case of Persons whose Income is less
than* 150*l. a Year ; and Abatement in case of Persons
whose Income is less than* 400*l. a Year.*—[1] This exemption, and abatement, respectively, may be claimed
in respect of duties charged under Schedule D., as
well as in respect of duties charged under Schedule
A.; and the mode of claiming the exemption or
abatement with reference to duties charged under
Schedule D. is similar to [2] that prescribed for claiming the same with reference to duties charged under
Schedule A.

*Abatement on Account of Life Assurance, or Purchase
of Deferred Annuity.*—The claim to this abatement, in

---

[1] 5 & 6 Vict. c. 35, ss. 163—170; 39 & 40 Vict. c. 16, s. 8.
[2] See *ante*, pp. 265—269, 271.

case the duty has been assessed without deduction on Chap. IV. that account and has been paid as assessed, is made in like manner as a similar [1] claim by a person charged under Schedule A.

Allowance on Account of Diminished Value of Machinery by Wear and Tear.—[2] In the case of any trade, manufacture, or concern in the nature of trade, chargeable under Schedule D., when any machinery or plant used for the purposes of the trade, &c., is let upon such terms that the burden of maintaining, and restoring, the same falls upon the lessor, he is entitled, upon claim made to the Special, or General, Commissioners in the manner prescribed by sect. 61 of 5 & 6 Vict. c. 35, to have repaid to him such a portion of the sum which has been assessed and charged in respect of the machinery or plant, and deducted by the lessee on payment of the rent, as represents the income tax upon such an amount as the Commissioners think reasonable, as representing the diminished value by reason of wear and tear of the machinery or plant during the year. But no such claim is allowed, unless it is made within twelve calendar months after the expiration of the year of assessment.

[1] See *ante*, pp. 271, 272.

[2] 41 & 42 Vict. c. 15, s. 12. We are dealing now, it will be observed, only with the claim to repayment made by the lessor of machinery, &c. As to the deduction for diminished value of machinery, &c., made upon assessment of any such trade, &c., as above mentioned, see *ante*, p. 60.

Chap. IV. *Appeal against Assessment made by Additional Commissioners, &c.—Notice of Day for.*—[1] If any person thinks himself aggrieved by an assessment made by the Additional Commissioners, or by any objection to such assessment made by any Surveyor, he may appeal to the General Commissioners, in the same district in which the assessment was made. Ten days' notice of the intention to appeal must be given to the Surveyor. [2] If the person assessed removes from the district in which he was assessed without appealing, and afterwards desires to appeal, the Board may, if they think fit, upon his application, authorize the General Commissioners for the district to which he has removed, to hear and determine his appeal, in like manner as if it had been prosecuted before the General Commissioners for the district in which he was assessed. The General Commissioners must from time to time appoint days for hearing appeals as soon after any assessment is returned to them by the Additional Commissioners as can conveniently be done; and the Assessors must give notice of the days so appointed to the different appellants. The meetings of the Commissioners for the purpose of hearing appeals are held from time to time, within the time limited by the Commissioners, [3] who cause a general notice to be fixed up

---

[1] 5 & 6 Vict. c. 35, s. 118.
[2] 16 & 17 Vict. c. 34, s. 55.
[3] 5 & 6 Vict. c. 35, s. 119.

in their office, or left with their clerk, and also
to be affixed on, or near to, the door of the church,
or chapel, of the parish or place; or, if such parish
or place has no church, or chapel, then on, or
near to, the door of the church, or chapel, of some
adjoining parish or place, limiting the time for
hearing all appeals. [1]No appeal can, as a general
rule, be received after the time so limited, except [2]on
account of diminution of income, [3]but if any person
is prevented by absence, sickness, or other reasonable
cause, to be allowed by the Commissioners, from
making, or proceeding upon, his appeal within the
time so limited, the Commissioners may give further
time for that purpose; or may admit the appeal to
be made by any agent, clerk, or servant, on behalf
of such appellant; and [4]if the appeal is made on
behalf of any person who is absent out of the realm,
or prevented by sickness from attending in person
within the time so limited, the Commissioners may
postpone such appeal from time to time, or admit
other proof than the oath of the appellant of the
truth of [5]the several matters required to be proved
by his oath.

[1] 5 & 6 Vict. c. 35, ss. 118 and 119.
[2] As to appeals on account of diminution of income, see
post, pp. 303—306.
[3] 5 & 6 Vict. c. 35, s. 118.
[4] 5 & 6 Vict. c. 35, s. 119.
[5] As to these matters, see *ante*, pp. 275—278.

Chap. IV. *Proceedings after Notice of Appeal given, and when*
Objection of Surveyor allowed.—[1] The General Commissioners, upon receiving notice of appeal against
any assessment made by the Additional Commissioners, and also whenever they see cause to allow an
objection of the Surveyor to such assessment, direct
their precept to the appellant to return to them,
within the time limited in the precept, a schedule
containing such particulars as the Commissioners
may demand respecting the property of the appellant,
or the trade, manufacture, adventure, or concern in
the nature of trade, or the profession, employment,
or vocation, carried on and exercised by the appellant,
and the amount of the balance of his profits and
gains, distinguishing the amounts received from each
[2]separate source, or respecting the particulars of the
deductions from any of such profits or gains made in
the statements or schedules delivered by him. The
Commissioners may demand such schedules at their
discretion, whenever they think them necessary, from
time to time, until a complete schedule satisfactory to
them of all the particulars required by them has
been delivered. The precept of the Commissioners
is delivered to the appellant, or left at his last, or
usual, place of abode; or, if the appellant has
removed from the jurisdiction of the Commissioners,
or cannot be found, is fixed on, or near to, the door

---

[1] 5 & 6 Vict. c. 35, s. 120.

[2] As to these sources, see *ante*, pp. 124, 154, 156, 158
and 162.

of the church, or chapel, of the place where the
Commissioners meet, and is thereupon binding upon
the appellant. The Surveyor has free access, at all
reasonable times, to any schedule delivered in pursuance of the precept of the Commissioners, and may
take such copies thereof, or extracts therefrom, as he
may think necessary. [1] He may within a reasonable
time after examining any such schedule, to be allowed
by the Commissioners, object to the schedule, or any
part thereof, and state his objection in writing; and
in such case he must deliver a notice in writing of
his objection, under cover, sealed up, and directed to
the appellant, or leave the same at his last, or usual,
place of abode, in order that the appellant may, if
he thinks fit, appeal from the objection to the Commissioners. No assessment can be confirmed, or
altered, until the appeal upon the objection, or the
assessment, has been heard and determined. [2] If
upon receiving the objection of the Surveyor to any
schedule the Commissioners see cause to disallow the
objection, or if upon hearing any appeal they are
satisfied with the assessment made by the Additional
Commissioners, or if after delivery of a schedule
they are satisfied therewith, and have received no
information of its insufficiency, the General Commissioners direct such assessment to be confirmed, or
altered, as the case requires. But if the General

---

[1] 5 & 6 Vict. c. 35, s. 121.
[2] 5 & 6 Vict. c. 35, s. 122.

Chap. IV. Commissioners think that the statement upon which the Additional Commissioners made their assessment, or the schedule delivered to themselves, should be verified, they direct the Assessor to give notice to the person charged to appear before them to verify the statement or schedule, and such person must appear accordingly and verify the contents of his statement or schedule on oath and sign the same; but he is at liberty to amend the statement or schedule before being required to take the oath. The Commissioners may also, if they are dissatisfied with any assessment returned to them by the Additional Commissioners, or with any schedule delivered to them, or if they require any further information, make the enquiries and proceed in the manner we have [1] before described. After such oath, and whenever the statement or schedule has not been objected to, and the Commissioners are satisfied therewith, they make an assessment according to the statement or schedule, which is final and conclusive as to the matters contained in the statement or schedule. [2] When any person has neglected, or refused, to return a schedule according to the exigency of the precept of the Commissioners, or any clerk, agent, or servant, of any such person, being summoned, has neglected, or refused, to appear before the Commissioners to be examined, or if any such person, or his clerk, agent, or servant, being

---

[1] *Ante,* pp. 238—240.
[2] 5 & 6 Vict. c. 35, s. 126.

summoned has declined to answer any question put
to him in writing, or *vivâ voce*, by the Commissioners,
or where any schedule delivered has been objected to
and the objection has not been appealed against, or
when any person being required to verify his statement or schedule, or his answers, or examination in
writing, shall have neglected, or refused, to do so,
or when the Commissioners agree to allow the objections, or any of them, made by the Surveyor, the
Commissioners settle and ascertain according to the
best of their judgment in what sums the person
chargeable ought to be charged, and make an assessment accordingly, which is final and conclusive. [1] In
every case in which the General Commissioners have
made any increased assessment upon the amount
contained in the statement or schedule of the person
to be charged, or at any time discover that any
increase ought to be made, whether upon the surcharge of the Surveyor, or from his information or
otherwise, they may charge such person in a sum
not exceeding treble the amount by which the duties
have been increased, unless he makes it appear to the
satisfaction of the Commissioners that the omission
complained of did not proceed from any fraud,
covin, act, or contrivance, or from gross, or wilful
neglect.

*Appeal may be to Special Commissioners instead of to
General Commissioners.*—[2] In any case in which an

---

[1] 5 & 6 Vict. c. 35, s. 127.
[2] 5 & 6 Vict. c. 35, s. 130.

Chap. IV. appeal is allowed to be made to the General Commissioners against any assessment under Schedule D., or against any objection of the Surveyor to such assessment, or against any surcharge of the duties, he may, if he thinks fit, instead of appealing to the General Commissioners, appeal to the Special Commissioners. In that case he must give notice in writing of his intention to the Surveyor, within the time limited for notice of appeal to the General Commissioners in similar cases. The appeal is then heard and determined by two or more of the Special Commissioners directed by the Board to hear appeals in the district in which the appellant is chargeable; and their determination is final and conclusive. But every appeal upon a claim to exemption on account of the appellant's income being less than 150*l.* a year, or [1] upon a claim to abatement on account of the appellant's income being less than 400*l.* a year, must be made to the General Commissioners.

Appeal in Case of Assessment by Special Commissioners on Application of Persons chargeable.—[2] An assessment made by the Special Commissioners upon the application of the person chargeable is subject to appeal by either the person charged, or the Surveyor; and the appeal is made in like manner, and

---

[1] 5 & 6 Vict. c. 35, s. 130; 16 & 17 Vict. c. 34, s. 28; 39 & 40 Vict. c. 16, s. 8.

[2] 5 & 6 Vict. c. 35, s. 131.

under like rules and regulations, as [1]an appeal Chap. IV. against an assessment made by the Additional Commissioners; but every such appeal is heard and determined by the Special Commissioners directed by the Board to hear appeals in the district. If either the person charged, or the Surveyor, thinks the determination of the Special Commissioners on any such appeal is wrong, and then expresses himself dissatisfied therewith, the Commissioners must, if required, state specially, and sign, the case upon which the question arises, with their determination thereon, and transmit the same to the Board for their opinion, who, with all convenient speed, state, and subscribe, their opinion on the case so transmitted, and according to the opinion of the Board, whose decision is final and conclusive, the assessment is altered or confirmed.

Relief on Account of Diminution of Income.—[2]If [3]within, or at the end of, the year current at the time of making any assessment, or at the end of any year when such assessment ought to have been made, any person charged to the duties under Schedule D.,

---

[1] See *ante*, pp. 296 *et seq.*

[2] 5 & 6 Vict. c. 35, s. 133.

[3] That is "in as short a time as, by using all reasonable and proper exertions, the party claiming can possibly have ascertained the fact and amount of the overpayment." Lord Esher, M. R., in *Reg.* v. *Commissioners of Income Tax, In re Cape Copper Mining Co.*, 21 Q. B. D. 313; 36 W. R. 776; 57 L. J., Q. B. 513; and see *Russell* v. *North of Scotland Bank*, 28 Sco. L. R. 389.

Chap. IV. finds, and proves to the satisfaction of the General Commissioners, that his profits and gains during such year fell short of the sum at which those profits and gains were computed, in respect of the same [1]source of profit as that upon which the computation was made, the Commissioners may amend the assessment for such current year as the case may require; and, if the sum assessed has been paid, they certify under their hands to the Special Commissioners, at the [2]Chief Office for Inland Revenue in England, the amount of the sum overpaid upon the assessment, and thereupon the Special Commissioners[3] issue an order for the repayment of the sum overpaid, directed to the Receiver General of Inland Revenue, or to an officer for receipt, or Collector, of the duties, or to a distributor, or sub-distributor, of stamps, as in the case of [4]allowances granted under No. 5 of Schedule A. [5]But no such reduction or repayment will be made in any case unless the profits of the year of assessment are proved to be less than the profits for one year on the average of the last three years, including the year of assessment; and no such

---

[1] As to the sources of profit, see *ante*, pp. 124, 154, 156, 158 and 162.

[2] 12 & 13 Vict. c. 1, s. 17.

[3] If the Special Commissioners wrongfully decline to issue an order for repayment, a mandamus will lie to compel them. *Reg.* v. *Commissioners of Income Tax, In re Cape Copper Mining Co., ubi sup.*

[4] As to these allowances, see *ante*, pp. 262—264, 275.

[5] 28 & 29 Vict. c. 30, s. 6.

relief will exceed in amount the difference between the sum on which the assessment has been made and such average profits for one year as aforesaid. [1]And in case any person charged to the duties under Schedule D. ceases to exercise the profession or to carry on the trade, employment, or vocation in respect of which the assessment was made, or dies, or becomes bankrupt or insolvent before the end of the year for making the assessment, or from any other specific cause, is deprived of, or loses, the profits or gains on which the computation of duty was made, such person, or his executors or administrators, may apply to the General Commissioners of the district within three calendar months after the end of such year; and upon proof of the facts to the satisfaction of the Commissioners, they may amend the assessment as the case may require, and give such relief to the person charged, or to his executors or administrators, as is just. In cases requiring the same, the Commissioners may order repayment to be made as above of the sum overpaid. But when any person has succeeded to the trade or business of the person charged, no abatement is made, unless the Commissioners are satisfied that the profits and gains of such trade or business have fallen short from some specific cause since such change or succession took place. [2]If a person who has sustained a loss in any

---

[1] 5 & 6 Vict. c. 35, s. 134.
[2] 53 & 54 Vict. c. 8, s. 23.

Chap. IV. trade, manufacture, adventure or concern, or profession, employment or vocation, carried on by him either solely or in partnership, seeks an adjustment of his liability by reference to the loss, and to the aggregate amount of his income for the year, he may obtain such adjustment in the manner [1] before stated.

Appeal against Surveyor's Charges and against Surcharges.—What [2] has been said of appeals against a Surveyor's charges, and against surcharges under Schedule A., applies equally to appeals against similar charges and surcharges under Schedule D.

Case for Opinion of High Court.—[3] Upon the determination of any appeal by the General Commissioners, or by the Special Commissioners, either the appellant or Surveyor may, if dissatisfied with the determination as being erroneous in point of law, require a case to be stated in the manner we have [4] before described. [5] An appeal lies from the decision of the High Court to Her Majesty's Court of Appeal, and from thence to the House of Lords.

Relief from Double Assessment.—[6] Whenever it appears to the Board that a person has been assessed

---

[1] See *ante*, pp. 303 *et seq.*

[2] *Ante*, pp. 282 *et seq.*

[3] 43 & 44 Vict. c. 19, s. 59.

[4] *Ante*, pp. 280, 282.

[5] 41 & 42 Vict. c. 15, s. 15 ; 43 & 44 Vict. c. 19, s. 59.

[6] 43 & 44 Vict. c. 19, s. 60.

more than once to the duties for the same cause and **Chap. IV.**
for the same year, they direct the whole, or such part,
of any assessment appearing to be an overcharge to
be vacated.

SECTION V.—SCHEDULE E.

*Claims of Exemption, Appeals, &c. upon Assessments
under Schedule E.*—There is not much to be said with
regard to claims of exemption, and abatement, and
appeals made upon assessments under Schedule E.
The necessity for making such claims or appeals can
rarely, if ever, arise in cases where the assessment is
made by the Commissioners for the particular office,
or department, in which the employment of profit,
which is the subject of assessment, is carried on.   In
cases where the assessment is made by the General
Commissioners of a district, much of what we have
said upon the subject of claims and appeals in dealing
with assessments made under the other schedules,
will be applicable to assessments under Schedule E.
We will add only the following provisions, which
have special reference to the last-mentioned assessments :—

1. [1] When a change has taken place during the
   year of assessment in any office or employment, chargeable under Schedule E., the
   assessment in respect of such office or employment is levied for the whole year, notwithstanding such change, without any new

[1] 5 & 6 Vict. c. 35, s. 146, r. 1.

assessment; but the person quitting such office or employment, or dying within the year, or his executors or administrators, is, or are, liable for the arrears due before, or at the time of, his so quitting such office or employment, or dying, and for such further period of time as shall then have elapsed, to be settled by the respective Commissioners; and his successor has a right to be repaid such sums as he has paid for duty on account of such portion of the year as aforesaid; and each such assessment remains in force for one whole year unless the office, or employment, or the annuity, pension, or stipend, payable in respect thereof ceases, or expires within the year by lapse, death, or otherwise, from which period the assessment is discharged.

2. [1]In every case in which any person holding any office or employment, or being entitled to any pension, or stipend, claims to be exempt from such assessment, the Commissioners must nevertheless set down in such assessment the name of such person, and the full and just value of such office, &c.; and the claim to such exemption must be preferred, and examined, and the merits thereof heard and determined, under the regulations in force with respect to other assessments.

[1] 5 & 6 Vict. c. 35, s. 152.

3. [1]In cases of claim to exemption on account of Chap. IV.
the claimant's income being less than 150*l.*
a year, where the whole income of the
claimant arises from an office, or employment
of profit, the duties whereon are cognizable
before the Commissioners of a department of
office, or from a pension, or stipend, the claim
may be made to, and allowed by, the Commissioners of the department in which the
duties are cognizable; and if the claimant is
out of Great Britain the facts required to be
stated in support of the claim may be stated
by affidavit taken before any person having
authority to administer an oath in the place
where the claimant resides.

[1] 5 & 6 Vict. c. 35, s. 169.

INDEX.

A.

ABATEMENT,
on account of life insurance or purchase of deferred annuity, 87—89, 96, 101, 128, 129, 169.
how claimed, 271, 294.
in respect of 120*l.* of income where yearly income is less than 400*l.* a year, 89, 90, 96, 97, 101, 102, 164, 170, 171.
how claimed, 265—270, 290, 294.
See also DEDUCTION AND ALLOWANCES—EXEMPTION.

ABSENTEES. *See* PERSONS RESIDING OUT OF GREAT BRITAIN.

ABSENTEES, temporary. *See* PERSONS WHO GO ABROAD FOR PURPOSES OF TEMPORARY RESIDENCE.

ACCOUNT,
by Collectors. *See* COLLECTORS.
of salaries chargeable under Schedule E. to be delivered on request of Assessor, 256, 257.
See also STATEMENT.

ACTIONS,
against Commissioners and other officers, limitation of, 38, 39.
against Collectors appointed by General Commissioners must be defended by Commissioners, 39.
for recovery of penalties exceeding 20*l.* imposed by Income Tax Acts, 39, 40.
See also RECOVERY OF DUTIES.

ADDITIONAL ASSESSMENT. *See* ASSESSMENT.

ADDITIONAL COMMISSIONERS. *See* COMMISSIONERS.

ANNUAL VALUE,
OF PROPERTY CHARGEABLE UNDER SCHEDULE A.,
general rule for ascertaining, 48.
extent of application of general rule, 49, 50.
special rules for ascertaining—
if owner pays rates and taxes, by law a charge upon
occupier, 49.
if occupier pays rates and taxes, by law a charge upon
owner, 49.
if rent depends on price of corn, &c., 50.
if whole or part of rent reserved in corn or grain, 50.
if rent depends on actual produce of land, 50.
of tithes taken in kind, 51.
of ecclesiastical dues, 51.
of compositions, rents, and money payments, in lieu
of tithes, other than tithe rentcharges, 51, 52.
of manors and other royalties, 52.
of fines upon demise, 53.
of other profits arising from land not in occupation
of person chargeable, and not before enumerated,
53.
if the possession, or interest, of the party to be
charged has commenced within the time for which
the average by which the annual value is to be
estimated is directed to be taken, 53, 71, 72.
of quarries of stone, slate, limestone, or chalk, 54.
of mines of coal, tin, lead, copper, mundic, iron and
other mines (except alum mines), 55, 56.
of iron works, gas works in England, salt springs,
alum mines or works, water works, streams of
water, canals, inland navigations, docks, drains
and levels, fishings, rights of market, fairs, tolls,
railways and other ways, bridges, ferries and other
like concerns, 59, 60.
of gas works on the continent of Europe, or in the
Colonies, 59, note 4.
UNDER SCHEDULE B.,
rules for ascertaining, generally the same as under
Schedule A., 92.
in case of land subject to tithe rentcharge, and lands
tithe free, 92.
in case of lands subject to modus, 93.
in case of lands subject to modus *and* tithe, 93.

ANNUAL VALUE of lands, &c., how estimated for purpose of
claiming exemption on ground of annual income being less
than 150*l*., 269, 270.

E.   P

P 2

ASSESSMENT—*continued.*

UNDER SCHEDULE D.—*continued.*
When assessment made by Special Commissioners,
procedure and powers of Special Commissioners, 245, 246.

UNDER SCHEDULE E.,
who are Commissioners for making, 252—254.
period for which made, 255.
proceedings in order to, 255—257.
additional, 259.
See also ASSESSORS—DUPLICATES OF ASSESSMENTS.

ASSESSORS,
how appointed by General Commissioners, 27, 28.
period for which appointment made, 28.
when appointed by magistrates, 28, 29.
when Surveyors may execute duties of, 29.
not appointed in the Metropolis, 29—31.
no persons inhabiting any city, &c., can be compelled to serve as, outside its limits, 31.
declaration to be made by, before acting, 31.
remuneration of, 31.
special provision for exercise of duties of, sometimes made in Annual Income Tax Act, 31, 32.
notices by, 174, 175, 191, 242, 274, 287, 296, 300.
lists to be delivered to, 177.
verification upon oath of fixing of general notices by, 185.
how assessment made by, 186—189.
may apply for instruction to Commissioners or Surveyor, 186.
may estimate value of house or land of less annual value than 10*l.* without return, 188.
may require tenant to produce lease or agreement of tenancy, 188.
if no lease or agreement, may make assessment upon written account by tenant, 189.
certificates of assessment by, 190, 191.
may inspect rate books, 191.
in case of failure to assess by, duties in arrear may be set *insuper*, 211.
may be appointed by Commissioners for assessing duties on interest on Exchequer Securities, 221.
may be directed by General Commissioners to give notice to person charged to appear and verify schedule, 242, 299, 300.
notice of desire to be assessed by Special Commissioners, in respect of profits chargeable under Schedule D., must be delivered to, 244.

C.

CITY,
 of London, within limits of "Chief Office of Excise," 4.
 of Westminster, within limits of "Chief Office of Excise," 4.
 when General Commissioners for County may act for,
 14, 15.
 in certain cities persons may be chosen to act as General
 Commissioners with the General Commissioners chosen in
 the ordinary way, 16, 17.
 qualification of General Commissioner for any. *See* COM-
 MISSIONERS FOR GENERAL PURPOSES.
 no person inhabiting any, can be compelled to be Assessor
 outside its limits, 31.
 profits of any office in, chargeable under Schedule E., 167.
 who are Commissioners for assessing offices in a, 253,
 note [3].

CLERGYMAN may deduct from profits of his profession expenses necessarily incurred in performance of duty, 72, note [1],
 97, note [2], 155, 156. *See also* GIFT OF MONEY.

CLERK TO GENERAL COMMISSIONERS,
 how appointed, 24.
 not removable except for just cause, 24.
 may not receive any fees, &c., except from person appointed
 by Board, 24.
 vacancy in office of, how filled up, 25.
 wilfully misconducting himself incurs penalty, 25.
 acts as Clerk to Additional Commissioners, 25.
 acting before taking oath incurs penalty, 25.
 Commissioners acting under Schedule E. may appoint a,
 255.

COAL MINES. *See* ANNUAL VALUE.

COLLECTION,
 of duties under Schedule A., 196—213.
 of duties under Schedule B., 213.
 of duties under Schedule C., 214—223.
 of duties under Schedule D., 247—252.
 of duties under Schedule E., 252—261.
 See also COLLECTORS.

COLLECTORS,
 how appointed, 32—35.
 nomination of, 32.
 acceptance of office by, not compulsory, 33.
 notice must be given by, if office declined, 33.

COLLECTORS—*continued.*
appointment of, 33.
appointment must be notified to, 33.
when power to appoint, vests in Board, 34, 35.
vacancy caused by death of, how filled, 34.
Board may require security to be given by, 34, 35.
Land Tax, and General, Commissioners may require security to be given by, 36.
two or more inhabitants of district may require security to be given by, 36.
parish answerable for, if security not given by, 37.
must take prescribed oath, 37.
remuneration of, 37, 38.
receipt given by, on payment of duty, 196, 197.
account by, 206, 207.
remittance of collection by, 207.
must answer lawful questions of Surveyor, or Collector of Inland Revenue, 208.
See also COLLECTION.

COLLECTORS OF INLAND REVENUE, 5.

COLLEGES,
repairs of. *See* DEDUCTIONS AND ALLOWANCES.
stock and dividends applicable to repairs of. *See* EXEMPTION.

COLLEGIATE CHURCHES, repairs of. *See* DEDUCTIONS AND ALLOWANCES.

COLONIAL COMPANIES, securities given by, chargeable under Schedule D., 158, 159.

COLONIAL POSSESSIONS, profits arising from, chargeable under Schedule D., 162.

COLONIAL REVENUES, annuities payable out of. *See* ANNUITIES.

COLONIAL SECURITIES, profits arising from, chargeable under Schedule D., 158.

COLONIES, gas works in, chargeable under Schedule D., 59, note 4. *See also* COLONIAL COMPANIES—COLONIAL POSSESSIONS—COLONIAL REVENUES—COLONIAL SECURITIES.

COMMISSARY COURT under her Majesty, Commissioners in relation to offices in any, 7, 8, 228, 229.

D.

F.

E.   Q

Q 2

O.

R.

RAILWAY COMPANY,
duties on railways paid under Schedule D., 54, note [1], 60, note [1].
assessed by Special Commissioners, 172, 194, 195.
collection of duties assessed on railways, 212, 213.
duties on offices under any, assessed by Special Commissioners, except in cases of persons paid weekly wages, 259, note [2], 260.
Special Commissioners notify particulars of assessment of offices under any, to secretary of, 259, 260.
may deduct amount of duty from wages, &c., of persons in their employment, 260.
See also SCHEDULE D.

RAILWAYS. *See* RAILWAY COMPANY.

RATE OF DUTY, variation in. *See* VARIATION IN RATE OF DUTY.

RATEABLE VALUE, meaning of, in Metropolis Valuation Act, 187.

RECEIPT, Collector's, for duty, 196, 197.
See also STAMP DUTY.

RECEIVER,
chargeable for persons for whom he receives profits, 179, 180.
in Chancery chargeable, 180.
being charged may retain duties, 181.
See also OFFICERS OF COMPANIES.

RECEIVER-GENERAL OF INLAND REVENUE, 5.

RECOVERY OF DUTY,
by distress, 202—204.
by committal of defaulter, 204.
by action, or suit, in High Court, 205, 206.

RELIEF,
to owners of land whose profits fall short of assessment. *See* DEDUCTIONS AND ALLOWANCES.
for losses caused by flood or tempest, 279, 280.
claim for, how made, 279, 280.

W.

WAREHOUSE occupied for purposes of trade or profession not charged under Schedule B., 91.

WATERWORKS. *See* ANNUAL VALUE.

WAYS, profits of, where charged, 173.
See also ANNUAL VALUE.

WEEKLY BILLS OF MORTALITY, 4, note [6].

WESTMINSTER. *See* CITY.

Y.

YEARLY INTEREST, meaning of (*Goslings* v. *Sharpe*), 198 note [5].

LONDON:

PRINTED BY C. F. ROWORTH, GREAT NEW STREET, FETTER LANE.

TELEGRAPHIC ADDRESS—
"RHODRONS, LONDON." June, 1901. TELEPHONE—
No. 1388 (HOLBORN).

CATALOGUE
OF
LAW WORKS
PUBLISHED BY
STEVENS AND SONS, LTD.
119 & 120, Chancery Lane, London.
(And at 14, Bell Yard, Lincoln's Inn.)

A Catalogue of Modern Law Works, *together with a complete Chronological List of all the English, Irish, and Scotch Reports, an Alphabetical Table of Abbreviations used in reference to Law Reports and Text Books, and an Index of Subjects.* Demy 8vo. Oct. 1900 (120 pp.), *limp binding, post free* 6d.

Acts of Parliament.—*Public and Local Acts from an early date may be had of the Publishers of this Catalogue, who have also on sale the largest collection of Private Acts, relating to Estates, Enclosures, Railways, Roads, &c., &c.*

ACCOUNT.—Williams' Law of Account.—Being a concise Treatise on the Right and Liability to Account, the taking of Accounts, and Accountants' Charges. By SYDNEY E. WILLIAMS, Esq., Author of "Law relating to Legal Representatives," &c. Demy 8vo. 1899. 10s.
"A well-arranged book, which should be very useful to receivers and accountants generally, as well as to both branches of the legal profession."— *Law Journal.*

ADMIRALTY.—Roscoe's Admiralty Practice.—Third Edition. By E. S. ROSCOE, Assistant Registrar, Admiralty Court, and T. LAMBERT MEARS, Esqrs., Barrister-at-Law. (*In preparation.*)

ADULTERATION.—Bartley's Adulteration of Food.—Statutes and Cases dealing with Coffee, Tea, Bread, Seeds, Food and Drugs, Margarine, Fertilisers and Feeding Stuffs, &c., &c., including the Food and Drugs Act, 1899. Second Edition. By DOUGLAS C. BARTLEY, Esq., Barrister-at-Law. Roy. 12mo. 1899. 8s.
"Not only concise but precise."—*Law Times.*

ADVOCACY.—Harris' Hints on Advocacy.—Conduct of Cases, Civil and Criminal. Classes of Witnesses and Suggestions for Cross-examining them, &c., &c. By RICHARD HARRIS, K.C. Eleventh Edition, with an Introduction. Royal 12mo. 1897. 7s. 6d.
"A very complete Manual of the Advocate's art in Trial by Jury."—*Sol. Jour.*
"Deserves to be carefully read by the young barrister whose career is yet before him."—*Law Magazine.*

AFFILIATION.—Bott's Manual of the Law and Practice in Affiliation Proceedings, with Statutes and Forms, Table of Gestation, Forms of Agreement, &c. By W. HOLLOWAY BOTT, Solicitor. Demy 12mo. 1894. 6s.

AGRICULTURAL LAW.—Dixon.—*Vide* "Farm."
Spencer's Agricultural Holdings (England) Acts, 1883—1900, with Explanatory Notes and General Forms; also the Board of Agriculture and County Court Rules and Forms, together with the Allotments and Cottage Gardens Compensation for Crops Act, 1887. —Second Edition. By AUBREY J. SPENCER, Esq., Barrister-at-Law. Demy 8vo. 1901. 7s. 6d.
"We do not hesitate to recommend this book. The value of the book is enhanced by the addition of a large number of useful forms. The Index has satisfactorily stood the test to which we subjected it."—*Law Jour.*, Mar. 23, 1901.

** All standard Law Works are kept in Stock, in law calf and other bindings.

A

ANNUAL COUNTY COURT PRACTICE.—The Annual County
Court Practice, 1901, with Supplement containing New
Rules, &c.—By His Honour Judge SMYLY, K.C., assisted by
W. J. BROOKS, Esq., Barrister-at-Law. 2 vols. Demy 8vo. 25s.

*** The Supplement may be had separately, sewed, 2s. 6d.

"The profession generally have gratefully recognized the very great value of
this book. It admirably fulfils the essential requisites of a practice book. It is
complete without being discursive or of unwieldy bulk; it is accurate and easy of
reference, and throughout bears the stamp of having been compiled by a man
who is thoroughly acquainted with his subject."—Law Times.

ANNUAL DIGEST.—Mews'.—Vide "Digest."

ANNUAL LIBRARY, THE LAWYER'S :—
(1) The Annual Practice.—SNOW, BURNEY, and STRINGER.
(2) The Annual Digest.—MEWS. (Also issued Quarterly.)
(3) The Annual Statutes.—LELY.
(4) The Annual County Court Practice.—SMYLY.

☞ Annual Subscriptions. For Complete Series, as above, delivered on
the day of publication, net, 2l. 5s. Nos. 1, 2, and 3 only, net, 1l. 15s.
Nos. 2, 3, and 4 only, net, 1l. 15s. (Carriage extra, 2s.)
Full prospectus forwarded on application.

ANNUAL PRACTICE.—The Annual Practice. 1901. Edited by
THOMAS SNOW, Barrister-at-Law; CHARLES BURNEY, a Master of
the Supreme Court; and F. A. STRINGER, of the Central Office.
2 vols. 8vo. Net 25s.

☞ Dr. Blake Odgers, K.C., has re-written the Notes to Orders XIX., XX.,
XXI.,XXV. and XXVIII., relating to Pleading, Statement of Claim, De-
fence and Counter-claim, Proceedings in Lieu of Demurrer, and Amendment.

"A book which every practising English lawyer must have."—Law Quarterly.
"It is only by the help of this established book of practice that a practitioner
can carry on his business."—Law Times.
"Every member of the bar, in practice, and every London solicitor, at all events,
finds the last edition of the Annual Practice a necessity."—Solicitors' Journal.

ANNUAL STATUTES.—Lely.—Vide "Statutes."

ARBITRATION.—Mozley-Stark's Duties of an Arbitrator under the
Workmen's Compensation Act, 1897.—With Notes on the Act
and Rules, and Appendices containing the Act, a selection from the
Workmen's Compensation Rules, 1898, and the Medical Referees'
Regulations. By A. MOZLEY-STARK, Solicitor. Roy. 12mo. 1898. 5s.

Russell's Treatise on the Power and Duty of an Arbitrator,
and the Law of Submissions and Awards; with an Appendix
of Forms, and of the Statutes relating to Arbitration. By FRANCIS
RUSSELL. Eighth Edition. By EDWARD POLLOCK, Esq., an Official
Referee of the Supreme Court of Judicature, and the late HERBERT
RUSSELL, Esq., Barrister-at-Law. Royal 8vo. 1900. 30s.

"The execution of the work leaves nothing to be desired."—Law Times.
"After a careful examination of the way in which the work has been done,
we may say that nothing which the practitioner will want to know seems to have
been omitted."—Law Journal.

ARCHITECTS.—Vide "Civil Engineers."

AVERAGE.—Hopkins' Hand-Book of Average.—Fourth Edition.
By MANLEY HOPKINS, Esq. Demy 8vo. 1884. 1l. 1s.

Lowndes' Law of General Average.—English and Foreign.
Fourth Edition. By RICHARD LOWNDES, Average Adjuster. Author
of "The Law of Marine Insurance," &c. Royal 8vo. 1888. 1l. 10s.

"The most complete store of materials relating to the subject in every particular."—Law Quarterly Review.

AUCTIONEERS.—Hart's Law relating to Auctioneers.—By HEBER
HART, Esq., LL.D., Barrister-at-Law. Demy 8vo. 1895. 7s. 6d.

BANKING.—Walker's Treatise on Banking Law.—Second Edition.
By J. D. WALKER, Esq., K.C. Demy 8vo. 1885. 15s.

*** All standard Law Works are kept in Stock, in law calf and other bindings.

BANKRUPTCY.—Lawrance's Precedents of Deeds of Arrangement between Debtors and their Creditors; including Forms, with Introductory Chapters, also the Deeds of Arrangement Acts, 1887 and 1890, with Notes. Fifth Ed. By ARTHUR LAWRENCE, Esq., Barrister-at-Law. Demy 8vo. 1900.   7s. 6d.
" Concise, practical, and reliable."—*Law Times.*

Williams' Law and Practice in Bankruptcy.—Comprising the Bankruptcy Acts, 1883 to 1890, the Bankruptcy Rules and Forms, 1886, 1890, the Debtors Acts, 1869, 1878, the Bankruptcy (Discharge and Closure) Act, 1887, the Deeds of Arrangement Act, 1887, and the Rules thereunder. By the Right Hon. Sir ROLAND L. VAUGHAN WILLIAMS, a Lord Justice of Appeal. Seventh Edition. By EDWARD WM. HANSELL, Esq., Barrister-at-Law. Roy. 8vo. 1898.   30s.
" The leading text-book on bankruptcy."—*Law Journal.*

BASTARDY.—Bott.—*Vide* "*Affiliation.*"

BILLS OF EXCHANGE.—Campbell's Ruling Cases. Vol. IV.— *Vide* " Digests,'' p. 10.

Chalmers' Digest of the Law of Bills of Exchange, Promissory Notes, Cheques and Negotiable Securities. Fifth Edition. By His Honour Judge CHALMERS, Draughtsman of the Bills of Exchange Act. Demy 8vo. 1896.   18s.
" The leading book on bills of exchange; it is well known, widely used, and highly appreciated."—*Law Journal.*
" Each section having appended to it illustrations in the nature of short statements of decided cases. These are prepared with that skilful conciseness of which the learned Judge is a master."—*Law Times.*

BILLS OF LADING.—Leggett's Treatise on the Law of Bills of Lading.—Second Edition. By EUGENE LEGGETT, Solicitor and Notary Public. Demy 8vo. 1893.   30s.

Pollock's Bill of Lading Exceptions.—By HENRY E. POLLOCK. Second Edition. Demy 8vo. 1896.   10s. 6d.

BOOK-KEEPING.—Matthew Hale's System of Book-keeping for Solicitors, containing a List of all Books necessary, with a comprehensive description of their objects and uses for the purpose of Drawing Bills of Costs and the rendering of Cash Accounts to clients; also showing how to ascertain Profits derived from the business; with an Appendix. Demy 8vo. 1884.   5s. 6d.
" The most sensible, useful, practical little work on solicitors' book-keeping that we have seen."—*Law Students' Journal.*

BUILDING SOCIETIES.—Wurtzburg on Building Societies.— The Law relating to Building Societies, with Appendices containing the Statutes, Regulations, Act of Sederunt, and Precedents of Rules and Assurances. Third Edition. By E. A. WURTZBURG, Esq., Barrister-at-Law. Demy 8vo. 1895.   15s.
" Will be of use not only to lawyers but also to secretaries and directors of building societies. It is a carefully arranged and carefully written book."— *Law Times.*

CARDINAL RULES.—*See* "Legal Interpretation."

CARRIERS.—Carver's Treatise on the Law relating to the Carriage of Goods by Sea.—Third Edition. By THOMAS GILBERT CARVER, Esq., K.C. Royal 8vo. 1900.   1l. 16s.
" A recognized authority."—*Solicitors' Journal.*
" Mr. Carver's work stands in the first rank of text-books written by living authors."—*Law Quarterly Review.*
   " The law of common carriers is nowhere better explained."—*Law Times.*

Macnamara's Digest of the Law of Carriers of Goods and Passengers by Land and Internal Navigation.—By WALTER HENRY MACNAMARA, Esq., Barrister-at-Law, Registrar to the Railway Commission. Royal 8vo. 1888.   1l. 8s.
" A complete *epitome* of the law relating to carriers of every class."—*Railway Press.*

⁎⁎ *All standard Law Works are kept in Stock, in law calf and other bindings.*
A 2

CHANCERY, *and Vide* "Equity."

Daniell's Chancery Practice.—The Practice of the Chancery Division of the High Court of Justice and on appeal therefrom. Seventh Edition. By CECIL C. M. DALE, C. W. GREENWOOD, SYDNEY E. WILLIAMS, Esqrs., Barristers-at-Law, and FRANCIS A. STRINGER, Esq., of the Central Office. 2 vols. (*In the press.*)

Daniell's Forms and Precedents of Proceedings in the Chancery Division of the High Court of Justice and on Appeal therefrom. Fifth Edition. By CHARLES BURNEY, Esq., B.A. (Oxon.), a Master of the Supreme Court. Royal 8vo. (*In the press.*)

CHARTER PARTIES.—Carver.—*Vide* "Carriers."

Leggett's Treatise on the Law of Charter Parties.—By EUGENE LEGGETT, Solicitor and Notary Public. Demy 8vo. 1894. 25*s.*

CHILDREN.—Hall's Law Relating to Children. By W. CLARKE HALL, Esq., Barrister-at-Law. Demy 8vo. 1894. 4*s.*

CHURCH LAW.—Whitehead's Church Law.—Being a Concise Dictionary of Statutes, Canons, Regulations, and Decided Cases affecting the Clergy and Laity. Second Edition. By BENJAMIN WHITEHEAD, Esq., Barrister-at-Law. Demy 8vo. 1899. 10*s.* 6*d.*
"A perfect mine of learning on all topics ecclesiastical."—*Daily Telegraph.*

The Statutes relating to Church and Clergy, with Preface and Index. By BENJAMIN WHITEHEAD, Esq., Barrister-at-Law. Royal 8vo. 1894. 6*s.*

CIVIL ENGINEERS.—Macassey and Strahan's Law relating to Civil Engineers, Architects and Contractors.—With a Chapter on Arbitrations. Second Edition. By L. LIVINGSTON MACASSEY and J. A. STRAHAN, Esqrs., Barristers-at-Law. Demy 8vo. 1897. 12*s.* 6*d.*

COLLISIONS.—Marsden's Treatise on the Law of Collisions at Sea.—Fourth Edition. By REGINALD G. MARSDEN, Esq., Barrister-at-Law. Demy 8vo. 1897. 1*l.* 8*s.*
"Mr. Marsden's book stands without a rival."—*Law Quarterly Review.*

COMMON LAW. — Chitty's Archbold's Practice. Fourteenth Edition. By THOMAS WILLES CHITTY, assisted by J. ST. L. LESLIE, Esqrs., Barristers-at-Law. 2 vols. Demy 8vo. 1885. (Published at 3*l.* 13*s.* 6*d.*) Reduced to *net*, 30*s.*

Chitty's Forms.—*Vide* "Forms."

Elliott's Outlines of Common Law.—By MARTIN ELLIOTT, Esq., Barrister-at-Law. Demy 8vo. 1898. 10*s.* 6*d.*
"Will prove of the greatest assistance to students."—*Law Times.*

Pollock and Wright's Possession in the Common Law.—Parts I. and II. by Sir F. POLLOCK, Bart., Barrister-at-Law. Part III. by R. S. WRIGHT, Esq., Barrister-at-Law. 8vo. 1888. 8*s.* 6*d.*

Shirley.—*Vide* "Leading Cases."

Smith's Manual of Common Law.—For Practitioners and Students. Comprising the Fundamental Principles, with useful Practical Rules and Decisions. Eleventh Edition. By C. SPURLING, Esq., Barrister-at-Law. Demy 8vo. 1898. 15*s.*
"The arrangement is clear and methodical, and will increase the usefulness of the work, not only for elementary study, but as a handy book of reference."—*Law Quarterly Review.*

COMPANY LAW.—Hamilton's Manual of Company Law. By W. F. HAMILTON, Esq., LL.D. Lond., K.C. Second Edition. By the Author, assisted by PERCY TINDAL-ROBERTSON, Esq., B.A., Barrister-at-Law. Demy 8vo. 1901. 21*s.*
"Everyone interested in the working of a company will find in this new edition all that is necessary from the legal point of view."—*The Stock Exchange.*
"It is difficult to conceive a question relating to the law affecting companies which cannot be answered by reference to this work."—*Southampton Times.*

** *All standard Law Works are kept in Stock, in law calf and other bindings.*

COMPANY LAW—*continued.*

Palmer's Company Law.—A Practical Handbook for Lawyers and Business Men. With an Appendix containing the Companies Acts, 1862 to 1900, and Rules. Third Edition. By FRANCIS BEAUFORT PALMER, Esq., Barrister-at-Law, Author of "Company Precedents," &c. Royal 8vo. 1901.   12s. 6d.

"The work is a marvel—for clearness, fulness, and accuracy, nothing could be better."—*Law Notes.*

"Of especial use to students and business men who need a clear exposition by a master hand."—*Law Journal.*

"The subject is dealt with in a clear and comprehensive manner, and in such a way as to be intelligible not only to lawyers but to others to whom a knowledge of Company Law may be essential."—*Law Students' Journal.*

"All the principal topics of company are dealt with in a substantial manner, the arrangement and typography are excellent, and the whole of the Statute Law—an indispensable adjunct—is collected in an appendix. **Perhaps what practising lawyers and business men will value most is the precious quality of practicality.**"—*Law Quarterly Review.*

"Popular in style, also accurate, with sufficient references to authorities to make the book useful to the practitioner."—*The Times.*

Palmer's Companies Act, 1900, with Explanatory Notes, and Appendix containing Prescribed and other Forms, together with Addenda to "Company Precedents." Second Edition. By FRANCIS BEAUFORT PALMER, Esq., Barrister-at-Law. Royal 8vo. 1901. 7s. 6d.

"It is essentially a book that all interested in companies or company law should procure."—*Law Times.*

"This book will be indispensable in considering the new requirements, and how they are to be met."—*Solicitors' Journal.*

Palmer's Company Precedents.—For use in relation to Companies subject to the Companies Acts.

Part I. COMPANY FORMS. Arranged as follows:—Promoters, Prospectuses, Underwriting, Agreements, Memoranda and Articles of Association, Private Companies, Employés' Benefits, Resolutions, Notices, Certificates, Powers of Attorney, Debentures and Debenture Stock, Banking and Advance Securities, Petitions, Writs, Pleadings, Judgments and Orders, Reconstruction, Amalgamation, Special Acts. With Copious Notes and an Appendix containing the Acts and Rules. Seventh Edition. By FRANCIS BEAUFORT PALMER, Esq., Barrister-at-Law, assisted by the Hon. CHARLES MACNAGHTEN, K.C., and ARTHUR JOHN CHITTY, Esq., Barrister-at-Law. Royal 8vo. 1898. 36s.

"No company lawyer can afford to be without it."—*Law Journal.*

Part II. WINDING-UP FORMS AND PRACTICE. Arranged as follows:—Compulsory Winding-Up, Voluntary Winding-Up, Winding-Up under Supervision, Arrangements and Compromises, with Copious Notes, and an Appendix of Acts and Rules. Eighth Edition. By FRANCIS BEAUFORT PALMER, assisted by FRANK EVANS, Esqrs., Barristers-at-Law. Royal 8vo. 1900. 32s.

"Palmer's 'Company Precedents' is the book *par excellence* for practitioners. There is nothing we can think of which should be within the covers which we do not find."—*Law Journal.*

Part III. DEBENTURES AND DEBENTURE STOCK, including Debentures, Trust Deeds, Stock Certificates, Resolutions, Prospectuses, Writs, Pleadings, Judgments, Orders, Receiverships, Notices, Miscellaneous. With Copious Notes. Eighth Edition. By FRANCIS BEAUFORT PALMER, Esq., Barrister-at-Law. Royal 8vo. 1900. 21s.

"The result of much careful study. . . . . . Simply invaluable to debenture-holders and to the legal advisers of such investors."—*Financial News.*

"Embraces practically the whole law relating to debentures and debenture stock. . . . Must take front rank among the works on the subject."—*Law Times.*

Palmer's Private Companies and Syndicates, their Formation and Advantages; being a Concise Popular Statement of the Mode of Converting a Business into a Private Company, and of establishing and working Private Companies and Syndicates for Miscellaneous Purposes. Sixteenth Edition. By F. B. PALMER, Esq., Barrister-at-Law. 12mo. 1901. *Net*, 1s.

✱✱ *All standard Law Works are kept in Stock, in law calf and other bindings.*

COMPANY LAW—*continued.*

Palmer's Shareholders, Directors, and Voluntary Liquidators Legal Companion.—A Manual of Every-day Law and Practice for Promoters, Shareholders, Directors, Secretaries, Creditors, Solicitors, and Voluntary Liquidators of Companies under the Companies Acts, 1862 to 1900, with Appendix of useful Forms. Twentieth Edit. By F. B. PALMER, Esq., Barrister-at-Law. 12mo. 1901.   *Net*, 2s. 6d.

COMPENSATION.—**Cripps' Treatise on the Principles of the Law of Compensation.** Fourth Edition. By C. A. CRIPPS, Esq., K.C.   Royal 8vo.   1900.   1l. 6s.
"An accurate and complete exposition of the law relating to compensation."
—*Law Journal,* June 9, 1900.
"Mr. Cripps' book is recognized as one of the best. . . . There are few men whose practical knowledge of the subject exceeds that of the learned author."—*Law Quarterly Review,* July, 1900.

COMPOSITION DEEDS.—**Lawrance.**—*Vide* "Bankruptcy."

CONDITIONS OF SALE.—**Webster.**—*Vide* "Vendors and Purchasers."

CONFLICT OF LAWS.—**Campbell's Ruling Cases.** Vol. V.—*Vide* "Digests," p. 10.

Dicey's Digest of the Law of England with reference to the Conflict of Laws.—By A. V. DICEY, Esq., K.C., B.C.L. With Notes of American Cases, by Professor MOORE. Royal 8vo. 1896. 1l. 10s.
"One of the most valuable books on English law which has appeared for some time. Thorough and minute in the treatment of the subject, cautious and judicial in spirit, this work is obviously the result of protracted labour."—*The Times.*

CONSTITUTION.—**Anson's Law and Custom of the Constitution.** By Sir WILLIAM R. ANSON, Bart., Barrister-at-Law. Demy 8vo.
Part I. Parliament. Third Edition. 1897.   12s. 6d.
Part II. The Crown. Second Edition. 1896.   14s.

CONTRACT OF SALE.—**Blackburn.**—*Vide* "Sales."

Moyle's Contract of Sale in the Civil Law.—By J. B. MOYLE, Esq., Barrister-at-Law. 8vo. 1892.   10s. 6d.

CONTRACTS.—**Addison on Contracts.**—A Treatise on the Law of Contracts. 9th Edit. By HORACE SMITH, Esq., Bencher of the Inner Temple, Metropolitan Magistrate, assisted by A. P. PERCEVAL KEEP, Esq., Barrister-at-Law. Royal 8vo. 1892.   2l. 10s.
"This and the companion treatise on the law of torts are the most complete works on these subjects, and form an almost indispensable part of every lawyer's library."—*Law Journal.*

Anson's Principles of the English Law of Contract.—By Sir W. R. ANSON, Bart., Barrister-at-Law. Ninth Edit. 1899. 10s. 6d.

Fry.—*Vide* "Specific Performance."

Leake's Law of Contracts.—A Digest of Principles of the Law of Contracts. Fourth Edition. By A. E. RANDALL, Esq., Barrister-at-Law.   (*In preparation.*)

Pollock's Principles of Contract.—Being a Treatise on the General Principles relating to the Validity of Agreements in the Law of England. Sixth Edition. By Sir FREDERICK POLLOCK, Bart., Barrister-at-Law, Author of "The Law of Torts," "Digest of the Law of Partnership," &c. Demy 8vo. 1894.   28s.
"A work which, in our opinion, shows great ability, a discerning intellect, a comprehensive mind, and painstaking industry."—*Law Journal.*

CONVEYANCING.—**Brickdale & Sheldon.**—*Vide* "Land Transfer."

Dart.—*Vide* "Vendors and Purchasers."

Dickins' Precedents of General Requisitions on Title, with Explanatory Notes and Observations. Second Edition. By HERBERT A. DICKINS, Esq., Solicitor. Royal 12mo. 1898.   5s.
"We cannot do better than advise every lawyer with a conveyancing practice to purchase the little book and place it on his shelves forthwith."—*Law Notes.*

*** *All standard Law Works are kept in Stock, in law calf and other bindings.*

CONVEYANCING—*continued.*

Eaton and Purcell.—*Vide* "Land Charges Acts."

Greenwood's Manual of the Practice of Conveyancing, showing the present Practice relating to the daily routine of Conveyancing in Solicitors' Offices. To which are added Concise Common Forms in Conveyancing.—Ninth Edit. Edited by HARRY GREENWOOD, M.A., LL.D., Esq., Barrister-at-Law. Roy. 8vo. 1897.   20*s.*

"The ninth edition will maintain the reputation which the work has long ago acquired of being one of the best expositions which the English lawyer possesses of the present practice relating to the daily routine of conveyancing in solicitors' offices."—*Literature.*

"We should like to see it placed by his principal in the hands of every articled clerk. One of the most useful practical works we have ever seen."—*Law Stu. Jo.*

Hood and Challis' Conveyancing and Settled Land Acts, and some other recent Acts affecting Conveyancing. With Commentaries. By H. J. HOOD and H. W. CHALLIS. Fifth Edition. By H. W. CHALLIS, assisted by J. I. STIRLING, Esqrs., Barristers-at-Law. Royal 8vo. 1898.   18*s.*

"That learned, excellent and useful work."—*Law Times.*

"This is the best collection of conveyancing statutes with which we are acquainted. . . . The excellence of the commentaries which form part of this book is so well known that it needs no recommendation from us."—*Law Journal.*

Jackson and Gosset's Precedents of Purchase and Mortgage Deeds.—By W. HOWLAND JACKSON and THOROLD GOSSET, Esqrs., Barristers-at-Law. Demy 8vo. 1899.   7*s.* 6*d.*

"Not the least merit of the collection is that each Precedent is complete in itself, so that no dipping about and adaptation from other parts of the book are necessary."—*Law Journal.*

*** This forms a companion volume to "Investigation of Title" by the same Authors, *vide* p. 17.

Palmer.—*Vide* "Company Law."

Prideaux's Precedents in Conveyancing—With Dissertations on its Law and Practice. 18th Edit. By JOHN WHITCOMBE and BENJAMIN LENNARD CHERRY, Esqrs., Barristers-at-Law. 2 vols. Royal 8vo. 1900.   3*l.* 10*s.*

"'Prideaux' is the best work on Conveyancing."—*Law Journal.*

"Accurate, concise, clear, and comprehensive in scope, and we know of no treatise upon Conveyancing which is so generally useful to the practitioner."—*Law Times.*

"Recent legislation has compelled the Editor to re-write some of the preliminary dissertations. He has evidently taken great pains to incorporate the effect of the Land Transfer Act of 1897."—*The Times.*

CORONERS.—Jervis on Coroners.—The Coroners Acts, 1887 and 1892. With Forms and Precedents. Sixth Edition. By R. E. MELSHEIMER, Esq., Barrister-at-Law. Post 8vo. 1898.   10*s.* 6*d.*

COSTS.—Johnson's Bills of Costs in the High Court of Justice and Court of Appeal, in the House of Lords and the Privy Council; with the Scales of Costs and Tables of Fees in use in the Houses of Lords and Commons, relative to Private Bills; Election Petitions, Parliamentary and Municipal. Inquiries and Arbitrations under the Lands Clauses Consolidation Act, the Light Railway Act and other Arbitrations. Proceedings in the Court of the Railway and Canal Commission, in the County Court and the Mayor's Courts. The Scales of Costs and Tables of Fees in use in the Court of Passage, Liverpool. Conveyancing Costs and Costs between Solicitors and their Clients; with Orders and Rules as to Costs and Court Fees, and Notes and Decisions relating thereto. By HORACE MAXWELL JOHNSON, Esq., Barrister-at-Law. Second Edition. Royal 8vo. 1901.   1*l.* 15*s.*

"A useful and sufficient guide to the subject."—*Law Quarterly Review.*

"It is difficult to conceive how any costs clerk or solicitor can go wrong with a work of this kind to guide him."—*Law Times.*

"We consider the book marvellously accurate, and we are able to commend it in all confidence. On the law of bills of costs the practitioner, let his business be as wide as it may, wants nothing but such a work as the one before us."—*Law Notes.*

*** *All standard Law Works are kept in Stock, in law calf and other bindings.*

COSTS—*continued.*
Summerhays and Toogood's Precedents of Bills of Costs.
Seventh Edition. By THORNTON TOOGOOD, THOMAS CHARLES SUMMER-HAYS, and C. GILBERT BARBER, Solicitors. Royal 8vo. 1896. 1*l.* 10*s.*

Webster's Parliamentary Costs.—Private Bills, Election Petitions, Appeals, House of Lords. Fourth Edition. By C. CAVANAGH, Esq., Barrister-at-Law. Post 8vo. 1881.   20*s.*

COUNTY COURTS.— The Annual County Court Practice, **1901.** With SUPPLEMENT containing New Rules, &c.—By His Honour Judge SMYLY, K.C., assisted by W. J. BROOKS, Esq., Barrister-at-Law. 2 vols. 8vo.   1*l.* 5*s.*
"Invaluable to the County Court practitioner."—*Law Journal.*

COVENANTS.—Hamilton's Concise Treatise on the Law of Covenants.—By G. BALDWIN HAMILTON, Esq., Barrister-at-Law. Demy 8vo. 1888.   7*s.* 6*d.*

CRIMINAL LAW.—Archbold's Pleading, Evidence and Practice in Criminal Cases.—With the Statutes, Precedents of Indictments, &c. Twenty-second Edition. By WILLIAM F. CRAIES and GUY STEPHEN-SON, Esqrs., Barristers-at-Law. Demy 8vo. 1900.   1*l.* 11*s.* 6*d.*
" Archbold ' is the one indispensable book for every barrister or solicitor who practises regularly in the criminal Courts."—*Solicitors' Journal,* March 3, 1900.

Chitty's Collection of Statutes relating to Criminal Law.—(Reprinted from "Chitty's Statutes.") With an Introduction and Index. By W. F. CRAIES, Esq., Barrister-at-Law. Royal 8vo. 1894.   10*s.*

Disney and Gundry's Criminal Law.—A Sketch of its Principles and Practice. By HENRY W. DISNEY and HAROLD GUNDRY, Esqrs., Barristers-at-Law. Demy 8vo. 1895.   7*s.* 6*d.*
"We think we have here just what students want."—*Law Times.*

Kershaw's Brief Aids to Criminal Law.—With Notes on the Procedure and Evidence. By HILTON KERSHAW, Esq., Barrister-at-Law. Royal 12mo. 1897.   3*s.*

Roscoe's Digest of the Law of Evidence in Criminal Cases.— Twelfth Edition. By A. P. PERCEVAL KEEP, Esq., Barrister-at-Law. Demy 8vo. 1898.   1*l.* 11*s.* 6*d.*
"To the criminal lawyer it is his guide, philosopher and friend. What Roscoe says most judges will accept without question."—*Law Times.*

Russell's Treatise on Crimes and Misdemeanors.—Sixth Edit. By HORACE SMITH, Esq., Metropolitan Police Magistrate, and A. P. PERCEVAL KEEP, Esq. 3 vols. Roy. 8vo. 1896.   5*l.* 15*s.* 6*d.*
"No library can be said to be complete without Russell on Crimes."—*Law Times.*
"Indispensable in every Court of criminal justice."—*The Times.*

Shirley's Sketch of the Criminal Law.—Second Edition. By CHARLES STEPHEN HUNTER, Esq., Barrister-at-Law. Demy 8vo. 1889. 7*s.* 6*d.*
Warburton.—*Vide* " Leading Cases."

DEATH DUTIES.—Freeth's Acts relating to the Estate Duty and other Death Duties, with an Appendix containing the Rules Regulating Proceedings in England, Scotland and Ireland in Appeals under the Acts and a List of the Estate Duty Forms, with copies of some which are only issued on Special Application. Third Edition. By EVELYN FREETH, Esq., Registrar of Estate Duties for Ireland, formerly Deputy-Controller of Legacy and Succession Duties. Demy 8vo. 1901.   12*s.* 6*d.*
" The official position of the Author renders his opinion on questions of procedure of great value, and we think that this book will be found very useful to solicitors who have to prepare accounts for duty."—*Solicitors' Journal.*

Harman's Finance Act, 1894, so far as it relates to the Death Duties. With an Introduction and Notes, and an Appendix of Forms. By J. E. HARMAN, Esq., Barrister-at-Law. Royal 12mo. 1894.   5*s.*

DECISIONS OF SIR GEORGE JESSEL.—Peter's Analysis and Digest of the Decisions of Sir George Jessel ; with Notes, &c. By APSLEY PETRE PETER, Solicitor. Demy 8vo. 1883.   16*s.*

** All standard Law Works are kept in Stock, in law calf and other bindings.

DEBENTURES AND DEBENTURE STOCK.—Palmer's Company Precedents.—For use in relation to Companies subject to the Companies Acts.
Part III. DEBENTURES AND DEBENTURE STOCK, including Debentures, Trust Deeds, Stock Certificates, Resolutions, Prospectuses, Writs, Pleadings, Judgments, Orders, Receiverships, Notices, Miscellaneous. With Copious Notes. Eighth Edition. By FRANCIS BEAUFORT PALMER, Esq., Barrister-at-Law. Royal 8vo. 1900. 21s.
"The result of much careful study. . . . . . Simply invaluable to debenture-holders and to the legal advisers of such investors."—*Financial News*, March 15.
"Embraces practically the whole law relating to debentures and debenture stock. . . . . . Must take front rank among the works on the subject."—*Law Times.*

DIARY.—Lawyers' Companion (The) and Diary, and London and Provincial Law Directory for 1901.—For the use of the Legal Profession, Public Companies, Justices, Merchants, Estate Agents, Auctioneers, &c., &c. Edited by EDWIN LAYMAN, Esq., Barrister-at-Law; and contains Tables of Costs in the High Court of Judicature and County Court, &c.; Monthly Diary of County, Local Government, and Parish Business; Oaths in Supreme Court; Summary of Statutes of 1900; Alphabetical Index to the Practical Statutes since 1820; Schedule of Stamp Duties; Legal Time, Interest, Discount, Income, Wages and other Tables; the New Death Duties; and a variety of matters of practical utility: together with a complete List of the English Bar, and London and Country Solicitors, with date of admission and appointments. PUBLISHED ANNUALLY. Fifty-fifth Issue. 1901.
Issued in the following forms, octavo size, strongly bound in cloth :—
1. Two days on a page, plain . . . . . . 5s.0d.
2. The above, INTERLEAVED with plain paper . . 7 0
3. Two days on a page, ruled, with or without money columns . 5 6
4. The above, with money columns, INTERLEAVED with plain paper 8 0
5. Whole page for each day, plain 7 6
6. The above, INTERLEAVED with plain paper 9 6
7. Whole page for each day, ruled, with or without money columns 8 6
8. The above, INTERLEAVED with plain paper . . . 10 6
9. Three days on a page, ruled blue lines, without money columns . 3 6
The Diary contains memoranda of Legal Business throughout the Year, with an Index for ready reference.
"The amount of information packed within the covers of this well-known book of reference is almost incredible. In addition to the Diary, it contains nearly 800 pages of closely printed matter, none of which could be omitted without, perhaps, detracting from the usefulness of the book. The publishers seem to have made it their aim to include in the Companion every item of information which the most exacting lawyer could reasonably expect to find in its pages, and it may safely be said that no practising solicitor, who has experienced the luxury of having it at his elbow, will ever be likely to try to do without it."—*Law Journal.*
"The legal Whitaker."—*Saturday Review.*

DICTIONARY.—The Pocket Law Lexicon.—Explaining Technical Words, Phrases and Maxims of the English, Scotch and Roman Law, to which is added a complete List of Law Reports, with their Abbreviations. Third Edit. By HENRY G. RAWSON and JAMES F. REMNANT, Esqrs., Barristers-at-Law. Fcap. 8vo. 1893. 6s. 6d.
"A wonderful little legal Dictionary."—*Indermaur's Law Students' Journal.*
Wharton's Law Lexicon.—Forming an Epitome of the Law of England, and containing full Explanations of the Technical Terms and Phrases thereof, both Ancient and Modern; including the various Legal Terms used in Commercial Business. Together with a Translation of the Latin Law Maxims and selected Titles from the Civil, Scotch and Indian Law. Ninth Edition. By J. M. LELY, Esq., Barrister-at-Law. Super-royal 8vo. 1892. 1l. 18s.
"On almost every point both student and practitioner can gather information from this invaluable book, which ought to be in every lawyer's office."—*Law Notes.*
"One of the first books which every articled clerk and bar student should procure."—*Law Students' Journal.*
*** *All standard Law Works are kept in Stock, in law calf and other bindings.*

B

DIGESTS.—Campbell's Ruling Cases.—Arranged, Annotated, and Edited by ROBERT CAMPBELL, of Lincoln's Inn, Esq., Barrister-at-Law, Advocate of the Scotch Bar, assisted by other Members of the Bar. With American Notes by IRVING BROWNE, formerly Editor of the American Reports, and the Hon. LEONARD A. JONES. Royal 8vo. 1894-1901.   *Half vellum, gilt top, net, each 25s.*

The following Volumes have been published :—

I.—Abandonment—Action.	XIII.—Infant—Insurance.
II.—Action—Amendment.	XIV.—Insurance—Interpretation.
III.—Ancient Light—Banker.	XV.—Judge—Landlord and Tenant
IV.—Bankruptcy—Bill of Lading.	XVI.—Larceny—Mandate.
V.—Bill of Sale—Conflict of Laws.	XVII.—Manorial Right—Mistake.
VI.—Contract.	XVIII.—Mortgage—Negligence.
VII.—Conversion—Counsel.	XIX.—Negligence—Partnership.
VIII.—Criminal Law—Deed.	XX.—Patent.
IX.—Defamation — Dramatic and Musical Copyright.	XXI.—Payment—Purchase for Value without Notice.
X.—Easement—Estate.	XXII.—Quo Warranto—Release.
XI.—Estoppel—Execution.	XXIII.—Relief—Sea.
XII.—Executor—Indemnity.	

XXIV.—Search Warrant—Telegraph.   (*Nearly ready.*)
XXV.—Tenant—Wills.   (*In the press.*)

** The Volumes are sold separately.

An Addendum, containing, under the appropriate title and rule, Notes of Cases published since the issue of Volume I., thus bringing all the Volumes up to date, also a complete Index of Cases and a general Index to the whole work.   (*In preparation.*)

PLAN OF THE WORK.

All the useful authorities of English Case Law, from the earliest period to the present time, on points of general application, are collected and arranged in alphabetical order of subjects.

The matter under each alphabetical heading is arranged in sections, in an order indicated at the commencement of the heading. The more important and Ruling Cases are set forth at length, subject only to abridgment where the original report is unnecessarily diffuse. The effect of the less important or subordinate cases is stated briefly in the Notes.

The aim of the Work is to furnish the practitioner with English Case Law in such a form that he will readily find the information he requires for ordinary purposes. The Ruling Case will inform him, or refresh his memory, as to the principles ; and the Notes will show in detail how the principles have been applied or modified in other cases.

"A Cyclopædia of law .... most ably executed, learned, accurate, clear, concise ; but perhaps its chief merit is that it impresses on us what the practising English lawyer is too apt to forget—that English law really is a body of principles."—*The British Review.*

"One of the most ambitious, and ought to be, when it is complete, one of the most generally useful legal works which the present century has produced."—*Literature.*

"A perfect storehouse of the principles established and illustrated by our case law and that of the United States."—*Law Times.*

"The general scheme appears to be excellent, and its execution reflects the greatest credit on everybody concerned. It may, indeed. be said to constitute, for the present, the high-water mark of the science of book-making."—*Sat. Rev.*

"The Series has been maintained at a high level of excellence."—*The Times.*

Marsden.—*Vide* "Shipping."

Mews' Digest of Cases relating to Criminal Law down to the end of 1897.—By JOHN MEWS, Esq., Barrister-at-Law. Royal 8vo. 1898.   25s.

** *All standard Law Works are kept in Stock, in law calf and other bindings.*

DIGESTS—*continued.*

MEWS' DIGEST OF ENGLISH CASE LAW.—Containing the Reported Decisions of the Superior Courts, and a Selection from those of the Irish Courts, to the end of 1897. (Being a New Edition of "Fisher's Common Law Digest and Chitty's Equity Index.") Under the general Editorship of JOHN MEWS, assisted by W. F. BARRY, E. E. H. BIRCH, A. H. BITTLESTON, B. A. COHEN, W. I. COOK, E. W. HANSELL, J. S. HENDERSON, A. LAWRENCE, J. M. LELY, R. C. MACKENZIE, E. MANSON, R. G. MARSDEN, H. J. NEWBOLT, A. E. RANDALL, J. RITCHIE, J. SMITH, J. F. WALEY, T. H. WALKER, and W. A. G. WOODS, Esqrs., Barristers-at-Law. In 16 vols. Royal 8vo. £20

(*Bound in half calf, gilt top, £3 net extra.*)

"A vast undertaking. . . . We have tested several parts of the work, with the result of confirming our impression as to the accuracy of a work which is indispensable to lawyers."—*The Times.*

** Lists of Cases followed, overruled, questioned, &c., have been omitted from this DIGEST, but a New Edition of DALE and LEHMANN'S "OVERRULED CASES" brought down to the end of 1900, by W. A. G. WOODS and J. RITCHIE, Esqrs., Barristers-at-Law, is nearly ready for the press.

The Annual Digest for 1898, 1899 and 1900. By JOHN MEWS, Esq., Barrister-at-Law. Royal 8vo. each 15*s.*

** This Digest is also issued quarterly, each part being cumulative. Price to Subscribers, for the four parts *payable in advance, net* 17*s.*

"The practice of the law without Mews' Annual would be almost an impossibility."—*Law Times.*

Law Journal Quinquennial Digest, 1890-95.—An Analytical Digest of Cases Published in the Law Journal Reports, and the Law Reports, from Michaelmas Sittings, 1890, to Trinity Sittings, 1895. By GEORGE A. STREETEN, Esq., Barrister-at-Law. 1896. 1*l.* 10*s.*

"Extremely well done, with abundance of headings and cross references . . . could not be done better."—*Law Times.*

Law Journal Quinquennial Digest, 1896-1900. (*In the press.*)

Talbot and Fort's Index of Cases Judicially noticed (1865—1890); being a List of all Cases cited in Judgments reported from Michaelmas Term, 1865 to the end of 1890, with the places where they are so cited.—By GEORGE JOHN TALBOT and HUGH FORT, Esqrs., Barristers-at-Law. Royal 8vo. 1891. 25*s.*

"This is an invaluable tool for the worker among cases."—*Solicitors' Journal.*

Woods and Ritchie's Digest of Cases, Overruled, Approved, or otherwise specially considered in the English Courts to the end of 1900; with Extracts from the Judgments dealing with the same. By W. A. G. WOODS and J. RITCHIE, Esqrs., Barristers-at-Law.—Being a New Edition of "Dale and Lehmann's Digest."

(*In preparation.*)

DISCOVERY.—Sichel and Chance's Discovery.—The Law relating to Interrogatories, Production, Inspection of Documents, and Discovery, as well in the Superior as in the Inferior Courts, together with an Appendix of the Acts, Forms and Orders. By WALTER S. SICHEL and WILLIAM CHANCE, Esqrs., Barristers-at-Law. Demy 8vo. 1883. 12*s.*

DISTRESS.—Oldham and Foster on the Law of Distress.—A Treatise on the Law of Distress, with an Appendix of Forms, Table of Statutes, &c. Second Edition. By ARTHUR OLDHAM and A. LA TROBE FOSTER, Esqrs., Barristers-at-Law. Demy 8vo. 1889. 18*s.*

DISTRICT COUNCILS.—Chambers' Digest of the Law relating to District Councils, so far as regards the Constitution, Powers and Duties of such Councils (including Municipal Corporations) in the matter of Public Health and Local Government. Ninth Edition. —By GEORGE F. CHAMBERS, Esq., Barrister-at-Law. Royal 8vo. 1895. 10*s.*

** *All standard Law Works are kept in Stock, in law calf and other bindings.*

DIVORCE.—Browne and Powles' Law and Practice in Divorce and Matrimonial Causes. Sixth Edition. By L. D. POWLES, Esq., Barrister-at-Law. Demy 8vo. 1897. 25*s.*

"The practitioner's standard work on divorce practice."—*Law Quar. Rev.*

Kelly's French Law.—*Vide* "Marriage."

DOGS.—Lupton's Law relating to Dogs.—By FREDERICK LUPTON, Solicitor. Royal 12mo. 1888. 5*s.*

DOMESDAY BOOK AND BEYOND.—Three Essays in the Early History of England. By Professor MAITLAND. 1897. 8vo. 15*s.*

EASEMENTS.—Campbell's Ruling Cases. Vol. X.—*Vide* "Digests."

Goddard's Treatise on the Law of Easements.—BY JOHN LEYBOURN GODDARD, Esq., Barrister-at-Law. Fifth Edition. Demy 8vo. 1896. 1*l.* 5*s.*

"Nowhere has the subject been treated so exhaustively, and, we may add, so scientifically, as by Mr. Goddard. We recommend it to the most careful study of the law student, as well as to the library of the practitioner."—*Law Times.*

Innes' Digest of the Law of Easements. Sixth Edition. By L. C. INNES, lately one of the Judges of Her Majesty's High Court of Judicature, Madras. Royal 12mo. 1900. 7*s.* 6*d.*

" Constructed with considerable care and pains."—*Law Journal.*

"We have only the pleasing duty remaining of recommending the book to those in search of a concise treatise on the law of Easements."—*Law Notes.*

ECCLESIASTICAL LAW.—Phillimore's Ecclesiastical Law of the Church of England. By the late Sir ROBERT PHILLIMORE, Bart., D.C.L. Second Edition, by his son Sir WALTER GEORGE FRANK PHILLIMORE, Bart., D.C.L., assisted by C. F. JEMMETT, B.C.L., LL.M., Barrister-at-Law. 2 vols. Royal 8vo. 1895. 3*l.* 3*s.*

"The task of re-editing Phillimore's ' Ecclesiastical Law ' was not an easy one. Sir Walter Phillimore has executed it with brilliant success. He has brought to the work all his father's subdued enthusiasm for the Church, he has omitted nothing that lent value to the original treatise, he has expunged from it what could be spared, and has added to it everything that the ecclesiastical lawyer can possibly need to know."—*Law Journal.*

Whitehead's Church Law.—Being a Concise Dictionary of Statutes, Canons, Regulations, and Decided Cases affecting the Clergy and Laity. Second Edition. By BENJAMIN WHITEHEAD, Esq., Barrister-at-Law. Demy 8vo. 1899. 10*s.* 6*d.*

" A perfect mine of learning on all topics ecclesiastical."—*Daily Telegraph.*

" Mr. Whitehead has amassed a great deal of information which it would be very difficult to find in any other book, and he has presented it in a clear and concise form. It is a book which will be useful to lawyers and laymen."—*Law Times.*

ELECTIONS.—Day's Election Cases in 1892 and 1893.—Being a Collection of the Points of Law and Practice, together with Reports of the Judgments. By S. H. DAY, Esq., Barrister-at-Law, Editor of "Rogers on Elections." Royal 12mo. 1894. 7*s.* 6*d.*

Hedderwick's Parliamentary Election Manual : A Practical Handbook on the Law and Conduct of Parliamentary Elections in Great Britain and Ireland, designed for the Instruction and Guidance of Candidates. Agents, Canvassers, Volunteer Assistants, &c. Second Edition. By T. C. H. HEDDERWICK, Esq., Barrister-at-Law. Demy 12mo. 1900. 10*s.* 6*d.*

" The work is pre-eminently practical, concise and clear."—*Solicitors' Journal.*
" One of the best books of the kind that we are acquainted with."—*Law Journal.*

Hunt's Metropolitan Borough Councils Elections : A Guide to the Election of the Mayor, Aldermen, and Councillors of Metropolitan Boroughs. By JOHN HUNT, Esq., Barrister-at-Law. Demy 8vo. 1900. 3*s.* 6*d.*

** *All standard Law Works are kept in Stock, in law calf and other bindings.*

ELECTIONS—*continued.*

Rogers' Law and Practice of Elections.—

Vol. I. REGISTRATION, including the Practice in Registration Appeals; Parliamentary, Municipal, and Local Government; with Appendices of Statutes, Orders in Council, and Forms. Sixteenth Edition; with Addenda of Statutes to 1900. By MAURICE POWELL, Esq., Barrister-at-Law. Royal 12mo. 1897.   1*l.* 1*s.*
"The practitioner will find within these covers everything which he can be expected to know, well arranged and carefully stated."—*Law Times.*

Vol. II. PARLIAMENTARY ELECTIONS AND PETITIONS; with Appendices of Statutes, Rules and Forms. Seventeenth Edition. Revised by S. H. DAY, Esq., Barrister-at-Law. Royal 12mo. 1900.   1*l.* 1*s.*
"The acknowledged authority on election law."—*Law Journal.*
"The leading book on the difficult subjects of elections and election petitions."—*Law Times.*
"We have nothing but praise for this work as a trustworthy guide for candidates and agents."—*Solicitors' Journal.*

Vol. III. MUNICIPAL AND OTHER ELECTIONS AND PETITIONS, with Appendices of Statutes, Rules, and Forms. Seventeenth Edit. By SAMUEL H. DAY, Esq., Barrister-at-Law. Royal 12mo. 1894. 1*l.* 1*s.*
This Volume treats of Elections to Municipal Councils (including the City of London), County Councils, Parish Councils, Rural and Urban District Councils; Boards of Guardians (within and without London), Metropolitan Vestries, School Boards.

EMPLOYERS' LIABILITY.—Mozley-Stark.—*Vide* "Arbitration."

Robinson's Employers' Liability under the Workmen's Compensation Act, 1897, and the Employers' Liability Act, 1880; with the Rules under the Workmen's Compensation Act, 1897. By ARTHUR ROBINSON, Esq., Barrister-at-Law   Second Edition. Including Precedents of Schemes of Compensation under the Workmen's Compensation Act, 1897, certified by the Registrar of Friendly Societies. By the Author and J. D. STUART SIM, Esq., Barrister-at-Law, Assistant Registrar of Friendly Societies. Royal 12mo. 1898.   7*s.* 6*d.*

ENGLISH LAW.—Pollock and Maitland's History of English Law before the time of Edward I.—By Sir FREDERICK POLLOCK, Bart., and FRED. W. MAITLAND, Esq., Barristers-at-Law.   Second Edition. 2 vols. roy. 8vo. 1898.   40*s.*

EQUITY, *and Vide* CHANCERY.

Seton's Forms of Judgments and Orders in the High Court of Justice and in the Court of Appeal, having especial reference to the Chancery Division, with Practical Notes. Sixth Edition. By C. C. M. DALE, Esq., Barrister-at-Law, and W. T. KING, Esq., a Registrar of the Supreme Court.   In 3 vols.   (*In the press.*)
"A monument of learned and laborious accuracy."—*Law Quarterly Review.*

Smith's Manual of Equity Jurisprudence.—A Manual of Equity Jurisprudence for Practitioners and Students, founded on the Works of Story and other writers, comprising the Fundamental Principles and the points of Equity usually occurring in General Practice. Fifteenth Edition. By SYDNEY E. WILLIAMS, Esq., Barrister-at-Law. 12mo. 1900.   12*s.* 6*d.*
"We can safely recommend 'Smith's Equity' in its new clothes to the attention of students reading for their Examinations."—*Law Notes.*
"Smith's Manuals of Common Law and Equity must be resorted to as the open sesames to the learning requisite in the Final Examination of the Incorporated Law Society."—*From Dr.* ROLLIT'S *Lecture.*

Smith's Practical Exposition of the Principles of Equity, illustrated by the Leading Decisions thereon. For the use of Students and Practitioners. Second Edition. By H. ARTHUR SMITH, M.A., LL.B., Esq., Barrister-at-Law. Demy 8vo. 1888.   21*s.*

⁎⁎⁎ All standard Law Works are kept in Stock, in law calf and other bindings.

EQUITY—*continued.*

Williams' Outlines of Equity.—A Concise View of the Principles of Modern Equity. By SYDNEY E. WILLIAMS, Esq., Barrister-at-Law. Author of "The Law relating to Legal Representatives," &c. Royal 12mo. 1900. 5s.

"The accuracy it combines with conciseness is remarkable."—*Law Magazine.*

ESTATE DUTIES.—Freeth.—*Vide* "Death Duties."

ESTOPPEL.—Everest and Strode's Law of Estoppel. By LANCELOT FIELDING EVEREST, and EDMUND STRODE, Esqrs., Barristers-at-Law. Demy 8vo. 1884. 18s.

Ewart's Exposition of the Principles of Estoppel by Misrepresentation.—By JOHN S. EWART, Esq., K.C. of the Canadian Bar. Demy 8vo. 1900. 25s.

EVIDENCE.—Campbell's Ruling Cases. Vol. XI.—*Vide* "Digests."

Wills' Theory and Practice of the Law of Evidence.—By WM. WILLS, Esq., Barrister-at-Law. Demy 8vo. 1894. 10s. 6d.

"It contains a large amount of valuable information, very tersely and accurately conveyed."—*Law Times.*
"We consider that Mr. Wills has given the profession a useful book on a difficult subject."—*Law Notes.*

EVIDENCE ON COMMISSION.—Hume-Williams and Macklin's Taking of Evidence on Commission : including therein Special Examinations, Letters of Request, Mandamus and Examinations before an Examiner of the Court. By W. E. HUME-WILLIAMS and A. ROMER MACKLIN, Barristers-at-Law. Demy 8vo. 1895. 12s. 6d.

EXAMINATION GUIDES.—Bar Examination Guide. By H. D. WOODCOCK, and R. C. MAXWELL, Esqrs., Barristers-at-Law. Vols. I. to V. (1895—1899). *Each, net* 7s. 6d.

Bar Examination Guide—Lecture Supplement, 1896. *Net* 2s.

Uttley's How to Become a Solicitor; or, Hints for Articled Clerks.—By T. F. UTTLEY, Solicitor. Royal 12mo. 1894. 5s.

EXECUTIONS.—Edwards' Law of Execution upon Judgments and Orders of the Chancery and Queen's Bench Divisions. By C. J. EDWARDS, Esq., Barrister-at-Law. Demy 8vo. 1888. 16s.

EXECUTORS.—Macaskie's Treatise on the Law of Executors and Administrators. By S. C. MACASKIE, Esq., Barrister-at-Law. 8vo. 1881. 10s. 6d.

Williams' Law of Executors and Administrators.—Ninth Edition. By the Right Hon. Sir ROLAND VAUGHAN WILLIAMS, a Lord Justice of Appeal. 2 vols. Roy. 8vo. 1893. 3l. 16s.

"We can conscientiously say that the present edition will not only sustain, but enhance the high reputation which the book has always enjoyed. The want of a new edition has been distinctly felt for some time, and in this work, and in this work only, will the practitioner now find the entire law relating to executors and administrators treated in an exhaustive and authoritative fashion, and thoroughly brought down to the present date."—*Law Journal.*

Williams' Law relating to Legal Representatives. — Real and Personal. By SYDNEY E. WILLIAMS, Esq., Author of "Law of Account," "Outlines of Equity," &c. Demy 8vo. 1899. 10s.

"We can commend to both branches of the profession, and more especially to solicitors."—*Law Times.*
"An excellent law book, excellently got up, and though it deals with a subject on which there is an ample literature, its existence is justified by its aim at being 'in as short a form as possible, a summary of the law of legal representatives as modified by the Land Transfer Act, 1897.'"—*Pall Mall Gazette.*

FARM, LAW OF.—Dixon's Law of the Farm : including the Cases and Statutes relating to the subject; and the Agricultural Customs of England and Wales. Fifth Edition. By AUBREY J. SPENCER, Esq., Barrister-at-Law. Demy 8vo. 1892. 26s.

"A complete modern compendium on agricultural matters."—*Law Times.*

*** *All standard Law Works are kept in Stock, in law calf and other bindings.*

FIXTURES.—Amos and Ferard on the Law of Fixtures and other Property partaking both of a Real and Personal Nature. Third Edition. By C. A. FERARD and W. HOWLAND ROBERTS, Esqrs., Barristers-at-Law. Demy 8vo. 1883.   18*s.*

FORMS.—Chitty's Forms of Practical Proceedings in the Queen's Bench Division.—Thirteenth Edition. By T. W. CHITTY and HERBERT CHITTY, Esqrs., Barristers-at-Law.   (*In preparation.*)

Daniell's Forms and Precedents of Proceedings in the Chancery Division of the High Court of Justice and on Appeal therefrom.—Fifth Edition. By CHARLES BURNEY, B.A., a Master of the Supreme Court. Royal 8vo.   (*In the press.*)
" The standard work on Chancery Procedure."—*Law Quarterly Review.*

Seton.—*Vide* " Equity."

FRAUD AND MISREPRESENTATION.—Moncreiff's Treatise on the Law relating to Fraud and Misrepresentation.—By the Hon. F. MONCREIFF, Barrister-at-Law. 8vo. 1891.   21*s.*

FRENCH LAW. — Cachard's French Civil Code. — By HENRY CACHARD, B.A., and Counsellor-at-Law of the New York Bar, Licencié en Droit de la Faculté de Paris. Demy 8vo. 1895.   20*s.*

Goirand's Treatise upon French Commercial Law and the Practice of all the Courts.—With a Theoretical and Practical Commentary. The text of the laws relating thereto, including the entire Code of Commerce, with a Dictionary of French Judicial Terms. Second Edition. By LEOPOLD GOIRAND, Licencié en droit. Demy 8vo. 1898.   1*l.*

Sewell's Outline of French Law as affecting British Subjects.— By J. T. B. SEWELL, M.A., LL.D., Solicitor. Demy 8vo. 1897.
10*s.* 6*d.*

GAME LAWS.—Warry's Game Laws of England. With an Appendix of the Statutes relating to Game. By G. TAYLOR WARRY, Esq., Barrister-at-Law. Royal 12mo. 1896.   10*s.* 6*d.*
" The author has treated the subject in a clear and lucid style."—*Law Times.*

GOLD COAST ORDINANCES.—Griffith's Ordinances of the Gold Coast Colony.—By Sir WILLIAM BRANDFORD GRIFFITH, Chief Justice of the Gold Coast Colony. 2 vols. Roy. 8vo. 1898.   3*l.*

GOODWILL.—Allan's Law relating to Goodwill.—By CHARLES E. ALLAN, M.A., LL.B., Esq., Barrister-at-Law. Demy 8vo. 1889. 7*s.* 6*d.*
Sebastian.—*Vide* " Trade Marks."

HACKNEY CARRIAGES.—*Vide* "Motor Cars."

HIGHWAYS.—Chambers' Law relating to Highways and Bridges. By GEORGE F. CHAMBERS, Esq., Barrister-at-Law. 1878.   7*s.* 6*d.*

HOUSE TAX.—Ellis' Guide to the House Tax Acts, for the use of the Payer of Inhabited House Duty in England.—By ARTHUR M. ELLIS, LL.B. (Lond.), Solicitor, Author of "A Guide to the Income Tax Acts." Royal 12mo. 1885.   6*s.*
" We have found the information accurate, complete and very clearly expressed."—*Solicitors' Journal.*

HUSBAND AND WIFE.—Lush's Law of Husband and Wife, within the jurisdiction of the Queen's Bench and Chancery Divisions. By C. MONTAGUE LUSH, Esq., Barrister-at-Law. Second Edition. By the Author and W. H. GRIFFITH, Esq., Barrister-at-
· Law. Demy 8vo. 1896.   1*l.* 5*s.*
"To the practising lawyer the work will be of the utmost importance."—*Law Times.*
" This book will certainly be consulted when difficulties arise relative to the position of married women."—*Law Journal.*

** *All standard Law Works are kept in Stock, in law calf and other bindings.*

INCOME TAX.—Ellis' Guide to the Income Tax Acts.—For the use of the English Income Tax Payer. Third Edition. By ARTHUR M. ELLIS, LL.B. (Lond.), Solicitor. Royal 12mo. 1893. 7s. 6d.
"Contains in a convenient form the law bearing upon the Income Tax."—*Law Times.*

Robinson's Law relating to Income Tax; with the Statutes, Forms, and Decided Cases in the Courts of England, Scotland, and Ireland.—By ARTHUR ROBINSON, Esq., Barrister-at-Law. Royal 8vo. 1895. 21s.
"The standard work on a complicated and difficult subject."—*Law Journal.*

INLAND REVENUE. — Highmore's Summary Proceedings in Inland Revenue Cases in England and Wales.—Second Edition. By N. J. HIGHMORE, Esq., Barrister-at-Law, and of the Solicitors' Department, Inland Revenue. Roy.12mo. 1887. 7s.6d.

Highmore's Inland Revenue Regulation Act, 1890, as amended by the Public Accounts and Charges Act, 1891, and the Finance Act, 1896, with other Acts; with Notes, Table of Cases, &c. By NATHANIEL J. HIGHMORE, Esq., Barrister-at-Law, Assistant Solicitor of Inland Revenue. Demy 8vo. 1896. 7s. 6d.

INSURANCE.—Arnould on the Law of Marine Insurance.—Seventh Edition. By EDWARD LOUIS DE HART and RALPH ILIFF SIMEY, Esqrs., Barristers-at-Law. 2 vols. Royal 8vo. (*In the press.*)

Campbell's Ruling Cases. Vols. XIII. and XIV.—*Vide* "Digests."

McArthur on the Contract of Marine Insurance.—Third Edit. By CHARLES McARTHUR, Average Adjuster. (*In preparation.*)

Marsden.—*Vide* "Shipping."

Tyser's Law relating to Losses under a Policy of Marine Insurance.—By CHARLES ROBERT TYSER, Esq., Barrister-at-Law. Demy 8vo. 1894. 10s. 6d.
"A clear, correct, full, and yet concise statement of the law."—*Law Times.*

INTERNATIONAL LAW.—Baker's First Steps in International Law. Prepared for the Use of Students. By Sir SHERSTON BAKER, Bart., Barrister-at-Law. Demy 8vo. 1899. 12s.

Dicey.—*Vide* "Conflict of Laws."

Hall's International Law.—Fourth Edit. Demy 8vo. 1895. 1l. 2s. 6d.

Hall's Treatise on the Foreign Powers and Jurisdiction of the British Crown. By W. E. HALL, Esq., Barrister-at-Law. Demy 8vo. 1894. 10s. 6d.

Holland's Studies in International Law.—By THOMAS ERSKINE HOLLAND, D.C.L., Barrister-at-Law. Demy 8vo. 1898. 10s. 6d.

Kent's Commentary on International Law.—Edited by J. T. ABDY, LL.D. Second Edition. Crown 8vo. 1878. 10s. 6d.

Nelson's Private International Law.—By HORACE NELSON, Esq., Barrister-at-Law. Roy. 8vo. 1889. 21s.
"The notes are full of matter, and avoid the vice of discursiveness, cases being cited for practically every proposition."—*Law Times.*

Rattigan's Private International Law.—By Sir WILLIAM HENRY RATTIGAN, LL.D., K.C., Vice-Chancellor of the University of the Punjab. Demy 8vo. 1895. 10s. 6d.
"Written with admirable clearness."—*Law Journal.*

Walker's Manual of Public International Law.—By T. A. WALKER, M.A., LL.D., Esq., Barrister-at-Law. Demy 8vo. 1895. 9s.

Walker's History of the Law of Nations.—Vol. I., from the Earliest Times to the Peace of Westphalia, 1648. By T. A. WALKER, M.A., LL.D., Esq., Barrister-at-Law. Demy 8vo. 1899. Net 10s.

Westlake's International Law.—Chapters on the Principles of International Law. By J. WESTLAKE, K.C., LL.D. Demy 8vo. 1894. 10s.

Wheaton's Elements of International Law; Third English Edition. Edited with Notes and Appendix of Statutes and Treaties. By A. C. BOYD, Esq., Barrister-at-Law. Royal 8vo. 1889. 1l. 10s.
"Wheaton stands too high for criticism."—*Law Times.*

*** *All standard Law Works are kept in Stock, in law calf and other bindings.*

INVESTIGATION OF TITLE.—Jackson and Gosset's Investigation of Title.—Being a Practical Treatise and Alphabetical Digest of the Law connected with the Title to Land, with Precedents of Requisitions. Second Edition. By W. HOWLAND JACKSON and THOROLD GOSSET, Barristers-at-Law. Demy 8vo. 1899. 12s. 6d.

"The new edition contains the following additional subjects—namely, boundaries, compromise, corporations, glebe lands, parcels, quit-rents and recitals; and the changes effected by the statute law of 1899 are noticed in their proper places. . . . Jackson and Gosset's book is well worth having."—*Law Times.*
"Will be of real help to the busy conveyancer."—*Law Notes.*

⁕ See "Conveyancing," p. 6, for companion volume, "Precedents of Purchase and Mortgage Deeds," by the same Authors.

JUDGMENTS AND ORDERS.—Seton.—*Vide* "Equity."

JURISPRUDENCE.—Holland's Elements of Jurisprudence.— Ninth Edition. By T. E. HOLLAND, D.C.L. 8vo. 1900. 10s. 6d.

Markby's Elements of Law. By Sir WILLIAM MARKBY, D.C.L. Demy 8vo. 1896. 12s. 6d.

JURY LAWS.—Huband's Practical Treatise on the Law relating to the Grand Jury in Criminal Cases, the Coroner's Jury, and the Petty Jury in Ireland.—By WM. G. HUBAND, Esq., Barrister-at-Law. Royal 8vo. 1896. *Net* 25s.

JUSTICE OF THE PEACE.—Magistrate's Annual Practice for 1900.—Being a Compendium of the Law and Practice relating to matters occupying the attention of Courts of Summary Jurisdiction, with an Appendix of Statutes and Rules, List of Punishments, Calendar for Magistrates, &c. By CHARLES MILNER ATKINSON, Esq., Stipendiary Magistrate for Leeds. Demy 8vo. 1900. 20s.

"An excellent magisterial guide."—*Law Journal.*
"Cannot fail to be of great service in any court of summary jurisdiction."— *Solicitors' Journal.*
"We can commend the use of the volume to all magisterial benches."—*The Field.*

Magistrates' Cases, 1893 to 1900.—Cases relating to the Poor Law, the Criminal Law, Licensing, and other subjects chiefly connected with the duties and office of Magistrates. 1894-1900. *Each Year, net 1l.*

⁕ These Reports, published as part of the Law Journal Reports, are also issued Quarterly. *Each Part, net 5s.*

Annual Subscription, payable in advance, 15s. post free.

Shirley's Magisterial Law.—An Elementary Treatise on Magisterial Law, and on the Practice of Magistrates' Courts. Second Edition. By LEONARD H. WEST, LL.D., Solicitor. Demy 8vo. 1896. 7s. 6d.

Wigram's Justice's Note-Book.—Containing a short account of the Jurisdiction and Duties of Justices, and an Epitome of Criminal Law. Seventh Edition. By HENRY WARBURTON and LEONARD W. KERSHAW, Esqrs., Barristers-at-Law. Royal 12mo. 1900. 10s. 6d.

"The information given is complete and accurate."—*Law Journal.*
"Contains a great deal of valuable information in a small compass, which has been brought well up to date."—*Law Times.*

LAGOS.—Ordinances, and Orders and Rules thereunder, in Force in the Colony of Lagos on December 31st, 1893.—By GEORGE STALLARD, Queen's Advocate, and E. H. RICHARDS, District Commissioner of Lagos. Royal 8vo. 1894. *Half-calf*, 42s.

LAND CHARGES ACTS.—Eaton and Purcell's Land Charges Acts, 1888 and 1900.—A Practical Guide to Registration and Searches. By ERNEST W. EATON, Esq., Senior Clerk, Land Charges Department, Land Registry, and J. POYNTZ PURCELL, Esq., of the same Department, Barrister-at-Law. Royal 12mo. 1901. *Net*, 2s. 6d.

LAND LAW.—Jenks' Modern Land Law. By EDWARD JENKS, Esq., Barrister-at-Law. Demy 8vo. 1899. 15s.

⁕ *All standard Law Works are kept in Stock, in law calf and other bindings.*

LAND TAX.—Bourdin's Land Tax.—An Exposition of the Land Tax. Including the Latest Judicial Decisions, and the Changes in the Law effected by the Taxes Management Act, &c. Fourth Edition. By the late FREDERICK HUMPHREYS, Deputy Registrar of Land Tax; and Digests of Cases decided in the Courts by CHARLES C. ATCHISON, Deputy Registrar of Land Tax. Royal 12mo. 1894. *7s. 6d.*

Atchison's Land Tax.—Changes Effected in the Processes of Assessment and Redemption by Part VI. of the Finance Act, 1896 (59 & 60 Vict. c. 28). By CHARLES C. ATCHISON, Deputy Registrar of Land Tax. Royal 12mo. 1897. (*A Supplement to above.*) *Net, 2s. 6d.*

LAND TRANSFER.—Brickdale and Sheldon's Land Transfer Acts, 1875 and 1897.—With a Commentary on the Acts, and Introductory Chapters explanatory of the Acts, and the Conveyancing Practice thereunder ; also the Land Registry Rules, Forms, and Fee Order, Orders in Council for Compulsory Registration, &c., with Forms of Precedents and Model Registers, &c. By C. FORTESCUE BRICKDALE, Registrar at the Land Registry, and W. R. SHELDON, Esqrs., Barristers-at-Law. Royal 8vo. 1899. *20s.*

" Not often is a statute so carefully edited."—*The Times.*

"Contains not only lengthy and valuable notes and annotations on the Land Transfer Acts and Rules, but also full and separate dissertations on the law, procedure, and practice thereunder."—*Law Times.*

LANDLORD and TENANT.—Campbell's Ruling Cases. Vol. XV. —*Vide* " Digests."

Redman's Law of Landlord and Tenant.—Including the Practice of Ejectment. Fifth Edition. By JOSEPH H. REDMAN, Esq., Barrister-at-Law. Demy 8vo. 1901. *25s.*

" We can confidently recommend the present edition."—*Law Journal*, April 6, 1901.

Woodfall's Law of Landlord and Tenant.—With a full Collection of Precedents and Forms of Procedure; containing also a collection of Leading Propositions. Sixteenth Edition, containing the Statutes and Cases down to Lady Day, 1898. By J. M. LELY, Esq., Barrister-at-Law. Roy. 8vo. 1898. *1l. 18s.*

" It stands pre-eminent as the chief authority amongst law books on the subject of landlord and tenant."—*Law Journal.*

" Nothing that we can say will add to the high reputation of ' Woodfall.' "— *Law Notes.*

LANDS CLAUSES ACTS.—Jepson's Lands Clauses Acts; with Decisions, Forms, and Tables of Costs. Second Edition. By J. M. LIGHTWOOD, Esq., Barrister-at-Law. Demy 8vo. 1900. *21s.*

" This work, in its new and practically re-written form, may be described as a handy and well-arranged treatise on the Lands Clauses Acts."—*Solicitors' Journal*, Feb. 16, 1901.

LAW JOURNAL REPORTS.—Edited by JOHN MEWS, Esq., Barrister-at-Law. Published monthly. *Annual Subscription :—*

Reports and Public General Statutes *Net, 3l. 4s.*

Reps. Stats. & Mews' Annual Digest (*Issued Quarterly*) *Net, 3l. 10s.*

Or, with the Law Journal weekly, 1l. extra.

LAW LIST.—Law List (The).—Comprising the Judges and Officers of the Courts of Justice, Counsel, Special Pleaders, Conveyancers, Solicitors, Proctors, Notaries, &c., in England and Wales; the Circuits, Judges, Treasurers, Registrars, and High Bailiffs of the County Courts; Metropolitan and Stipendiary Magistrates, Official Receivers under the Bankruptcy Act, Law and Public Officers in England and the Colonies, Foreign Lawyers with their English Agents, Clerks of the Peace, Town Clerks, Coroners, &c., &c., and Commissioners for taking Oaths, Conveyancers Practising in England under Certificates obtained in Scotland. Compiled, so far as relates to Special Pleaders, Conveyancers, Solicitors, Proctors and Notaries, by ERNEST CLEAVE, Controller of Stamps, and Registrar of Joint Stock Companies, and Published by the Authority of the Commissioners of Inland Revenue and of the Incorporated Law Society. 1901. (Postage 6d. extra.) *Net, 10s. 6d.*

** *All standard Law Works are kept in Stock, in law calf and other bindings.*

LAW QUARTERLY REVIEW—Edited by Sir FREDERICK POLLOCK, Bart., M.A., LL.D. Vols. I.—XVI. (with General Indices to Vols. I. to XV.) Royal 8vo. 1885-1900. *Each*, 12s.

☞ *Annual Subscription post free* 12s. 6d., *net.* *Single numbers, each* 5s.

"A little criticism, a few quotations, and a batch of anecdotes, afford a sauce that makes even a quarter's law reporting amusing reading."—*Law Journal.*

"The greatest of legal quarterly reviews . . . the series of 'Notes' always so entertaining and illustrative, not merely of the learning of the accomplished jurist (the Editor) but of the grace of language with which such learning can be unfolded."—*Law Jour.*

LAWYER'S ANNUAL LIBRARY—
(1) The Annual Practice.—SNOW, BURNEY, and STRINGER.
(2) The Annual Digest.—MEWS. (*Also Issued Quarterly.*)
(3) The Annual Statutes.—LELY.
(4) The Annual County Court Practice.—SMILY.

☞ *Annual Subscriptions. For* Complete Series, as above, delivered on the day of publication, *net*, 2l. 5s. Nos. 1, 2, and 3 only, *net*, 1l. 15s. Nos. 2, 3, and 4 only, *net*, 1l. 15s. (*Carriage extra*, 2s.) *Full prospectus forwarded on application.*

LAWYER'S COMPANION.—*Vide* "Diary."

LEADING CASES.—Ball's Leading Cases. *Vide* "Torts."

Shirley's Selection of Leading Cases in the Common Law. With Notes. By W. S. SHIRLEY, Esq., Barrister-at-Law. Sixth Edition. By RICHARD WATSON, Esq., Barrister-at-Law. Demy 8vo. 1900. 16s.

"A sound knowledge of common law can be gleaned from Shirley."—*Law Notes.*
"The selection is very large, though all are distinctly 'Leading Cases,' and the notes are by no means the least meritorious part of the work."—*Law Journal.*
"Calculated to be of great service to students."—*Law Students' Journal.*
"Will so long as Mr. Watson remains the Editor retain its hold on the student world."—*Law Notes.*

Warburton's Selection of Leading Cases in the Criminal Law. With Notes. By HENRY WARBURTON, Esq., Barrister-at-Law. [Founded on "Shirley's Leading Cases."] Second Edition. Demy 8vo. 1897. 10s. 6d.

"The cases have been well selected, and arranged. . . . We consider that it will amply repay the student or the practitioner to read both the cases and the notes."—*Justice of the Peace.*

LEGAL INTERPRETATION.—Beal's Cardinal Rules of Legal Interpretation.—Collected and Arranged by EDWARD BEAL, Esq., Barrister-at-Law. Royal 8vo. 1896. 12s. 6d.

"Invaluable to the student. To those with a limited library, or a busy practice, it will be indispensable."—*Justice of Peace.*

LEGAL PROCEDURE.—Greenidge's Legal Procedure of Cicero's Time.—By A. H. J. GREENIDGE, Esq. Demy 8vo. 1901. 21s.

LEGISLATIVE METHODS.—Ilbert's Legislative Methods and Forms.—By Sir COURTENAY ILBERT, K.C.S.I., C.I.E., Parliamentary Counsel to the Treasury. Demy 8vo. 1901. 16s.

LEXICON.—*Vide* "Dictionary."

LIBEL AND SLANDER.—Odgers on Libel and Slander.—A Digest of the Law of Libel and Slander: with the Evidence, Procedure, Practice, and Precedents of Pleadings, both in Civil and Criminal Cases. Third Edition. By W. BLAKE ODGERS, LL.D., one of His Majesty's Counsel. Royal 8vo. 1896. 32s.

"The best modern book on the law of libel."—*Daily News.*
"The most scientific of all our law books. . . . . In its new dress this volume is secure of an appreciative professional welcome."—*Law Times.*
"The general opinion of the profession has always accorded a high place to Mr. Blake Odgers' learned work, and the new edition cannot but enhance that opinion."—*Law Journal.*

** *All standard Law Works are kept in Stock, in law calf and other bindings.*

LICENSING.—Lathom's Handy Guide to the Licensing Acts.
By H. W. LATHOM, Solicitor. Royal 12mo. 1894.   5s.
"This book is arranged in dictionary form, with especial regard to ease of reference, and should prove an immense saving of time and labour to the large class to whom it is addressed. The mass of confusing statute and case law on this wide subject has been most ably codified."—*Law Times.*

Talbot's Law and Practice of Licensing.—Being a Digest of the
Law regulating the Sale by Retail of Intoxicating Liquor. With
a full Appendix of Statutes and Forms. With Addendum containing
the decision of the House of Lords in *Boulter* v. *Justices of Kent.* By
GEORGE JOHN TALBOT, Esq., Barrister-at-Law. 12mo. 1896. 7s. 6d.
"His method gives professional men a guide to the legislation afforded by no other book."—*Law Journal.*

LOCAL AND MUNICIPAL GOVERNMENT.—Bazalgette and
Humphreys' Law relating to County Councils.—Third Edition.
By GEORGE HUMPHREYS, Esq. Royal 8vo. 1889.   7s. 6d.

Bazalgette and Humphreys' Law relating to Local and Muni-
cipal Government. Comprising the Statutes relating to Public
Health, Municipal Corporations, Highways, Burial, Gas and Water,
Public Loans, Compulsory Taking of Lands, Tramways, Electric
Lighting, &c. With Addenda. By C. NORMAN BAZALGETTE and
G. HUMPHREYS, Esqrs., Barristers-at-Law. Sup. royal 8vo. 1888. 3l. 3s.

Chambers.—*Vide* "District Councils."

Humphreys.—*Vide* "Parish Law."

LONDON LOCAL GOVERNMENT. — Hunt's London Local
Government. The Law relating to the London County Council,
the Vestries and District Boards elected under the Metropolis
Management Acts, and other Local Authorities. By JOHN HUNT,
Esq., Barrister-at-Law. 2 vols. Royal 8vo. 1897.   3l. 3s.
"This very comprehensive and well-arranged code of London Local Govern-
ment will be invaluable to local authorities, the legal profession and others
directly interested in the subject."—*London.*
"Concise, accurate and useful."—*Law Journal.*
"We heartily recommend Mr. Hunt's work."—*County Council Times.*

LUNACY.—Heywood and Massey's Lunacy Practice.—By ARTHUR
HEYWOOD and ARNOLD MASSEY, Solicitors. Demy 8vo. 1900. 7s. 6d.
"A very useful little handbook, which contains a clear account of the practice
in lunacy."—*Law Journal.*
"An exceedingly useful handbook on lunacy practice."—*Law Notes.*
"A clear and able handbook. . . . A feature of the work are the precedents
given, which have nearly all stood the test of actual practice."—*Law Times.*

MAGISTRATES' PRACTICE and **MAGISTERIAL LAW.**— *Vide*
"Justice of the Peace."

MARINE INSURANCE.—*Vide* "Insurance."

MARITIME DECISIONS.—Douglas' Maritime Law Decisions.—
Compiled by ROBT. R. DOUGLAS. Demy 8vo. 1888.   7s. 6d.

MARRIAGE.—Kelly's French Law of Marriage, Marriage Contracts, and Divorce, and the Conflict of Laws arising therefrom. Second Edition. By OLIVER E. BODINGTON, Esq., Barrister-at-
Law, Licencié en Droit de la Faculté de Paris. Roy. 8vo. 1895. 21s.

MARRIED WOMEN'S PROPERTY.—Lush's Married Women's
Rights and Liabilities in relation to Contracts, Torts, and
Trusts. By MONTAGUE LUSH, Esq., Barrister-at-Law, Author of
"The Law of Husband and Wife." Royal 12mo. 1887.   5s.

MASTER AND SERVANT.—Macdonell's Law of Master and
Servant. Second Edition. By JOHN MACDONELL, Esq., LL.D., M.A.,
C.B., a Master of the Supreme Court.   (*In preparation.*)

MEDICAL PARTNERSHIPS.—Barnard and Stocker's Medical
Partnerships, Transfers, and Assistantships.—By WILLIAM
BARNARD, Esq., Barrister-at-Law, and G. BERTRAM STOCKER, Esq.,
Managing Director of the Scholastic, Clerical and Medical Associa-
tion (Limited). Demy 8vo. 1895.   10s. 6d.

** All standard Law Works are kept in Stock, in law calf and other bindings.

MERCANTILE LAW.—Smith's Compendium of Mercantile Law.
—Tenth Edition. By JOHN MACDONELL, Esq., C.B., a Master of
the Supreme Court of Judicature, assisted by GEO. HUMPHREYS, Esq.,
Barrister-at-Law. 2 vols. Royal 8vo. 1890.   2*l.* 2*s.*

"Of the greatest value to the mercantile lawyer."—*Law Times.*
"One of the most scientific treatises extant on mercantile law."—*Sol. Jl.* .

Tudor's Selection of Leading Cases on Mercantile and Maritime
Law.—With Notes. By O. D. TUDOR, Esq., Barrister-at-Law.
Third Edition. Royal 8vo. 1884.   2*l.* 2*s.*

Wilson's Mercantile Handbook of the Liabilities of Merchant,
Shipowner, and Underwriter on Shipments by General Vessels.—By A. WILSON, Solicitor and Notary. Royal 12mo. 1883. 6*s.*

MERCHANDISE MARKS ACT.—Payn's Merchandise Marks
Act, 1887.—By H. PAYN, Barrister-at-Law. Royal 12mo. 1888. 3*s.*6*d.*
"A safe guide to all who are interested in the Act."—*Law Times.*

METROPOLIS BUILDING ACTS.—Craies' London Building Act,
1894; with Introduction, Notes, and Index, and a Table showing
how the Former Enactments relating to Buildings have been dealt
with.—By W. F. CRAIES, Esq., Barrister-at-Law. Royal 8vo. 1894. 5*s.*

MORALS AND LEGISLATION.—Bentham's Introduction to the
Principles of Morals and Legislation.—By JEREMY BENTHAM,
M.A., Bencher of Lincoln's Inn. Crown 8vo. 1879.   6*s.* 6*d.*

MORTGAGE.—Beddoes' Concise Treatise on the Law of Mortgage.—By W. F. BEDDOES, Esq., Barrister-at-Law. 8vo. 1893. 10*s.*

"Compiled carefully and with discretion."—*Law Times.*
"A useful addition to the literature of its subject."—*Law Journal.*
"We commend the work as a reliable and useful little manual."—*Law Students' Journal.*
"We can cordially recommend this work to a practitioner who likes to have small compact books at hand on all subjects."—*Law Notes.*

Robbins' Treatise on the Law of Mortgages, Pledges and
Hypothecations.—By L. G. GORDON ROBBINS, Assisted by F. T.
MAW, Esqrs., Barristers-at-Law. Founded on "Coote's Law of
Mortgage." 2 vols. Royal 8vo. 1897.   3*l.*

"It is not a patched-up edition of an old work; it is a new book, containing of the old what is good and is still law, with the advantage of the work of a modern editor."—*Law Journal.*
"The practising lawyer will find in detail everything that he can possibly want."—*Solicitors' Journal.*
"A complete treatise on the law of mortgages."—*Law Quarterly Review.*

MOTOR CARS.—Bonner's Law of Motor Cars, Hackney and other
Carriages.—An Epitome of the Law, Statutes, and Regulations.
By G. A. BONNER, Esq., Barrister-at-Law. Demy 8vo. 1897. 7*s.* 6*d.*

"The book is full of useful information, and will undoubtedly prove of service to those who require advice on this subject."—*Law Times.*

MUNICIPAL CORPORATIONS.—Bazalgette and Humphreys.—
Vide "Local and Municipal Government."

NAVY.—Manual of Naval Law and Court Martial Procedure;
in which is embodied Thring's Criminal Law of the Navy, together
with the Naval Discipline Act and an Appendix of Practical
Forms.—By J. E. R. STEPHENS, Esq., Barrister-at-Law, C. E.
GIFFORD, Esq., C.B., Fleet Paymaster, Royal Navy, and F.
HARRISON SMITH, Esq., Staff Paymaster, Royal Navy. Demy 8vo.
1901.   15*s.*

NEGLIGENCE.—Smith's Treatise on the Law of Negligence.
Second Edition. By HORACE SMITH, Esq., Barrister-at-Law, Editor
of "Addison on Contracts, and Torts," &c. 8vo. 1884. 12*s.* 6*d.*

⁎⁎ All standard Law Works are kept in Stock, in law calf and other bindings.

NISI PRIUS.—Roscoe's Digest of the Law of Evidence on the Trial of Actions at Nisi Prius.—Seventeenth Edition. By MAURICE POWELL, Esq., Barrister-at-Law. 2 vols. Demy 8vo. 1900. 2*l.* 2*s.*

" Continues to be a vast and closely packed storehouse of information on practice at Nisi Prius."—*Law Journal.*

" Almost invaluable to a Nisi Prius practitioner. . . . We have nothing but praise for the new edition."—*Law Quarterly Review.*

NOTARY.—Brooke's Treatise on the Office and Practice of a Notary of England.—With a full collection of Precedents. Sixth Ed. By JAMES CRANSTOUN, Esq., Barrister-at-Law. Demy 8vo. 1901. 25*s.*

OATHS.—Stringer's Oaths and Affirmations in Great Britain and Ireland; being a Collection of Statutes, Cases, and Forms, with Notes and Practical Directions for the use of Commissioners for Oaths, and of all Courts of Civil Procedure und Offices attached thereto. By FRANCIS A. STRINGER, of the Central Office, Royal Courts of Justice, one of the Editors of the "Annual Practice." Second Edition. Crown 8vo. 1893.   4*s.*

" Indispensable to all commissioners."—*Solicitors' Journal.*

OTTOMAN CIVIL LAW.—Grigsby's Medjellé, or Ottoman Civil Law.—Translated into English. By W. E. GRIGSBY, LL.D., Esq., Barrister-at-Law. Demy 8vo. 1895.   21*s.*

PARISH LAW.—Humphreys' Parish Councils.—The Law relating to Parish Councils, being the Local Government Act, 1894 : with an Appendix of Statutes, together with an Introduction, Notes, and a Copious Index. Second Edition. By GEORGE HUMPHREYS, Esq., Barrister-at-Law, Author of "The Law relating to County Councils," &c. Royal 8vo. 1895.   10*s.*

Steer's Parish Law. Being a Digest of the Law relating to the Civil and Ecclesiastical Government of Parishes and the Relief of the Poor. Sixth Edition. By W. H. MACNAMARA, Esq., Assistant Master of the Supreme Court, Registrar of the Court constituted under the Benefices Act, 1898. Demy 8vo. 1899.   20*s.*

" Of great service both to lawyers and to parochial officers."—*Solicitors' Jour.*

" A most useful book of reference on all matters connected with the parish, both civil and ecclesiastical."—*Law Journal.*

PARTNERSHIP.—Pollock's Digest of the Law of Partnership. Seventh Edition. With an Appendix of Forms. By Sir FREDERICK POLLOCK, Bart., Barrister-at-Law, Author of "Principles of Contract," "The Law of Torts," &c. Demy 8vo. 1900.   10*s.*

" We are confident this book will be most popular as well as extremely useful."—*Law Times.*

" Of the execution of the work we can speak in terms of the highest praise. The language is simple, concise, and clear."—*Law Magazine.*

" Praiseworthy in design, scholarly and complete in execution."—*Sat. Review.*

PATENTS.—Campbell's Ruling Cases, Vol. XX.—*Vide* " Digests," p. 10.

Edmunds on Patents.—The Law and Practice of Letters Patent for Inventions. By LEWIS EDMUNDS, K.C. Second Edition. By T. M. STEVENS, Esq., Barrister-at-Law. Roy. 8vo. 1897.   1*l.* 12*s.*

" We have nothing but commendation for the book."—*Solicitors' Journal.*

" It would be difficult to make it more complete."—*Law Times.*

Edmunds' Patents, Designs and Trade Marks Acts, 1883 to 1888, Consolidated with an Index. Second Edition. By LEWIS EDMUNDS, K.C., D.Sc., LL.B. Imp. 8vo. 1895.   *Net* 2*s.* 6*d.*

Gordon's Monopolies by Patents and the Statutable Remedies available to the Public. By J. W. GORDON, Esq., Barrister-at-Law. Demy 8vo. 1897.   18*s.*

" A treatise which we think must take a unique place in our legal literature." —*Law Times.*

Gordon's Compulsory Licences under the Patents Acts. By J. W. GORDON, Esq., Barrister-at-Law, Author of " Monopolies by Patent." Demy 8vo. 1899.   15*s.*

** *All standard Law Works are kept in Stock, in law calf and other bindings.*

PATENTS—*continued.*

Johnson's Patentees' Manual.—A Treatise on the Law and Practice of Patents for Inventions. Sixth Edition. By JAMES JOHNSON, Esq., Barrister-at-Law ; and J. HENRY JOHNSON, Solicitor and Patent Agent. Demy 8vo. 1890. 10*s.* 6*d.*

Johnson's Epitome of Patent Laws and Practice. Third Edition. Crown 8vo. 1900. *Net,* 2*s.* 6*d.*

Morris's Patents Conveyancing.—Being a Collection of Precedents in Conveyancing in relation to Letters Patent for Inventions. With Dissertations and Copious Notes on the Law and Practice. By ROBERT MORRIS, Esq., Barrister-at-Law. Royal 8vo. 1887. 1*l.* 5*s.*

Thompson's Handbook of Patent Law of all Countries.—By WM. P. THOMPSON. Tenth Edition, with Addendum. 12mo. 1899. *Net,* 2*s.* 6*d.*

Thompson's Handbook of British Patent Law. Eleventh Edition. 12mo. 1899. *Net,* 6*d.*

PAWNBROKING.—**Attenborough's Law of Pawnbroking,** with the Pawnbrokers Act, 1872, and the Factors Act, 1889, and Notes thereon. By CHARLES L. ATTENBOROUGH, Esq., Barrister-at-Law. Post 8vo. 1897. *Net,* 3*s.*

PERSONAL PROPERTY.—Smith.—*Vide* "Real Property."

PLEADING.—**Bullen and Leake's Precedents of Pleadings,** with Notes and Rules relating to Pleading. Fifth Edition. Revised and Adapted to the Present Practice in the Queen's Bench Division of the High Court of Justice. By THOMAS J. BULLEN, Esq., Barrister-at-Law, CYRIL DODD, Esq., K.C., and C. W. CLIFFORD, Esq., Barrister-at-Law. Demy 8vo. 1897. 38*s.*

"The standard work on modern pleading."—*Law Journal.*
"A very large number of precedents are collected together, and the notes are full and clear."—*Law Times.*
"The Editors have in every way preserved the high standard of the work, and brought it down to date effectively and conscientiously."—*Law Magazine.*

Odgers' Principles of Pleading, Practice and Procedure in Civil Actions in the High Court of Justice.—Fourth Edition. By W. BLAKE ODGERS, LL.D., K.C., Recorder of Plymouth, Author of "A Digest of the Law of Libel and Slander." Demy 8vo. 1900. 12*s.* 6*d.*

"The student or practitioner who desires instruction and practical guidance in our modern system of pleading cannot do better than possess himself of Mr. Odgers' book."—*Law Journal.*
"Includes a careful outline of the procedure in an ordinary action at law. This sketch will be of the utmost value to students, and ought to win the approval also of examining bodies, as it is remarkably free from any adaptability to the purposes of the mere crammer."—*Literature.*
"Of immense assistance to junior counsel."—*Law Notes.*
"Terse, clear and pointed."—*Law Quarterly Review.*

POISONS.—**Reports of Trials for Murder by Poisoning.**—With Chemical Introductions and Notes. By G. LATHAM BROWNE, Esq., Barrister-at-Law, and C. G. STEWART, Senior Assistant in the Laboratory of St. Thomas's Hospital, &c. Demy 8vo. 1883. 12*s.* 6*d.*

POWERS.—**Farwell on Powers.**—A Concise Treatise on Powers. Second Edition. By the Hon. Sir GEORGE FARWELL, a Justice of the High Court, assisted by W. R. SHELDON, Esq., Barrister-at-Law. Royal 8vo. 1893. 1*l.* 5*s.*

"We have looked through the volume with some care, and we believe that the practitioner and the judge will find it comprehensive and complete."—*Law Times.*
"Of great service to the conveyancing lawyer."—*Law Gazette.*

PRINCIPAL AND AGENT.—**Wright's Law of Principal and Agent.** By E. B. WRIGHT, Esq., Barrister-at-Law. Demy 8vo. 1894. 18*s.*

"Clearly arranged and clearly written."—*Law Times.*
"May with confidence be recommended to all legal practitioners as an accurate and handy text book on the subjects comprised in it."—*Solicitors' Journal.*

*** *All standard Law Works are kept in Stock, in law calf and other bindings.*

PRIVY COUNCIL LAW.—Wheeler's Privy Council Law: A Synopsis of all the Appeals decided by the Judicial Committee (including Indian Appeals) from 1876 to 1891. Together with a précis of the Cases from the Supreme Court of Canada. By GEORGE WHEELER, Esq., Barrister-at-Law, and of the Judicial Department of the Privy Council. Royal 8vo. 1893.   31s. 6d.

PROBATE.—Nelson's Handbook on Probate Practice (Non-Contentious), with Rules, Forms, Costs, and General Instructions to Solicitors and their Assistants in Extracting Grants of Probate and Administration (in the High Court of Justice, Ireland).—By HOWARD A. NELSON, Esq., Barrister-at-Law, District Probate Registrar, Londonderry. Demy 8vo. 1901.   12s. 6d.

Powles and Oakley's Law and Practice relating to Probate and Administration. By L. D. POWLES, Barrister-at-Law, and T. W. H. OAKLEY, of the Probate Registry. (Being a Third Edition of "Browne on Probate.") Demy 8vo. 1892.   1l. 10s.

PROPERTY.—*See also* "Real Property."

Raleigh's Outline of the Law of Property.—Demy 8vo. 1890. 7s. 6d.

Strahan's General View of the Law of Property.—Second Edit. By J. A. STRAHAN, assisted by J. SINCLAIR BAXTER, Esqrs., Barristers-at-Law. Demy 8vo. 1895.   12s. 6d.
"The student will not easily find a better general view of the law of property than that which is contained in this book."—*Solicitors' Journal.*
"We know of no better book for the class-room."—*Law Times.*

PUBLIC MEETINGS.—Chambers' Handbook for Public Meetings, including Hints as to the Summoning and Management of them. Second Edition. By GEORGE F. CHAMBERS, Esq., Barrister-at-Law. Demy 8vo. 1888.   *Net,* 2s. 6d.

QUARTER SESSIONS.—*See* "Criminal Law."

RAILWAY RATES.—Darlington's Railway Rates and the Carriage of Merchandise by Railway; including the Provisional Orders of the Board of Trade as sanctioned by Parliament, containing the Classification of Traffic and Schedule of Maximum Rates and Charges applicable to the Railways of Great Britain and Ireland. By H. R. DARLINGTON, Esq., Barrister-at-Law. Demy 8vo. 1893.   1l. 5s.

RAILWAYS.—Browne and Theobald's Law of Railway Companies.—Being a Collection of the Acts and Orders relating to Railway Companies in Great Britain and Ireland, with Notes of all the Cases decided thereon. Third Edition. By J. H. BALFOUR BROWNE, Esq., one of His Majesty's Counsel, and FRANK BALFOUR BROWNE, Esq., Barrister-at-Law. Royal 8vo. 1899.   2l. 2s.
"Contains in a very concise form the whole law of railways."—*The Times.*
"It is difficult to find in this work any subject in connection with railways which is not dealt with."—*Law Times.*
"Practitioners who require a comprehensive treatise on railway law will find it indispensable."—*Law Journal.*

Campbell's Ruling Cases. Vol. XXII.—*Vide* "Digests," p. 10.

RATES AND RATING.—Castle's Law and Practice of Rating.—Third Edition. By EDWARD JAMES CASTLE, Esq., one of His Majesty's Counsel. Demy 8vo. 1895.   25s.
"A sure and safe guide."—*Law Magazine.*
"Mr. Castle's book has hitherto held a very high place, and the success that has attended it seems assured to the new edition."—*Law Journal.*
"A compendious treatise, which has earned the goodwill of the Profession on account of its conciseness, its lucidity, and its accuracy."—*Law Times.*

Chambers' Law relating to Local Rates; with especial reference to the Powers and Duties of Rate-levying Local Authorities, and their Officers; comprising the Statutes in full and a Digest of 718 Cases. Second Edition. By G. F. CHAMBERS, Esq., Barrister-at-Law. Royal 8vo. 1889.   10s. 6d.

REAL PROPERTY.—Digby's History of the Law of Real Property. Fifth Edition. Demy 8vo. 1897.   12s. 6d.

*** *All standard Law Works are kept in Stock, in law calf and other bindings.*

REAL PROPERTY—*continued.*

Lightwood's Treatise on Possession of Land : with a chapter on the Real Property Limitation Acts, 1833 and 1874.—By JOHN M. LIGHTWOOD, Esq., Barrister-at-Law. Demy 8vo. 1894.   15*s.*

Shearwood's Real Property.—A Concise Abridgment of the Law of Real Property and an Introduction to Conveyancing. Designed to facilitate the subject for Students preparing for examination. By JOSEPH A. SHEARWOOD, Esq., Barrister-at-Law. Third Edition. Demy 8vo. 1885.   8*s.* 6*d.*

Shelford's Real Property Statutes. — Comprising the principal Statutes relating to Real Property passed in the reigns of King William IV. and Queen Victoria, with Notes of Decided Cases. Ninth Edition. By THOMAS H. CARSON, Esq., K.C., assisted by HAROLD B. BOMPAS, Esq., Barrister-at-Law. Royal 8vo. 1893.   30*s.*
" Absolutely indispensable to conveyancing and equity lawyers."

Smith's Real and Personal Property.—A Compendium of the Law of Real and Personal Property, primarily connected with Conveyancing. Designed as a Second Book for Students, and as a Digest of the most useful learning for Practitioners. Sixth Edition. By the AUTHOR and J. TRUSTRAM, LL.M., Barrister-at-Law. 2 vols. Demy 8vo. 1884.   2*l.* 2*s.*
" A book which he (the student) may read over and over again with profit and pleasure."—*Law Times.*
" Will be found of very great service to the practitioner."—*Solicitors' Journal.*
" A really useful and valuable work on our system of Conveyancing."—*Law Students' Journal.*

Strahan.—*Vide* " Property."

REGISTRATION.—Rogers.—*Vide* " Elections."

Fox and Smith's Registration Cases. (1886—1895). Royal 8vo.   *Calf, net,* 2*l.* 10*s.*

Smith's (C. Lacey) Registration Cases. Part I. (1895-96). *Net,* 6*s.* 6*d.* Part II. (1896), 5*s.* Part III. (1897), 4*s.* Part IV. (1898-9), 6*s.* Part V. (1899-1900), 4*s.*

Lawson's Notes of Decisions under the Representation of the People Acts and the Registration Acts, 1885—1893, inclusive.—By WM. LAWSON, Barrister-at-Law. Demy 8vo. 1894.   24*s.*
Ditto, ditto, for 1894, 1895, 1896 and 1897.   *Each net* 4*s.* 6*d.*
Ditto, ditto, for 1898.   *Net,* 7*s.* 6*d.*
Ditto, ditto, for 1899.   *Net,* 4*s.* 6*d.*

REQUISITIONS ON TITLE.—Dickins.—*Vide* "Conveyancing."

RIVERS POLLUTION.—**Haworth's Rivers Pollution.**—The Statute Law relating to Rivers Pollution, containing the Rivers Pollution Prevention Acts, 1876 and 1893, together with the Special Acts in force in the West Riding of Yorkshire and the County of Lancaster. By CHARLES JOSEPH HAWORTH, Solicitor, B.A. (Cantab.), LL.B. (London). Royal 12mo. 1897.   6*s.*

ROMAN LAW.—**Abdy and Walker's Institutes of Justinian,** Translated, with Notes, by J. T. ABDY, LL.D., and the late BRYAN WALKER, M.A., LL.D. Crown 8vo. 1876.   16*s.*

Abdy and Walker's Commentaries of Gaius and Rules of Ulpian. With a Translation and Notes, by J. T. ABDY, LL.D., late Regius Professor of Laws in the University of Cambridge, and the late BRYAN WALKER, M.A., LL.D. New Edition by BRYAN WALKER. Crown 8vo. 1885.   16*s.*

Buckler's Origin and History of Contract in Roman Law down to the end of the Republican Period. By W. H. BUCKLER, B.A., LL.B. Post 8vo. Second Edition.   (*In the press.*)

** *All standard Law Works are kept in Stock, in law calf and other bindings.*

ROMAN LAW—*continued.*

Goodwin's XII. Tables.—By FREDERICK GOODWIN, LL.D. London. Royal 12mo. 1886.　　　　　3*s.* 6*d.*

Greene's Outlines of Roman Law.—Consisting chiefly of an Analysis and Summary of the Institutes. For the use of Students. By T. WHITCOMBE GREENE, Barrister-at-law. Fourth Edition. Foolscap 8vo. 1884.　　　　　7*s.* 6*d.*

Grueber's Lex Aquilia.—The Roman Law of Damage to Property: being a Commentary on the Title of the Digest "Ad Legem Aquiliam" (ix. 2). With an Introduction to the Study of the Corpus Iuris Civilis. By ERWIN GRUEBER, Dr. Jur., M.A. 8vo. 1886.· 10*s.* 6*d.*

Holland's Institutes of Justinian.—Second Edition. Extra fcap. 8vo. 1881.　　　　　5*s.*

Holland and Shadwell's Select Titles from the Digest of Justinian.—Demy 8vo. 1881.　　　　　14*s.*

Holland's Gentilis Alberici, I.C.D., I.C.P.R., de Iure Belli Libri Tres.—Edidit T. E. HOLLAND, I.C.D. Small 4to., half-morocco. 21*s.*

Monro's Digest IX. 2. Lex Aquilia. Translated, with Notes, by C. H. MONRO, M.A. Crown 8vo. 1898.　　　　　5*s.*

Monro's Digest XIX. 2, Locati Conducti. Translated, with Notes, by C. H. MONRO, M.A. Crown 8vo. 1891.　　　　　5*s.*

Monro's Digest XLVII. 2, De Furtis. Translated, with Notes, by C. H. MONRO, M.A. Crown 8vo. 1893.　　　　　5*s*

Monro's Digest XLI. 1, De Adquirendo Rerum Dominio. Translated, with Notes, by C. H. MONRO, M.A. Crown 8vo. 1900. 5*s.*

Moyle's Imperatoris Justiniani Institutiones.—Third Edition. 2 vols. Demy 8vo. 1896.　　　　　1*l.* 2*s.*

Poste's Elements of Roman Law.—By Gaius. With a Translation and Commentary. Third Edition. By EDWARD POSTE, Esq., Barrister-at-Law. Demy 8vo. 1890.　　　　　18*s.*

Roby's Introduction to the Study of Justinian's Digest, containing an account of its composition and of the Jurists used or referred to therein. By H. J. ROBY, M.A. Demy 8vo. 1886. 9*s.*

Roby's Justinian's Digest.—Lib. VII., Tit. I. De Usufructu, with a Legal and Philological Commentary. By H. J. ROBY, M.A. Demy 8vo. 1884.　　　　　9*s.*
Or the Two Parts complete in One Volume. Demy 8vo.　18*s.*

Sohm's Institutes of Roman Law.—Second Edition. Demy 8vo. 1901.　　　　　18*s.*

Walker's Selected Titles from Justinian's Digest.—Annotated by the late BRYAN WALKER, M.A., LL.D.

　　Part I. Mandati vel Contra. Digest XVII. 1. Crown 8vo. 1879. 5*s.*

　　Part III. De Condictionibus. Digest XII. 1 and 4—7, and Digest XIII. 1—3. Crown 8vo. 1881.　　　　　6*s.*

Walker's Fragments of the Perpetual Edict of Salvius Julianus. Collected and annotated by BRYAN WALKER, M.A., LL.D. Crown 8vo. 1877.　　　　　6*s.*

Whewell's Grotius de Jure Belli et Pacis, with the Notes of Barbeyrac and others ; accompanied by an abridged Translation of the Text, by W. WHEWELL, D.D. 3 vols. Demy 8vo. 1853.　12*s.*

.*** All standard Law Works are kept in Stock, in law calf and other bindings.*

RULING CASES.—Campbell.—*Vide* "Digests," p. 10.

SALES.—Blackburn on Sales. A Treatise on the Effect of the Contract of Sale on the Legal Rights of Property and Possession in Goods, Wares, and Merchandise. By Lord BLACKBURN. 2nd Edit. By J. C. GRAHAM, Esq., Barrister-at-Law. Royal 8vo. 1885. 1*l.* 1*s.*
"We have no hesitation in saying that the work has been edited with remarkable ability and success."—*Law Quarterly Review.*

SALVAGE.—Kennedy's Treatise on the Law of Civil Salvage.—By the Hon. Sir WILLIAM R. KENNEDY, a Justice of the High Court. Royal 8vo. 1891. 12*s.*
"The best work on the law of salvage. It is a complete exposition of the subject, and as such is accurate and exhaustive."—*Law Times.*

SHERIFF LAW.—Mather's Compendium of Sheriff Law, especially in relation to Writs of Execution.—By PHILIP E. MATHER, Solicitor and Notary, formerly Under Sheriff of Newcastle-on-Tyne. Royal 8vo. 1894. 25*s.*
"We think that this book will be of very great assistance to any persons who may fill the positions of high sheriff and under-sheriff from this time forth. The whole of the legal profession will derive great advantage from having this volume to consult."—*Law Times.*

SHIPPING.—Carver.—*Vide* "Carriers."

Marsden's Digest of Cases relating to Shipping, Admiralty, and Insurance Law, down to the end of 1897.—By REGINALD G. MARSDEN, Esq., Barrister-at-Law, Author of "The Law of Collisions at Sea." Royal 8vo. 1899. 30*s.*

Pulling's Merchant Shipping Act, 1894.—With Introduction, Notes, and Index. By ALEXANDER PULLING, Esq., Barrister-at-Law. Royal 8vo. 1894. *Net* 6*s.*

Pulling's Shipping Code; being the Merchant Shipping Act, 1894 (57 & 58 Vict. c. 60); With Introduction, Notes, Tables, Rules, Orders, Forms, and a Full Index.—By ALEXANDER PULLING, Esq., Barrister-at-Law. Royal 8vo. 1894. *Net* 7*s.* 6*d.*

Temperley's Merchant Shipping Act, 1894 (57 & 58 Vict. c. 60). With an Introduction ; Notes, including all Cases decided under the former enactments consolidated in this Act ; a Comparative Table of Sections of the Former and Present Acts ; an Appendix of Rules, Regulations, Forms, etc., and a Copious Index.—By ROBERT TEMPERLEY, Esq., Barrister-at-Law. Royal 8vo. 1895. 25*s.*
"A full, complete, and most satisfactory work."—*Law Quarterly Review.*
"A monument of well-directed industry and knowledge directed to the elucidation of the most comprehensive and complicated Act."—*Law Journal.*

SLANDER.—Odgers.—*Vide* "Libel and Slander."

SOLICITORS.—Cordery's Law relating to Solicitors of the Supreme Court of Judicature. With an Appendix of Statutes and Rules, the Colonial Attornies Relief Acts, and Notes on Appointments open to Solicitors, and the Right to Admission to the Colonies, to which is added an Appendix of Precedents. Third Edition. By A. CORDERY, Esq., Barrister-at-Law. Demy 8vo. 1899. 21*s.*
"The leading authority on the law relating to solicitors."—*Law Journal.*
"A complete compendium of the law."—*Law Times.*
"Thoroughly up to date in every respect."—*Law Quarterly Review.*

Turner.—*Vide* "Conveyancing" and "Vendors and Purchasers."

SPECIFIC PERFORMANCE.—Fry's Treatise on the Specific Performance of Contracts. By the Right Hon. Sir EDWARD FRY. Third Edition. By the Author and E. PORTSMOUTH FRY, Esq., Barrister-at-Law. Royal 8vo. 1892. 1*l.* 16*s.*

** *All standard Law Works are kept in Stock, in law calf and other bindings.*

STAMP LAWS.—Highmore's Stamp Laws.—Being the Stamp Acts of 1891 : with the Acts amending and extending the same, including the Finance Act, 1899, together with other Acts imposing or relating to Stamp Duties, and Notes of Decided Cases ; also an Introduction, and an Appendix containing Tables showing the comparison with the antecedent Law. By NATHANIEL JOSEPH HIGHMORE, Assistant-Solicitor of the Inland Revenue. Demy 8vo. 1900. 10s. 6d.

"Will be found of the greatest use to solicitors, the officers of companies, and all men of business."—*Law Journal,* Feb. 10, 1900.

"This work is not only complete up to the present year, but is excellently arranged."—*Irish Law Times,* Feb. 10, 1900.

"A very comprehensive volume, fulfilling every requirement. . . . The various notes to the sections of the several Acts incorporated in the volume are fully and accurately set out, the points of the decided cases clearly expressed, and the effect and object of the enactment indicated ; and what must be of especial value to the practitioner, the practice at Somerset House with regard to all matters coming before that institution is stated."—*Justice of the Peace,* Feb. 24, 1900.

"Mr. Highmore's 'Stamp Laws' leaves nothing undone."—*The Civilian,* March 3, 1900.

STATUTE LAW.—Wilberforce on Statute Law. The Principles which govern the Construction and Operation of Statutes. By E. WILBERFORCE, Esq., a Master of the Supreme Court. 1881. 18s.

STATUTES, and *vide* "Acts of Parliament."

Chitty's Statutes.—New Edition.—The Statutes of Practical Utility, from the earliest times to 1894 inclusive. Arranged in Alphabetical and Chronological Order ; with Notes and Indexes. Fifth Edition. By J. M. LELY, Esq., Barrister-at-Law. Royal 8vo. *Complete with Index. In 13 Volumes.* 1894–1895.   13l. 13s.

Annual Supplements. By J. M. LELY, ESQ. 1895, 5s. 1896, 10s. 1897, 5s. 1898, 7s. 6d. 1899, 7s. 6d. 1900, 7s. 6d.

"It is a book which no public library should be without."—*Spectator.*

"A work of permanent value to the practising lawyer."—*Solicitors' Journal.*

"The profession will feel grateful both to the editor and the publishers of a work which will be found of the highest value."—*Law Journal.*

"A legal work of the very highest importance. . . . Few besides lawyers will, we suspect, realise the amount of work which such an undertaking involves to the editor, who appears to have spared no pains to give a clear, orderly, and methodical character to the compilation."—*Daily News.*

"This collection has fulfilled a purpose of usefulness only to be understood by those who are acquainted with the amazing complexity of English statute law, with its bewildering incoherence and painful heterogeneity."—*Pall Mall Gazette.*

"Indispensable in the library of every lawyer."—*Saturday Review.*

"To all concerned with the laws of England, Chitty's Statutes of Practical Utility are of essential importance, whilst to the practising lawyer they are an absolute necessity."—*Law Times.*

"It is apparently the belief of some popular novelists that lawyers in their difficulties still uniformly consult daily Coke upon Littleton and Blackstone. Those who know better are aware that the lawyer's Bible is the 'Statutes of Practical Utility'—that they are his working tools, even more than accredited text-books or 'authorised reports.' More than one judge has been heard to say that with the 'Statutes of Practical Utility' at his elbow on the bench he was apprehensive of no difficulties which might arise."—*The Times.*

.*.* *All standard Law Works are kept in Stock, in law calf and other bindings.*

SUCCESSION.—Holdsworth and Vickers' Law of Succession, Testamentary and Intestate. Demy 8vo. 1899.   10*s*. 6*d*.

SUMMARY CONVICTIONS.—Paley's Law and Practice of Summary Convictions under the Summary Jurisdiction Acts, 1848—1884; including Proceedings Preliminary and Subsequent to Convictions, and the Responsibility of Convicting Magistrates and their Officers, with the Summary Jurisdiction Rules, 1886, and Forms.—Seventh Edition. By W. H. MACNAMARA, Esq., Barrister-at-Law. Demy 8vo. 1892.   24*s*.

TAXPAYERS' GUIDES.—*Vide* "House," "Income," & "Land Tax."

THEATRES AND MUSIC HALLS.—Geary's Law of Theatres and Music Halls, including Contracts and Precedents of Contracts.—By W. N. M. GEARY, J.P. With Historical Introduction. By JAMES WILLIAMS, Esqrs., Barristers-at-Law. 8vo. 1885.   5*s*.

TITLE.—Jackson and Gosset.—*Vide* "Investigation of Title."

TORTS.—Addison on Torts.—A Treatise on the Law of Torts; or Wrongs and their Remedies. Seventh Edition. By HORACE SMITH, Esq., Bencher of the Inner Temple, Metropolitan Magistrate, Editor of "Addison on Contracts," &c., and A. P. PERCEVAL KEEP, Esq., Barrister-at-Law. Royal 8vo. 1893.   1*l*. 18*s*.

"As an exhaustive digest of all the cases which are likely to be cited in practice it stands without a rival."—*Law Journal*.

"As now presented, this valuable treatise must prove highly acceptable to judges and the profession."—*Law Times*.

"An indispensable addition to every lawyer's library."—*Law Magazine*.

Ball's Leading Cases on the Law of Torts, with Notes. Edited by W. E. BALL, LL.D., Esq., Barrister-at-Law, Author of "Principles of Torts and Contracts." Royal 8vo. 1884.   1*l*. 1*s*.

Bigelow's Elements of the Law of Torts.—A Text-Book for Students. By MELVILLE M. BIGELOW, Ph.D., Lecturer in the Law School of the University of Boston, U.S.A. Crown 8vo. 1889. 10*s*. 6*d*.

Innes' Principles of the Law of Torts.—By L. C. INNES, lately one of the Judges of the High Court, Madras, Author of "A Digest of the Law of Easements." Demy 8vo. 1891.   10*s*. 6*d*.

"A useful addition to any law library."—*Law Quarterly Review*.

Pollock's Law of Torts: a Treatise on the Principles of Obligations arising from Civil Wrongs in the Common Law. Sixth Edition. By Sir FREDERICK POLLOCK, Bart., Barrister-at-Law. Author of "Principles of Contract," "A Digest of the Law of Partnership," &c. Demy 8vo. 1901.   25*s*.

"Concise, logically arranged, and accurate."—*Law Times*.

"Incomparably the best work that has been written on the subject."—*Literature*.

"A book which is well worthy to stand beside the companion volume on 'Contracts.' Unlike so many law-books, especially on this subject, it is no mere digest of cases, but bears the impress of the mind of the writer from beginning to end."—*Law Journal*.

"The work is one 'professing to select rather than to collect authorities,' but the leading cases on each branch of the subject will be found ably dealt with. A work bearing Mr. Pollock's name requires no recommendation. If it did, we could heartily recommend this able, thoughtful, and valuable book . . . . as a very successful and instructive attempt to seek out and expound the principles of duty and liability underlying a branch of the law in which the Scottish and English systems do not materially differ."—*Journal of Jurisprudence*.

*** *All standard Law Works are kept in Stock, in law calf and other bindings.*

TRADE MARKS.—Sebastian on the Law of Trade Marks and their Registration, and matters connected therewith, including a chapter on Goodwill; the Patents, Designs and Trade Marks Acts, 1883-8, and the Trade Marks Rules and Instructions thereunder; with Forms and Precedents; the Merchandize Marks Acts, 1887-94, and other Statutory Enactments; the United States Statutes, 1870-82, and the Rules and Forms thereunder; and the Treaty with the United States, 1877. By LEWIS BOYD SEBASTIAN, Esq., Barrister-at-Law. Fourth Edition. By the Author and HARRY BAIRD HEMMING, Esq., Barrister-at-Law. Royal 8vo. 1599.   1*l*, 10*s*.

"Stands alone as an authority upon the law of trade-marks and their registration."—*Law Journal.*
"It is rarely we come across a law book which embodies the results of years of careful investigation and practical experience in a branch of law, or that can be unhesitatingly appealed to as a standard authority. This is what can be said of Mr. Sebastian's book."—*Solicitors' Journal.*

Sebastian's Digest of Cases of Trade Mark, Trade Name, Trade Secret, Goodwill, &c., decided in the Courts of the United Kingdom, India, the Colonies, and the United States of America. By LEWIS BOYD SEBASTIAN, Esq., Barrister-at-Law. 8vo. 1879. 1*l*. 1*s*.

"Will be of very great value to all practitioners who have to advise on matters connected with trade marks."—*Solicitors' Journal.*

TRAMWAYS.—Sutton's Tramway Acts of the United Kingdom; with Notes on the Law and Practice, an Introduction, including the Proceedings before the Committees, Decisions of the Referees with respect to Locus Standi, and a Summary of the Principles of Tramway Rating, and an Appendix containing the Standing Orders of Parliament. Rules of the Board of Trade relating to Tramways, &c. Second Edition. By HENRY SUTTON, assisted by ROBERT A. BENNETT, Barristers-at-Law. Demy 8vo. 1883.   15*s*.

TRUSTS AND TRUSTEES.—Ellis' Trustee Act, 1893, including a Guide for Trustees to Investments. By ARTHUR LEE ELLIS, Esq., Barrister-at-Law. Fifth Edit. Roy. 12mo. 1894.   6*s*.

"The entire Act is annotated, and the way in which this is done is satisfactory."—*Law Journal.*
"Mr. Arthur Lee Ellis gives many valuable hints to trustees, not only with regard to the interpretation of the measure, but also with regard to investments."

Godefroi's Law Relating to Trusts and Trustees.—Second Edit. By HENRY GODEFROI, of Lincoln's Inn, Esq., Barrister-at-Law. Royal 8vo. 1891.   1*l*. 12*s*.

"The second edition of this work which lies before us is a model of what a legal text-book ought to be. It is clear in style and clear in arrangement."—*Law Times.*

VENDORS AND PURCHASERS.—Dart's Vendors and Purchasers.—A Treatise on the Law and Practice relating to Vendors and Purchasers of Real Estate. By the late J. HENRY DART, Esq., one of the Six Conveyancing Counsel of the High Court of Justice, Chancery Division. Sixth Edition. By the late WILLIAM BARBER, Q.C., RICHARD BURDON HALDANE, K.C., and WILLIAM ROBERT SHELDON, Esq., Barrister-at-Law. 2 vols. Royal 8vo. 1888.   3*l*. 15*s*.

Turner's Duties of Solicitor to Client as to Sales, Purchases, and Mortgages of Land.—Second Edition. By W. L. HACON, Esq., Barrister-at-Law. Demy 8vo. 1893.   10*s*. 6*d*.

"The most skilled in practical conveyancing would gain many useful hints from a perusal of the book, and we recommend it in all confidence."—*Law Notes.*

⁎⁎ *All standard Law Works are kept in Stock, in law calf and other bindings.*

VENDORS AND PURCHASERS—*continued.*

Webster's Law Relating to Particulars and Conditions of Sale on a Sale of Land.—With Appendix of Forms. Second Edition. By W. F. WEBSTER, Esq., Barrister-at-Law. Royal 8vo, 1896.   25*s.*

" This is the Second Edition of a well arranged and useful book, and the usefulness will not be impaired by the fact that the authority for each proposition and the reference to such authority are cited in the text itself instead of being relegated to a footnote."—*Law Journal.*

Webster's Conditions of Sale under the Land Transfer Acts, 1875 and 1897. Being a Supplement to above. Royal 8vo. 1899.   *Net* 2*s.*

WAR, DECLARATION OF.—Owen's Declaration of War.—A Survey of the Position of Belligerents and Neutrals, with relative considerations of Shipping and Marine Insurance during War. By DOUGLAS OWEN, Esq., Barrister-at-Law. Demy 8vo. 1889.   21*s.*

Owen's Maritime Warfare and Merchant Shipping.—A Summary of the Rights of Capture at Sea. By DOUGLAS OWEN, Esq., Barrister-at-Law. Demy 8vo. 1898.   *Net* 2*s.*

WILLS.—Theobald's Concise Treatise on the Law of Wills.— Fifth Edition. By H. S. THEOBALD, Esq., one of His Majesty's Counsel. Royal 8vo. 1900.   32*s.*

" Comprehensive though easy to use, and we advise all conveyancers to get a copy of it without loss of time."—*Law Journal.*

" Of great ability and value. It bears on every page traces of care and sound judgment."—*Solicitors' Journal.*

" The work is, in our opinion, an excellent one, and of very great value, not only as a work of reference, but also for those who can afford to give special time to the study of the subject with which it deals."—*Law Student's Journal.*

Weaver's Precedents of Wills.—A Collection of Concise Precedents of Wills, with Introduction, Notes, and an Appendix of Statutes. By CHARLES WEAVER, B.A.   Post 8vo. 1882.   5*s.*

WINDING UP.—Palmer's Company Precedents.—For use in relation to Companies, subject to the Companies Acts, 1862—1890. Part II. WINDING-UP FORMS AND PRACTICE. Arranged as follows:— Compulsory Winding-Up, Voluntary Winding-Up, Winding-Up under Supervision, Arrangements and Compromises, with copious Notes, and an Appendix of Acts and Rules. Eighth Edition. By FRANCIS BEAUFORT PALMER, assisted by FRANK EVANS, Esqrs., Barristers-at-Law. Royal 8vo. 1900.   32*s.*

" Palmer's ' Company Precedents' is the book *par excellence* for practitioners. . . . . . It is needless to recommend Mr. Palmer's book to the profession, for it is already known and appreciated. We advise those who have any doubts to consult it, and they will be in agreement with us."—*Law Journal.*

" Simply invaluable, not only to company lawyers, but to everybody connected with companies."—*Financial News.*

WORKMEN'S COMPENSATION ACT.—*Vide* " Employers' Liability."

WRECK INQUIRIES.—Murton's Law and Practice relating to Formal Investigations in the United Kingdom, British Possessions and before Naval Courts into Shipping Casualties and the Incompetency and Misconduct of Ships' Officers. With an Introduction. By WALTER MURTON, Solicitor to the Board of Trade. Demy 8vo. 1884.   1*l.* 4*s.*

WRONGS.—Addison, Ball, Bigelow, Pollock.—*Vide* " Torts."

PREPARING FOR PUBLICATION.

Arnould on the Law of Marine Insurance.—Seventh Edition. By EDWARD LOUIS DE HART and RALPH ILIFF SIMEY, Esqrs., Barristers-at-Law. (*In the press.*)

Campbell's Ruling Cases.—Arranged, Annotated and Edited by R. CAMPBELL, Esq., Barrister-at-Law; with American Notes by the Hon. LEONARD A. JONES.
Vol. XXIV. "Search Warrant" to "Telegraph." (*Nearly ready.*)
Vol. XXV. "Tenant" to "Wills." (*In the press.*)
An Addendum, containing, under the appropriate title and rule, Notes of Cases published since the issue of Volume I., thus bringing all the Volumes up to date, also a complete Index of Cases and a general Index to the whole work. (*In preparation.*)

Chitty's Forms of Practical Proceedings in the Queen's Bench Division.—Thirteenth Edition. By T. W. CHITTY and HERBERT CHITTY, Esqrs., Barristers-at-Law. (*In preparation.*)

Daniell's Chancery Practice.—Seventh Edition. By CECIL C. M. DALE, C. W. GREENWOOD, SYDNEY E. WILLIAMS, Esqrs., Barristers-at-Law, and FRANCIS A. STRINGER, Esq., of the Central Office. (*In the press.*)

Daniell's Chancery Forms.—Fifth Edition. By CHARLES BURNEY, Esq., a Master of the Supreme Court. (*In the press.*)

Digest of Cases, Overruled, Approved, or otherwise specially considered in the English Courts to the end of 1900. With extracts from the Judgments dealing with the same. By W. A. G. WOODS and J. RITCHIE, Esqrs., Barristers-at-Law. Being a new edition of "DALE and LEHMANN's Digest." (*In preparation.*)

Highmore's Summary Proceedings in Inland Revenue Cases in England and Wales.—Third Edition. By N. J. HIGHMORE, Esq., Barrister-at-Law, and of the Solicitors' Department, Inland Revenue. (*In the press.*)

Hood and Challis' Conveyancing and Settled Land Acts, and some other recent Acts affecting Conveyancing. With Commentaries. By H. J. HOOD and H. W. CHALLIS. Sixth Edition. By PERCY F. WHEELER, assisted by J. I. STIRLING, Esqrs., Barristers-at-Law. (*In the press.*)

Law Journal Quinquennial Digest, 1896—1900. (*In the press.*)

Leake's Digest of Principles of the Law of Contracts.—Fourth Edition. By A. E. RANDALL, Esq., Barrister-at-Law. (*In preparation.*)

Macdonell's Law of Master and Servant.—Second Edition. By JOHN MACDONELL, Esq., a Master of the Supreme Court. (*In preparation.*)

Seton's Forms of Judgments and Orders in the High Court of Justice and in the Court of Appeal, having especial reference to the Chancery Division, with Practical Notes. Sixth Edition. By CECIL C. M. DALE, Esq., Barrister-at-Law, and W. T. KING, Esq., a Registrar of the Supreme Court. (*In the press.*)

Smith's Compendium of Mercantile Law.—Eleventh Edition. By JOHN ANDREW HAMILTON, Esq., K.C., and GEO. HUMPHREYS, Esq., Barrister-at-Law. (*In preparation.*)

Smith's Practical Exposition of the Principles of Equity, illustrated by the Leading Decisions thereon. For the use of Students and Practitioners. Third Edition. By H. ARTHUR SMITH, Esq., Barrister-at-Law. (*In preparation.*)

Wright's Law of Principal and Agent.—Second Edition. By E. BLACKWOOD WRIGHT, Esq., Barrister-at-Law. (*In the press.*)

Wurtzburg on Building Societies.—The Law relating to Building Societies, with Appendices containing the Statutes, &c. Fourth Edition. By E. A. WURTZBURG, Esq., Barrister-at-Law. (*In preparation.*)